Eating Locally and Seasonally

A Community Food Book
For Lopez Island

(and All Those Who Want to Eat Well)

Elizabeth Simpson & Henning Sehmsdorf — Transition Lopez Island

Printed by Applied Digital Imaging Inc, Bellingham, WA
ISBN 978-0-578-84887-7

Cover: Watercolor by Kelley Palmer-McCarty, 2009. All drawings in the book are by this artist.
Photographs by Henning Sehmsdorf.

Contents:

Preface

Hood River Valley, Oregon, is bounded by the Columbia River to the north (with a splendid view of Mt. Adams in Washington), Mt. Hood to the south, the Cascade Range to the west, and dry foothills to the east that are a geographic border to Eastern Oregon. It is a charming valley, filled with fruits that grow easily in that part of the Northwest, such as apples, pears, cherries, peaches, plums, grapes, and strawberries.

Elizabeth was born and grew up in that valley, where her parents owned a small farm with a Concord grape arbor, Bartlett and Anjou pear trees, Striped and Red Delicious apple trees, peach trees, plum trees, and two Bing cherry trees, 60 feet tall. Elizabeth's brother Bill used to climb to the tops of those trees and saw off branches to drop down to her to harvest. What wealth!

Her parents planted strawberries and, during the season, would harvest twelve flats early in the morning which they delivered to the Apple Blossom Cafe in the town of Hood River. The garden they planted produced fresh vegetables, fresh and canning tomatoes, and raspberries. Blackberries and Oregon grape were abundant in the nearby woods.

Canning tomatoes and fresh fruits, making jam, jelly, and juice, were summer projects. By winter, shelves in the cellar were filled with canned foods that would see the family through the winter. There were Bantam chickens that provided meat, eggs, and broth. Elizabeth's parents purchased beef from a neighbor.

And yet…there were poisons in Paradise. In the 1940s, 50s, and 60s, orchardists sprayed their trees with Paris green, an arsenic-laced pigment that had been previously marketed as paint, and with copper solutions, lead arsenate, lime sulfur, and DDT. Since then, the number of pesticides, herbicides and fungicides has risen. None of the news for human, water, or environmental health is good.

During Elizabeth's childhood, people in the valley saw speed sprayers spew white dust between rows of fruit trees. Even more exciting were the "crop dusters" — spray planes that dipped into the valley, dropping pesticides from their bellies onto orchards, and people, and into soil and water, before swooping out again.

People were ignorant of the health effects of toxins then; Elizabeth and her brother used to pick an apple, wipe the white residue on their sleeves, and eat.

Cooking in America from the 1950s through the 1970s was marked by the rise of "convenience foods" — boxed, canned, processed — that were supposed to ease the burden of the housewife. So Elizabeth was fed not only homemade foods from garden and orchard, raw milk from a neighbor's cow, and fresh eggs from the farm, but also from pudding and cake mixes and cans of soup and spaghetti. She calls her childhood eating experience "half homegrown, half Betty Crocker."

Elizabeth received her bachelor's and master's degrees from the University of Oregon and her PhD from the University of Washington, where she and Henning met. They taught at the University, and on weekends, vacations and during summers, they grew food on the farm Henning had developed on Lopez Island. In 1994 they made the switch to full-time farming. Both left their teaching jobs at the University, and Elizabeth took a job teaching English, Spanish, and sustainable farming at the local high school.

Henning's childhood experience was both similar and different. His lifelong dream to be a farmer began with growing up in a large family in economically distressed post-war Germany. He and his siblings survived by growing vegetables and fruit in a sizable home garden and by gleaning surrounding fields in exchange for food. Later in high school, he participated in "harvest vacations," where groups of schoolchildren worked the fields and the farmer delivered produce to the school kitchen in return. At age nineteen he came to America to work his way through school, eventually earning a PhD at the University of Chicago. His first job, at a meat processing plant in Indiana, taught him, as he puts it, "everything I didn't want to know about how animals were treated in a massive slaughter facility and how poor the quality of the food was that came out of such factories." When he got his first teaching position, at the University of Washington, a trip to Lopez Island brought him back to his dream of farming. Starting with 10 acres in 1970, Henning began to build the infrastructure of the farm while he continued to work at the UW. In 1994, when their youngest child was 18 and ready to stand on his own feet, Henning became a full-time farmer. He joined Washington State University as an adjunct professor at the Center for Sustaining Agriculture and Natural Resources in 1999. Over the years he served on numerous boards and committees related to sustainable agriculture, farming, land stewardship, and education. From the start, he and Elizabeth planned to transition the farm to community ownership. Since 2012, Henning has been a Mentor Farmer under the apprenticeship program offered by the Biodynamic Farming Association.

Until the early 1990s, all the food the farm provided was grown in an orchard, and Henning had built a shelter in the woods for the family and a storage shed nearby. Now the farm boasts a family home, two orchards, three gardens, four large pastures, a chicken house and run, a barn, a pole barn used as a milking parlor, a processing kitchen, a greenhouse, two hoop houses, a wood shop, a 750,000 gallon pond that supplies water for the gardens and the animals, and solar installations on the roofs of the barn, the wood shop, and the pump house by the pond. Beef and dairy cows, sheep, pigs, chickens and turkeys provide food for the family and fertility for the gardens and pastures. Farm surplus is sold to the community through a CSA, local stores, and direct sales.

The farm has been a teaching site for all the years Henning and Elizabeth have lived here full time: annual workshops, farm classes for local high school and middle school students, and interns (staying for 3-12 months) and apprentices (staying for two years). Here they learned how to garden, harvest, process and cook the food, milk the cow, produce a variety of dairy products from her milk, and bake bread from grain grown on the farm. They learned animal husbandry, pasture management, water cycling, and sound business practices by selling produce at the Farmers Market and through the CSA. They learned how to think biodynamically, and to husband and care for resources, machines, and tools. They read and

wrote, and met in weekly discussion groups. Some went on to run their own farms; others went into environmental studies, social service, or ecological sciences. All of them, we hope, continue to eat locally and seasonally.

The practice of eating locally and seasonally, which impacts the health of people and the environment, is one that Henning and Elizabeth embrace and wish to pass on to others. That practice is reflected in this book. We deeply believe that everyone should be able to eat healthy foods produced on local farms; that our environment will be strengthened by sound agricultural practices that do not change the climate for the worse; that people should be aware of how the food they put in their bodies is raised; and, especially, that young people should learn how to produce food and how to live sustainably.

All the recipes in this book are sized for a family, and all are ones we prepare at home. We have sourced them over many years: some we created ourselves, some came from our families, some from friends and neighbors, some from cookbooks of many backgrounds, some from online. All of the recipes we adapted to what we grow on the farm and how we prepare foods. In this sense, the food book represents *terroir*: it reflects the soil and climate of Lopez Island. When asked how to plan meals, we say, "Look in the garden; look on the shelves; look in the freezer. Make a meal plan for the week, and purchase only what you can't produce."

Eating locally and seasonally does not mean being deprived of coffee, olive oil and lemons, or doing without staples such as rice and flour. It does mean that in the non-growing season strawberries can be taken out of the freezer, tomatoes pulled off the shelf, or bread baked with grain from nearby farms.

Visitors to the farm often shake their heads and say, "I could *never* do this!" We remind them that our farm was fifty years in the making, and we developed it at a reasonable pace. Everyone can start with a garden, such as containers on a deck, and grow from there. Everyone can procure food from local producers, and thereby eat well, support their neighbors, and sustain the environment.

How to use this book: As farmers and gardeners, we recommend that you start by reading the first two chapters, *Why Eat Locally and Seasonally?* and *A*

Seasonal Calendar For Farmers, Gardeners, and Eaters.
These chapters build on the idea that eating locally
and seasonally is fundamental to personal and
environmental health, and show how to implement
nutritionally whole and ecologically benign eating.
As cooks, we recommend that you consult the
Recipe List to make your daily or weekly food plan.

We take this opportunity to thank the organizations
and individuals who have made this book possible.
We thank the board of Transition Lopez Island for
adopting the book as a means for moving the food
culture and economy of the island toward the goal
of a fossil-free future. We thank Lopez Locavores
and the Heller Foundation for endorsing the book.
We thank all the interns, apprentices, and students
in the Lopez Island School District farm class who
came to the farm for many years to learn and help
us learn about sustainable agriculture. We thank the
Lopez Community Land Trust for holding our
vision of an island commons of farmland
supporting a local food system.

We thank Washington State University County
Extension for years of support of on-farm
workshops and farm-based research into the
feasibility of regenerative agriculture and, most
recently, for implementing a county-wide survey
that measures how local consumers make food
choices.

We thank Learner Limbach, manager of Orcas
Food Co-op, Faith van der Putte representing the
Agricultural Resource Committee, Taproot Lopez
Island Community Kitchen, and all the farmers and
gardeners on the island who believe in the future of
a resilient island-based food system.

We especially thank Evelyn Adams and Jack Hartt
of Transition Fidalgo & Friends for their generosity
in providing tireless editorial feedback and
proofreading and, as important, carrying the book
project to the various Transition groups around the
Salish Sea. We also thank David Sather for technical
help in wrestling with recalcitrant computers and
publishing software. Finally, we thank Ben Vahl,
manager of Digital Imaging in Bellingham who
guided us with great patience and skill toward
publishing this book on S&S Homestead Press.

Elizabeth Simpson and Henning Sehmsdorf
Lopez Island, 2021

For more information about biodynamic farming,
visit our website www.sshomestead.org.

Why Eat Locally and Seasonally?

FLOSS is our acronym for Fresh, Local, Organic, Seasonal, and Sustainable. Since eating is one of the most intimate acts we perform, putting food in our bodies at least three times a day, the foods we choose make a big difference in our daily pleasure, and our physical and moral health. "Fresh" speaks for itself. Fresh foods have a bright flavor and crisp texture. The first strawberry, warm from the bush, the first peas from the pod, the first ripe tomato, provide a delight to the senses we can't get from imported food. Our CSA customers pick up vegetables that are, at most, three hours out of the soil. We have folks call us in the middle of their meals to tell us how great the food tastes.

Moreover, "fresh" also means nutritional wholeness. The longer the vegetables are out of the soil, the greater the loss of vitamins. Three days after spinach is harvested, it will have lost 30% of its vitamins. The staying power of nutritional content does vary: brassicas, such as cabbage and broccoli, keep their nutritional value much longer than succulents, like leafy greens. Just watch the wilt factor, and you can tell how soon a vegetable loses its vitamin content.

Fresh Means Local

Truly fresh foods come from your own garden, or your CSA grower, or a store that carries local produce. As you can tell from the notations in this book, most of the fruits, vegetables and meats grown in America originated in another part of the world, and have been naturalized to America's regional climates and soils. Why, then, does the U.S. import any of the foods we are able to raise here? Obviously, the answer is that it is often cheaper to buy the foods grown in far away places than to source them locally. However, any food that has traveled more than a few miles is almost certainly inferior in quality to food grown where it is consumed. Foods raised for shipping are bred to have a long shelf life and endure packing and long-distance travel. Typically, imported fruits and vegetables are picked green so that they can "ripen" on the road. Since natural sugars develop only when the plants take in solar energy on the vine, long-distance foods are inferior in taste and nutrition to foods grown and distributed locally. One of our interns did a presentation at the local Farmers Market. She sliced some of our homegrown tomatoes and put them next to sliced tomatoes from the grocery store, which had been grown in Israel. She invited people to taste them. The result? We had a barrage of phone calls and visits from people wanting to buy our tomatoes. We understood, since we have never wanted to eat foods that are better traveled than we are.

Because commercial crops have been chosen for their ability to withstand long journeys and many days in the produce section and your refrigerator, nutritional value, crop variety, taste, and scent have been sidelined in order to privilege staying power.

The cost of imported foods has serious consequences. A typical morsel of food travels 1400 miles from field to plate, changing hands six times at great environmental cost. Food miles – the number of miles it takes for a food to get to market – are very important. One kilo of asparagus from California uses four kilos of aviation fuel to get to Maine. "It takes about 10 fossil fuel calories to produce and transport each food calorie in the average American diet."[1] The use of fuels in the production, processing, and distribution of foods is a primary source of the greenhouse gases that are changing the global climate. Much of the beef served by fast-food restaurants in the U.S. is raised in Latin America, requiring that rain forests burn to create pasture for cattle, and that indigenous farmers are dispossessed of ancestral lands by

---

[1] Center for Ecoliteracy, June 29, 2009. *https://www.ecoliteracy.org/article/fossil-food-consuming-our-future*. Retrieved 1/1/2020.

foreign corporate owners, thereby losing the ability to feed themselves as they had for centuries. And, while there are few enough controls on the use of hormones and antibiotics in cattle raised in the U.S., there are even fewer in Latin America; in the flesh of imported animals, we import chemical substances that are illegal in our own country.

We contribute to waste and pollution even if we import food from other regions of the U.S. Every time we buy pork or corn products from the Midwest we contribute to the dead sea (now larger than New Jersey) that lies in the Gulf of Mexico. Toxic chemical effluents from huge pig farms and endless cornfields flow into the Mississippi, destroying life all the way up the food chain, and emptying poisons into the Gulf. In factory farms everywhere, animals are raised in appalling conditions, massed in feedlots so close together that the inevitable spread of disease has to be controlled through antibiotics. Those drugs end up in markets and on plates far away.

Transporting food over long distances contributes to waste, because a substantial portion is delivered past the date for freshness. According to the U.S. Department of Agriculture, one-fifth of America's food goes to waste each year, with an estimated 130 pounds of food per person ending up in landfills. Foods that outlive their cosmetic profiles in grocery stores or are scraped off plates in homes or restaurants are usually not composted, but become garbage. The food that goes into landfills — often wrapped in plastic — contributes eight percent of carbon emissions, almost three times more than air travel. Released into the atmosphere, these emissions exacerbate climate change.

When you buy local foods, you learn to accept some oddly shaped tomatoes, or a few bugs in the cabbage — evidence of organic practices — because you know that the food is good tasting and wholesome.

Crop variety, and the biodiversity it depends on, are seriously undermined by commercial growers'

selection of foods that will withstand shipping. Since they must choose fruits and vegetables for shipping and shelf life, large growers generally do not raise heirloom varieties that may be delicious and nutritious when harvested ripe and sold quickly in local markets, but will turn to mush in long-distance transport. Heirloom varieties are therefore disappearing, and with them, the genetic diversity that protects cultivars when attacked by pests or disease. The Irish Potato Famine in the 1800s, for example, was caused by planting a single variety — the Irish Lumper — instead of diverse strains that would have protected the potatoes from the blight that destroyed the entire crop and starved a nation.

Fifty years ago, there were 5000 different varieties of seeds available in catalogs. Today, there are 500. This is because large seed companies are buying up smaller ones and reducing the range of available seeds. If you are a gardener, you probably get ten different catalogs per season. The names of the catalogs differ, but the seeds offered come from the same company. The parent company gets its seeds — mostly patented hybrids developed for high productivity with chemical inputs, from a single source, which may be in Europe, India, or China, and its primary goal is to sell seeds used by large commercial growers. A limited number of catalogs, however, do offer heirloom (non-hybrid) varieties, and these must be grown out every year if the varieties are to survive and remain available to future growers. Gardeners who save and share their own (non-commercial) seed are also able to grow heirloom varieties, thereby helping to preserve genetic diversity, and providing foods that are flavorful and nutritionally dense.

Not only seed production, but food production, is being consolidated into fewer and fewer hands. Five corporations control the world's grain supply, for example. A recent study of the food processing industry showed that no more than 138 men and women sit on the boards of directors of the ten firms that account for over half of all commercially raised food in America. Just as with seed catalogs, the names and labels are misleading. A hundred different brand names can be owned and controlled by a single company — Phillip Morris, tobacco manufacturer, among them.

Just as names of seed catalogs may mislead us about who controls and distributes the seed, so labels about the origin and contents of processed foods also mislead us. Elizabeth grew up with ads for the Jolly Green Giant, and naively believed that he grew and distributed the vegetables in the fields pictured behind him. Originally, there was a real corporation that controlled the fields and foods that came from them. But today, Green Giant grows, produces, and distributes nothing. Its farms and factories were sold off years ago, and only the brand name remains and is marketed. The consumer has no way of knowing where the peas come from and how they are grown, at what nutritional, social and ecological cost.

More troubling is what labels don't tell us. Companies that produce and market genetically modified foods spend billions of dollars to keep labeling laws from being passed. They don't want us to know about the fish gene in tomatoes or the genetically modified corn in taco shells: we might choose not to buy the product. And, if consumers have an allergic reaction to the foreign gene, or to the bacterium, antibiotic or protein used to carry the gene into the seed — the cause of allergic reaction or illness can't be traced to the producer of the genetically altered product. So the biodiversity we depend upon for our food security, health and ecological sustainability, is best assured by growing our own, or buying locally. Small farms that sell to local folks can grow heirloom varieties for their flavor, nutrition, color, and size. Compare the lettuce or apples from the supermarket with those from your own garden, at a local farmers market or your CSA, and taste the difference.

In Summary, Why Buy Local Foods?

If you buy local foods:

~The food travels from the farmer's hand to your hand, not thousands of miles.

~You have a personal relationship with the farmer and you can see how the food is grown — most small farms on Lopez Island use organic methods.

~You help preserve a local farming economy and culture.

~You strengthen the food security of your community.

~You maintain plant diversity.

~You preserve open spaces and the complex ecology that farms create.

~You avoid unforeseen, toxic consequences for human and environmental health from genetic alteration of plants and animals.

~You have a great place to take guests and children! We have guided up to ten formal tours of our farm each year, and in the summer we typically host weekly visits from customers' children, grandchildren, and guests who love to see the pigs, hold the chickens, cuddle the lambs, pet the milk cow, and wander around the gardens, flower beds, orchards, barns, and pond. If this sounds trivial, think about the number of young people who have no idea where their food comes from, and whose closest contact with animals may be a pet, or a petting zoo.

Does Organic Mean Nutritious?

According to *Organic Gardening,* "Fruit and vegetables grown organically contain, on average, 27% more vitamin C, 21% more iron, 29% more magnesium, 14% more phosphorus, and 15% fewer nitrates than conventional produce."[2] We need to add a caveat here, however. According to the USDA, "organic" means only that the food was raised free of chemical pesticides, herbicides, fertilizers, sewage sludge or genetic modification. Nutritional health, however, comes from soil health, which is more than absence of man-made inputs. Soil is the nutritional source and digestive system of the plant. The biological sources of vitamins, minerals, enzymes, proteins and phytonutrients are

---

[2] *Organic Gardening* (Sept/Oct 2003).

in the soil – or not. If the soil has been leached by water, its micro-organic life killed by chemicals or mechanical compaction, thus depleting soil organic matter, essential nutritional elements will be absent. Even if they are present, their transfer from soil to plant has to take place, a process requiring bacteria and other microorganisms, which absorb the nutritional elements from the soil into their bodies, move them to the roots of the plant, and exchange the nutrition they carry for carbohydrates. This exchange requires a layered soil structure, air, moisture, light and warmth. A brief example: Ten years ago, we had a cold spring. Very little grew, and overwintering plants, such as leeks, developed purple leaves. A visiting soil biologist, Steve Fransen, explained that the plants suffered from a lack of phosphorus. Tests showed that there was plenty of phosphorus in the soil, but the vehicular microorganisms were dormant because of the cold. Once the weather improved and warmed the ground, the soil fauna became active and the alliums thrived.

Healthy soil structure means not only that the soil is loose and friable, but that the natural texture resulting from the work of bacteria, fungi, earthworms and other soil organisms is left undisturbed as much as possible — one reason that our rototiller that causes soil compaction and destruction of the fungi holding the soil together, has been retired. Instead of a rototiller, or even a shovel or spading fork, we use "Big Bertha," a huge fork-like tool with 2-foot tines (built by a local welder) that loosens the soil without disturbing the layers, air spaces, and crumb structure created by fungal and bacterial action.

If the soil they were grown in is lacking in micro-organic life, or if the transfer of nutrients cannot happen due to disturbed soil structure, or if the soil is insufficiently warm or moist, vegetables will produce fiber but not much else. Therefore, while "organic" foods are certainly preferable to those that come laden with poisons and synthetic chemicals, more is required for foods to be nutritionally whole.

The health value of organic foods can also be compromised by transport, processing and packaging. You will note in the section on carrots, for example, that the organic "baby carrots" sold in many stores are often large carrots that have been peeled down to a uniform size, and thus robbed of most of the vitamins residing in the skin. And, as food researcher Buck Levin notes: "An organically grown food might escape toxic contamination by pesticides, heavy metals, and other sewage sludge components, only to be packaged in thin-film plastics that subsequently migrate into the food." We return to the issue of buying local foods. You can visit the farmers and their compost piles. You can sift the soil in your hands, smell it, and taste it — it sounds odd, but it's a traditional way for farmers to ascertain the health of their soils. You can ask questions. You can buy directly from the farmer, and you can even help the farmer produce and harvest good vegetables and other foods for yourself, family, and neighbors. In other words, you can, even without a garden of your own, contribute directly to the health of your foods and thereby, your own health.

Seasonal

Ah, this is the tough issue. Americans are so accustomed to the variety of imported foods that "choice" comes second only after price in decision-making. We buy California strawberries in March, even though they come laden with up to fifty-two different pesticides and herbicides and taste like styrofoam. We insist on oranges in December, even though fresh kale and a crisp apple from storage provide the same food value.

To show how marketing and advertising mislead consumers, recall *Moscow on the Hudson*, the film starring Robin Williams as a Russian musician who defects to the U.S. and faints at the apparent range of "choice" of coffees at the supermarket, not realizing they are uniformly of poor quality and, most likely, raised and harvested under conditions unhealthful for land, growers, and consumers.

Seasonal foods are whole foods. An apple is a whole food – commercially processed apple juice is not, because it lacks most of the fiber, and all of the enzymes, and some of the vitamins have been destroyed by pasteurization. Most processed foods have had at least some of their nutritional value stripped away. For example, whole grain wheat, whose products account for 18% of caloric intake for U.S. adults, provides at least 17 nutrients contained in the endosperm, germ, and bran. By contrast, in refined grains only the endosperm is retained. More than half of the nutrients are lost in flour extraction, of which only four are replaced by "enrichment." Unfortunately, the multi-million dollar weight loss industry promotes the idea that whole foods are somehow unwholesome. We are urged to buy foods for what they don't contain — fat, sodium, sugar, carbohydrates — rather than for what they do. Processed foods replace nutrients with artificial flavors, colors, and stabilizers, such as trans-fatty acids, which may be carcinogenic.

Buying seasonal, local, whole foods requires knowing how to cook, and being willing to eat them. Liver is a good case in point. Many of our beef customers do not want the liver, because they learned that, as organ meat, liver contains concentrated toxins — in non-organic beef, it does; in organic, grass-fed beef, it does not. Or their memory of liver is of a hard-fried, nasty brown slab served up by Mom when finances were tight. Or the idea of eating liver vaguely bothers them. As a result, we keep most of the liver from our slaughtered animals for ourselves. It is firm, deep red in color, and delicious fried with onions and a bit of lemon peel. We also keep the heart, oxtail, tongue, and hanging tender. Baked, in soup, pickled, fried, or made into sausage, these are the most flavorful and nutritious parts of the animal.

Teaching people how to prepare seasonal foods lies at the heart of this book. Elizabeth had never eaten kale, chard, kohlrabi or savoy cabbage until Henning — who had enjoyed these foods since childhood — started a Fall/Winter CSA. Since kale and other winter vegetables' being "good for you"

won't put them on anybody's plate, we developed recipes that featured the week's vegetables and passed them on to our CSA members. And yes, we enjoy these dishes ourselves. Last night, for example, we served kale cooked with potatoes and a few herbs. Lacking fresh tomatoes, we softened some dried tomatoes in olive oil, and then sautéed them together with fresh onion. We topped the dish with homemade feta cheese, and fought over the last scraps. (For the recipe, see *Kale* in *Vegetables*.)

Being willing to cook is also a challenge. Dollars spent on food from restaurants match dollars spent on food eaten at home, and most of that is not prepared from scratch or from fresh ingredients. But people still dream of home cooked food. Recipes abound in magazines, and cookbooks are among the most popular books sold. Cooking shows are available 24 hours a day on media, and draw huge audiences – mostly teenagers hungering for a "kitchen culture." The reasons for eating out or ordering in usually have to do with the assumed need for two incomes and the perceived lack of time. After a full day on the job, coming home to children and chores may put cooking last on the list of priorities. But it seems sad to watch a TV chef prepare a meal and then go out to dinner, and the economics may deserve some reconsideration. Our friend Susan reluctantly left homemaking to get a job, intending to add to the savings account. But she found that, during her working years, the family "simply hemorrhaged money," eating in restaurants and the school cafeteria. Too tired to cook after a full day's work, Susan would order pizza or Chinese food, or the family ate out. After figuring the costs and benefits, which included their time together as a family, Susan quit her job. The next year, she found that the family had more money than before. They had moved to a lower income tax bracket, and had spent half the money on groceries than they had on food prepared outside the home.

Sustainable

When you buy locally, you contribute to a

sustainable ecology. For us, "sustainable" means that our intricate farm system can go on forever. The farm is a self-sufficient organism that provides for most of its own needs, including animal feed and soil fertility. We do not exhaust the soil: our pasture management is designed so animals do not overgraze but fertilize the pastures, trample seed into the ground, and do not require antibiotics or vermifuges. We do not import fertility: kitchen and garden wastes, animal manures and slaughter offal are composted, and, together with cover crops, renew the soil every year. We save seed. Our animals live in closed herds, cows and bull, ewes and ram, chickens and rooster, turkey hens and tom, producing calves, lambs, chicks and poults every year. "Sustainable" also means that we produce most of the foods we eat: meat, herbs, vegetables, fruit, grain, and dairy products. We have no need for commercially produced vitamins, supplements, or medications. We go to the store for toilet paper, cleaning supplies, coffee, spices, and olive oil. We minimize the use of fossil fuels and maximize solar inputs. To buy your food from a sustainable, organic farm or grow it in your own garden means that you become part of saving soil and water, fostering animal husbandry to produce contented animals and healthy meat, and contributing that much less to climate change.

Health

According to a recent article in *The New York Times,* Americans now spend more on health care than on food, not including money spent on health insurance, medications, or supplements, which many people consider necessary to compensate for the nutritional deficiencies of conventionally produced foods. According to a note in *Acres USA,* a government study that tracked the nutrient levels in fruits and vegetables for 50 years found that today's offerings are less abundant in key nutrients than those of the 1950s. The USDA monitored 13 major nutrients in fruits and vegetables from 1950 to 1999 with six showing noticeable drop-offs — protein, calcium, phosphorus, iron, riboflavin and

vitamin C. The declines ranged from 6 percent for protein, 15 percent for iron, 20 percent for vitamin C, to 38 percent for riboflavin.[3] The decline in nutritive value is partially due to industrial growers' choosing varieties that will grow rapidly. Fast-growing vegetables cannot acquire the nutrients that slower-growing plants can, from photosynthesis and the soil. As a local physician quipped, "In 1950, Popeye could get all the strength he needed from a can of spinach. Today he would have to eat a bathtub of spinach to get the same power."

So what are the repercussions? One out of three Americans is clinically obese. Seven out of ten develop cancer. Diabetes, allergies, colitis, and asthma are on the rise. Developmental, learning and behavior problems in children, such as autism, ADD and ADHD, are growing rapidly. Our local physician is seeing children in elementary school with early-onset diabetes or at risk for heart disease. Although there are other possible causes, all of these illnesses are related to a diet of processed and denatured foods. The connection between illness and diet is well established. Some physicians hold that the Covid-19 outbreak is the result of world-wide nutritional deficiencies that weaken the immune system. The solution to weakened health is as simple as it is daunting, given today's fast-paced, fast food culture: Buy fresh, local, organic foods, and eat seasonally. Physical health is part of a larger issue. As Barbara Kingsolver writes in *Animal, Vegetable, Miracle:* "Modern American culture is fairly empty of any suggestion that one's relationship to the land, to consumption and food, is a religious matter. But it's true; the decision to attend to the health of one's habitat and food chain is a spiritual choice; it is also a political choice, and scientific one, a personal and a convivial one."

For example, envision a farm in Kansas before World War II. There was a farmhouse, surrounded by trees, a picnic table under them. There were barns for hay, a corral for horses that pulled the plows and harrows, chickens for eggs, pigs and a few cows for meat and dairy. Now those family

---

[3] *Acres USA* (August, 2006).

farms are gone, as are the towns with churches and stores and community halls that served them. The farms have been replaced with agribusinesses, supported by government subsidies, growing one crop, mostly corn or soybeans, which become unhealthy additives for commercially processed food or are fed to animals, such as cows, that cannot properly digest them. The soil and water are polluted with pesticides, herbicides, and fungicides. Birds and wild animals are gone, because there is no habitat to support them. There are only acres of corn or soybeans as far as the eye can see.

What happened to the farm animals? They were moved into CAFOs (Confined Animal Feeding Operations). "Factory farms" is a more common term, although the word "farm" is misused here. "Factory" is appropriate, since animals are treated like machines, called "production units" and are unable to live anything like the lives they lived on that Kansas farm.

Laying hens are crammed five or six to a cage. The stress caused by overcrowding and the frustration of every natural instinct causes them to rub their breasts against the cage wire until they are featherless and bleeding. They cannibalize their cage mates, so as chicks they are "debeaked" with a hot knife. When their egg production begins to fall off, they are starved of food, water, and light for several days. As the hen begins to die, she tries to produce life, and will give a few more eggs before the end.

Broiler chickens, a breed specialized for rapid growth, are not kept in cages because they might scar the breast meat if they rubbed against the wire. Unless organically raised, they are given antibiotics, hormones, and even arsenic (which increases their appetite). They are slaughtered at seven weeks of age, because their growth is so rapid that their hearts would stop and their legs would break if they lived longer. We once raised some Cornish cross hens. Because our chickens run around all day, they are muscular; they make excellent broth, but their meat is tough. Hungry for fried chicken, we got a dozen Cornish cross chicks, and tried to raise them

naturally. Because these chickens are bred to grow fast and be slaughtered while the meat is still tender, they have weakened immune systems, so commercial growers routinely put antibiotics in their feed. We did not. We fed them the same as our laying hens: ground barley, fresh vegetables, cooked potatoes, and table scraps. These chicks were the sweetest birds we'd ever raised. They had trusting, gentle natures, and funny croaky little voices. But they did not act like chickens. They did not forage for food. They did not run around. They did not establish hierarchies among themselves. They did not take sun baths or dust baths, or have much to say to each other. And, sadly, some of them could not defecate. It was awful to watch their beaks and combs grow pale, and see how listless they became. They were unable to survive in a natural environment. We managed to get six through to maturity. We have no memory of eating them. The whole experience was too sad.

The overall picture of CAFOs is an ugly one. Thousands of pigs crowded into a single building, or each in a cage so narrow the pig cannot turn around. Because they are bred to produce lean meat — a big selling point in fat-conscious America — their natural hardiness has been bred out of them. When strangers enter the building — in hazmat suits to protect the immunity-deficient animals from disease — they are met with the screams of terrified, overstressed animals.

CAFO cows, like Cornish cross hens and factory-farmed pigs, are treated as producers of marketable food, and as "animal units." It begins with feed. Cows evolved to eat grass. Their stomachs have four chambers that allow them to convert cellulose into protein. Under natural circumstances, cows graze, ruminate, and fertilize pastures with their manure. CAFO cows are fed corn-based concentrates and in some instances cardboard, stale pastry, or brewery wastes. They stand crowded in feedlots up to their knees in manure, do not move in pastures, raise their young, or in any other way live out their lives as cows should. They, too, are given antibiotics to prevent the spread of disease and the illnesses caused by their diet.

Indeed, about 80% of the antibiotics in America are consumed by dairy cows, chickens and pigs. Consumers take in the residues of the antibiotics in milk, eggs, and meat, causing the general population to become increasingly immune to antibiotics. As a result, the effectiveness of antibiotics against infections in humans is greatly diminished.

Feeding antibiotics has produced superbugs that are difficult to control. The lethal strain of e-coli bacteria that appeared in the 1980s — in beef, apple juice, and spinach, for example — evidently evolved in the guts of feedlot cattle from e-coli bacteria that survived the antibiotics. Grass-fed cattle do not carry this e-coli strain because in the absence of antibiotics, the virulent bacteria never develop. The Center for Disease Control and Prevention estimates that our commercial food supply now sickens 76 million Americans every year, putting more than 300,000 in the hospital and killing 5,000.

Social justice is another issue to consider when sourcing your food. Take the meat industry, for example: people employed in slaughterhouses have dangerous jobs. Because of the speed of their work, and the repetitive motions they must use, they suffer lacerations, loss of limbs, broken bones, torn muscles, slipped discs, pinched nerves. Every year one quarter of the meatpacking workers in this country — about forty thousand men and women — are recorded to suffer from a work-related injury or illness. Thousands go unrecorded. Workers avoid reporting injuries for fear of being fired or deported.

According to Eric Schlosser's *Fast Food Nation* (2002), by 1980 government oversight of plant safety was so minimal that a single plant could expect a visit from the Occupational Safety and Health Administration (OSHA) once every eighty years. Since March 2020, there have been only 61 federal and state inspections of American meat processing plants. Inspections have yielded little help for workers in meat plants during Covid 19. By July 2020 workers had filed 7,943 complaints regarding the lack of adequate protective gear and safe distancing, but OSHA issued only four citations.[4] Similar conditions circumscribe the work of harvesters picking field crops. Harvesters in non-organic fields take in pesticides and herbicides through their skin, and they and their children get sick from eating the foods they pick. Working and living in close quarters, they now are also subject to the Corona virus. The federal government has not made safety rules mandatory, leaving it to farmers' discretion to enact protective measures. Some farms have rebuilt workers' housing to lessen overcrowding, and installed hand-washing stations and imposed mask requirements. But efforts are inconsistent, allowing the virus to spread as harvesters move from place to place.

The health, environmental, ethical, and social costs of an industrialized, corporate-run food system are high. But each of us has a choice. "Eating is an agricultural act," Wendell Berry writes. What we choose to buy will be grown and sold. Not only can we purchase local foods, but we can change the system. Consumer demand puts organic milk and meats and fruits and vegetables on the shelves of grocery stores and locally sourced foods in our schools, hospitals, and restaurants. We have many examples right here on Lopez Island.

In our island stores the first section is organic produce, some of it locally sourced. The natural foods store carries many local fruits and vegetables, and those obtained from elsewhere are nearly all organic. The store features raw milk from the nearby mainland, as well as island-made raw milk cheeses.

Culture shift is possible. When Henning arrived on Lopez Island fifty years ago with a pickup full of shovels and hoes, and said to the attendant at a gas

---

[4] *The Washington Post*, 7/23/2020. https://www.washingtonpost.com/business/2020/07/23/lawsuit-osha-safety-coronavirus/. Retrieved 8/25/2020.

station that he had come here to farm, he was told "Farming is dead in the islands." San Juan County farms, which until WWII had fed the islands and provided the near mainland with dairy products, fruit, vegetables, grain and fish, had been supplanted by farms east of the mountains made possible by government-built dams on the Columbia River. In 1970 there remained only a couple of farms on the island, raising mostly grain and beef and exporting their products to the mainland instead of feeding the island.

The 2019-2020 *Farm Products Guide* (produced by the Lopez Community Land Trust), now lists nearly 30 farms on Lopez Island, and this count does not include every farmer or market gardener. Products listed in the guide include goat and cow milk cheeses; vegetables, flowers, herbs and seedlings; beef, pork, and lamb; eggs, broiler chickens, and turkeys; tree fruits, berries, and wine; grain; hay; shellfish; walnuts and hazelnuts; breads and pastries; skin care and herbal products. Many are carried by local stores and restaurants. Many people on the island grow food in gardens, and raise animals for their own use and for sale to neighbors; local fishers supply salmon, cod, halibut, rock cod, and other seafood, seasonally.

There are several CSAs on the island, where people can subscribe for a basket of fruits, vegetables, herbs, (sometimes cheeses, bread, eggs, and meat) distributed on a weekly basis. One of these, Lopez Community Farm on S&S Homestead, raises money every year from The Lions Club, The Thrift Store, and four faith communities to supply a healthy diet to families chosen by the Family Resource Center. This year, the *San Juan Islands Food Hub* (SJIFH) was established to coordinate the sales and distribution of products from the San Juan Islands and thereby make locally grown food readily available to local eaters.

A star in the crown of the local food system is the L.I.F.E. Program (Lopez Island Farm Education) at the Lopez Island School District. It began in 2002 as a joint project of the Heller Family Foundation

and S&S Homestead Farm, to supply students with heathy food and teach them how to grow it sustainably.

Today, the school garden is comprised of an orchard, multiple vegetable beds, and four hoop houses. Students' work in the garden is integrated with their academic curriculum, including geography, mathematics, history, language, social studies, art, and music. Students are fully engaged in growing, processing, serving and eating what they grow. The yearly monetary value of food from the garden served in the school cafeteria is about $30,000; the educational and health benefits are beyond measure. The program has become internationally known, and is featured in the book *Smart by Nature —Schooling for Sustainability*.

Inspired by the L.I.F.E. Program, and originally sponsored by the Heller Foundation, the Lopez Locavores, a group of farmers, chefs, and volunteers, host monthly Evening Meals at School. The delicious dinners, made from foods purchased from local farmers, and served in the school cafeteria, bring people together over a great meal. One menu featured ratatouille with local goat chèvre, toasted millet pilaf, slaw of seasonal greens, chocolate beet brownies, and island herb tea. Admission is by donation, and families sit at tables decked with flowers, and visit with friends they might see only on these occasions. There is often music, a slide presentation, or a tour of the school gardens.

During the shut down due to Covid 19, when schools were closed and the Senior Center unable to continue their usual lunches, the Center switched to Meals on Wheels, delivering lunches to seniors and shut-ins. The Locavores took on Grow-A-Row produce distribution, and packaged the fresh food donated by local farmers to be sent with Meals on Wheels or picked up at the Center.
The Family Resource Center gathers donations to purchase locally grown foods for distribution to families in need, and works with churches, the Locavores, and other groups to see that fresh and

processed food gets to the people who need it. During the summer, they delivered the weekly shares for Lopez Community Farm CSA, for example, and they house Lopez Fresh stocked with donations from farmers and gardeners. Churches and individuals supply the Food Bank with non-perishable foods, and the local Lutheran Church contributes funds to purchase dairy and eggs for Lopez Fresh.

These examples speak clearly to the power of a community to sustain and feed itself, and care for those in need. When Henning and Elizabeth talked to their apprentice about the fact that, during the Covid 19 outbreak, pig farmers in the Midwest were having to slaughter their pigs and piglets because slaughterhouses were closing, he said, "That wouldn't be a problem if animal raising and small slaughterhouses were local."

Indeed, the islands and Skagit County have the service of the Mobile Slaughter Unit, based in Bow, Washington. Previously, local farmers had to ship their livestock hundreds of miles away in order to have federal meat inspection — an expensive undertaking, and stressful to the animals. Henning conceived of a local, mobile unit that could come to individual farms with a federal inspector, slaughter the animals where they had been born and lived, take the carcass in a refrigerated truck to the processing facility, to be cut and wrapped to the buyers' specifications.

Henning spent two years talking with people from the USDA, who said such a project was impossible. Then he found a federal law from 1928 that all Americans are entitled to free meat inspection. He took the project to the Lopez Island Community Land Trust. With a major grant, a lot of planning and design, the Mobile Unit — now adopted by several states in the U.S. — came into being.

As the world faces the conundrum of simultaneous hunger and food waste, pandemics, climate change, depletion of natural resources, species extinction, water, soil, and air pollution, chronic illnesses, we

see that individuals can make an enormous difference by the way they live, eat, and treat the world around them. Eating local and seasonally produced food is probably the most important step, because it is a step all of us can take.

A Seasonal Calendar For Farmers, Gardeners, and Eaters

The key to eating locally and sustainably is eating seasonally. Farmers, gardeners, and consumers live by the weather and rhythms of each season — often in anticipation of the next — so we divide this chapter into Winter (December to March), Spring (March to June), Summer (June to September), and Fall (September to December), and discuss what happens in garden and field, the kitchen and the table throughout the agricultural year.

Winter (December to March)

In anticipation of the growing season to come, December is a time to tend your compost pile. Compost is waste turned into a money-saving, effective resource that contributes to farm and household self-sufficiency. Compost is not only a source of fertility for the gardens, but also a key to the inter-connectedness of the whole farm organism: what table scraps cannot be fed to the dog, chickens, pigs, and cows go into the compost pile; so does litter from the chicken and turkey pens and the hay and manure from the night stall of the dairy cow and calf; shredded twigs and branches from the fruit trees and berry bushes, and offal from slaughtered animals are composted; compost turns into planting soil, and the vegetables growing in that soil feed the animals, the farm household, and the community.

We maintain five separate compost piles for different purposes: hay and garden waste mixed with manure and slaughter offal for soil fertility; spoiled hay for mulching garden beds; mineral-rich deciduous leaves for mulching flower beds; high-nitrogen dairy and poultry composts for potting soil and seedlings; chipped twigs and tree branches for animal bedding, pathways between flower beds, and the muddier parts of the farm.

Winter is the time to build cold frames. (Elliot Coleman in *The Four Season Garden* gives specific instructions for building these boxes.) It is also the time to maintain and repair buildings, machines, fences and tools, to slaughter cows, goats, pigs,

lambs, turkeys, chickens, geese, rabbits, and tend the animals you will carry over until the next year. If you purchase meat from a local farmer, now is the time to put in your order. It is time to mulch and put gardens to bed, and clear them of crops and weeds to prepare the soil for spring planting; to sow cover crops; store dried beans and root crops, such as potatoes, winter squash, onions, garlic, and shallots, and mulch those left in the soil for fresh harvest throughout the fall and winter, such as beets, kale, winter broccoli, Brussels sprouts, red cabbage, parsnips, rutabaga, turnips, celeriac, carrots, chard, and herbs. We store sugar beets in a clamp in the ground (see *Keeping the Harvest*).

January and February are the months to prune your fruit trees and berry bushes before they bud. There are many books and local gardeners to show you how, if you are unsure of what to do.

In the greenhouse, start the artichoke plants that will provide fruit for years. With plenty of compost, fertilize the asparagus bed you have dug in the fall, and purchase male and female crowns — male crowns produce thicker and larger spears — planting them two months before your last frost date. Like artichokes, these are permanent plantings. Both are harvested in spring and early summer. Plant garlic in fall or early winter, choosing the best bulbs from the year before. Check seed catalogs for the best planting date for our region.

In January, seed catalogs begin to arrive. You may have saved your own seed, but if you order it, be sure it is non-GMO, and suited to our climate and soils. Plan your garden, making sure that in order to prevent club root, you don't plant brassicas in the same bed as the year before, and that nitrogen-fixing crops, such as legumes, follow high-nitrogen using crops, such as corn. We have kept records of garden plans for many years so that we know what has been planted in each bed the years before. We recommend that you consult John Jeavons, *How to Grow More Vegetables, and Fruits, Nuts, Berries, Grains, and Other Crops Than You Ever Thought Possible on Less Land with Less Water Than You Can Imagine, 9th edition.*

Another basic source we recommend for both new and experienced gardeners, is *Rodale's Basic Organic Gardening: A Beginner's Guide to Starting a Healthy Garden*. We especially rely on the 1947 edition, which we call "Our Green Bible." If you are interested in biodynamic management, consult our website at sshomestead.org.

Eating seasonally in winter means making use of root crops in storage, vegetables in garden and freezer — our favorite frozen winter vegetables are peas and corn — or from farm stands or stores that provide local produce. It means using the fermented and canned foods you put up in the summer, and getting to the bottom of the freezer to make room for the meats, vegetables, berries and fruits you have coming. Splendid December dinners might be made from dried beans, meat, and fresh and fermented winter vegetables. For example, try *Beans with Attitude, Braised Pork Chops,* and *Sauerkraut* for a dinner (recipes in this book).

Winter is also a time to sit by a bright fire with a friend, a good book, a cup of tea or glass of wine, and plan for the coming year. Don't forget to celebrate Winter Solstice during this dark time of the year.

In February, that coming year is upon us. Seeds have arrived, and can be put into pots or a growing pit in the greenhouse as soon as warmth and light are sufficient. You can start seeds in a window in your house, and transplant them as soon as they are hardy. Your first crops will be the early greens, such as lettuce, spinach, chard, arugula, corn salad, and early radishes. Leafy greens are filled with vitamins, minerals, and phytonutrients, and are the first line of defense against the common cold as well as macular degeneration. Many of these crops are "cut and come again" — take off the larger leaves from the outside or cut a whole plant, leaving two inches at the bottom. They will regrow, and you will have a steady supply. Plant seeds of brassicas, such as broccoli and cauliflower.

Consult a planting calendar (many seed catalogs have them) for the right time to begin seeding peas, beans, and other summer crops. Putting seeds or seedlings in the ground at the right time depends on the soil — it needs to be relatively dry and friable — and the last frost date. With the changing climate, these crucial times have been changing in our region, so be patient. Seed will rot if planted too soon.

Gain access to bones from pork, beef, chicken, turkey, lamb, or goat, and make broth. We add onion, garlic, carrots, celery and peppercorns to the cooking water, and simmer slowly for three days, which releases the bone marrow. Process the broth in a pressure canner, and use for soups, stews, and for cooking beans and rice all the rest of the year. These broths are among the most healthful foods you can eat, due to their collagen, plentiful vitamins and minerals. Time to get the bones out of the freezer and onto the shelves.

Spring (March to June)

First plantings in the garden! The soil should be dry and friable, and the date past your last frost — around April 15 on Lopez Island. Take the greens and brassica seedlings you have grown and hardened off — putting them outside during the day in a sheltered place to toughen up against wind and rain, and taking them in at night. Seed sugar peas, shelling peas, beets, turnips, parsnips, kohlrabi, carrots, leeks, onions, herbs, and potatoes. Beans, pumpkins, squash, cucumbers, and corn follow once the soil has warmed to 50 degrees.

In the greenhouse, start the crops that need special warmth for germination: melons, peppers, tomatoes, and basil, for example. Transplant them when the weather is warm enough into a sheltered place that has been mulched and fertilized — we put ours into a high tunnel hoop house.

Turn the cover crops you planted in the fall into the soil deeply enough that no green remains showing above the soil. They will provide tilth and nitrogen for the vegetables to follow. In a couple of weeks, the coarse greens from the cover crops will be absorbed into the soil, devoured by the micro-organic life there. When you are ready to plant, simply rake the soil; no rototilling required.

Raise flowers from seed or purchased pots. Many flowers, such as nasturtiums, are edible, and really dress up a salad. Nasturtiums also attract aphids and keep them off your tomato plants. Marigolds secrete a mild toxin that wards off moles and voles and mice, and thereby protect your brassicas. Other flowers nurture pollinators. Lavender, cerinthe, borage and rosemary, among other herbs and flowers, feed the bees, butterflies, and hummingbirds.

Put in an herb garden. Some plants, such as basil and cilantro, are annuals, but bushes of rosemary, sage, thyme, marjoram and oregano, will last for many years in the bed you dug and fertilized for them in the fall. Plant rhubarb in a place it can grow every year. One plant will serve you nicely. It can reside in a corner of your yard. The deer will not eat it, because the leaves contain an acid they avoid and you should not consume or give to your animals.

Seed a second round of greens, especially those you eat every day, such as lettuce and arugula. Plan on needing more greens than the "cut and come again" method will supply. Lettuce and other tender greens should be planted every three or four weeks. Succession planting is hard to remember, but it is painful to cut the last head of lettuce from your garden, and think, "Whoops! Where's the next one?" Put reseeding and transplanting on your calendar and stay on top of it.

Start making your own salad dressing. Bottled dressings are full of trans fats, sugars, and preservatives, and their artificial flavors overwhelm the subtle, complex taste of your greens. A simple vinaigrette, composed of olive oil, white balsamic vinegar, a pinch of sugar, salt, pepper, dried basil, mustard and garlic takes only a minute to make, and is wonderful over salads, on French bread, rice, or potatoes. (See *Lettuce* in *Vegetables* for other dressings for salad.)

Springtime means new life: chicks, turkey poults, calves, lambs, pigs. We purchase the chicks and pigs, because the brooding instinct has been bred out of the egg layers, and we don't breed the pigs because we don't have winter shelter for them. So we purchase egg-laying chicks every three years, raise them in the greenhouse under a heat lamp, and move them into the chicken run when old enough. We purchase heritage Guinea Hogs from a neighbor, and rotate them through runs to keep them on fresh grass. We feed them organic barley, whey, apples, cooked potatoes and other vegetables and fruits, to produce succulent pork. The turkeys hatch poults in spring, the cows calve, and the ewes lamb close to our house, so that we can observe them in labor and assist if needed. Soon there are lamb games, climbing onto the ram or chasing each other around the chestnut tree. Nothing in spring is more fun than watching lamb games.

In the kitchen, it is time for salads with sugar peas, lettuce, spinach, and radishes; freezing peas; making sauerkraut. Ham, chicken, beef, pork, lamb, and turkey make for celebratory meals — for Easter, Midsummer, birthday and outdoor parties.

Spring is the time to gain access to raw milk. If you don't have your own cow or goat, find someone on the island who does and will sell you milk. Because of the abundance of fresh grass in spring, cows give milk rich with cream, and milk from a grass-fed cow will give you butter, buttermilk, ice cream, yogurt, sour cream, whey, mozzarella, cottage cheese, cheddar, ricotta, and other homemade cheeses. This is the time to produce extra butter and cheese to eat later during the year when the grass is no longer abundant. (See *Dairy* for a full discussion of the benefits of raw milk, and for recipes for dairy products.)

Harvest garlic. June to August is the best time. Garlic scapes can be cut before then, and are a great addition to salads and casseroles. We grow soft neck garlic, which means that the stalks are pliable and can be braided. Brush off any dirt and cure the garlic on the warm soil. When cured, we braid the garlic and hang it in a shady, dry corner just outside our kitchen door, so we can snip off a bulb at a time — we use on average a head of garlic every day in some form. We also grow Elephant garlic, much larger and not suitable for storage, but wonderful fresh out of the garden.

Summer (July-September)

By July it is already time to plant overwintering crops, such as carrots, turnips, parsnips, rutabagas, and beets, kale and chard and another round of greens and annual herbs. It's hard to remember to do this because of the bounty you harvest every day now, but keep in mind how you will enjoy the winter crops all through the non-growing season.

Start preserving foods for the winter. Freeze the strawberries, raspberries, blueberries and currants you can't eat immediately. You can have peas and corn in December, salsa in February, blueberry muffins and strawberry shortcake and apple and blackberry pie all winter. If you aren't raising the foods you want to preserve, you can contract for them. Farmers who sell to grocery stores, at farmers markets, and to restaurants will always have fruits and vegetables that are cosmetically imperfect, and will be happy to sell them to you at a discount.

The basic equipment, such as freezer bags and a water bath canner, is inexpensive. The food dehydrator, juicing equipment, and pressure canner are more costly, but if you regard them as lifelong tools, the expense spreads over many years, and they are a good investment. Before you purchase any of these new, look around. Many people have canning jars that they no longer use, or a pressure canner that is just sitting in the attic. Really expensive items, like a cider press, can be shared. You can have a community "pressing" where everyone brings apples and pears, share the work and the cider.

Every year, we freeze:
- Strawberries, raspberries, blackberries, red and black currants, blueberries
- Corn
- Rhubarb
- Peas
- Sugar peas
- Green beans
- Marinated artichokes
- Leeks
- Pesto from basil, cilantro, and parsley

We make juice from:
- Apples
- Red and black currants
- Grapes
- Plums
- Pears

We dry:
- Apples
- Pears
- Plums
- Tomatoes (sprinkled with dried basil)
- Hot peppers

We can tomatoes as:
- Basil and tomato sauce
- Salsa
- Chili sauce
- Whole and crushed canned tomatoes
- Tomato soup
- Ketchup

We can or ferment cucumbers, zucchini, red peppers and onions as:

- Dill pickles
- Vegetable pickles
- Sweet pickles

We ferment cabbage as:
- Sauerkraut
- Kimchi

Yes, it's a lot of work. We call it "the race with rot," as the pickling cucumbers get large, the tomatoes soft. But it is well worthwhile. The berries can be eaten fresh for their own sweet sakes, or frozen, or made into jam. Marinated artichokes adorn salads, focaccia or pizza, or become a wonderful addition to quiche. Pesto is an instant pasta sauce, thinned with a little white wine and topped with homemade cheese. It is also great on sourdough rye bread.

In winter, we are grateful for the race with rot — all the canning, freezing, pickling, fermenting, jamming and juicing — when we can take a jar off the shelf or a package out of the freezer and have half the meal done. We only have to read the labels on most commercially canned foods to be glad we make our own.

Make fermented foods, such as sauerkraut and kimchi. Fermentation is one of the oldest forms of food preservation and one of the best.

Fermentation preserves food without cooking it, so all the enzymes — which carry the life force in the food — remain. Fermentation also breaks foods down into easily digested forms, enhances the availability of minerals in the food, and creates new nutrients. (See *Keeping the Harvest* for recipes and suggestions.)

Roast and freeze garlic, cook and freeze squash.

Make your own pumpkin pie filling for the holidays. Be sure that the pumpkin you grow or purchase is for eating, not carving. Cut the pumpkin into large pieces, cleaning out the seeds and saving them for roasting in olive oil and salt as a special treat, or to use as a topping for soups. Roast the pumpkin in a baking dish with a little water, and bake at 350 until the flesh is tender and the shell can be peeled off. Puree the flesh and freeze in one-cup servings in plastic freezer bags.

Elizabeth resisted this procedure when Henning first presented her with a pumpkin and had that pie gleam in his eye. She argued that you could buy canned pumpkin, so why bother to prepare your own? But then we were invited to Mark and Lois Brown's house for dinner, and Lois served a pumpkin pie that was golden and fragrant and delicious, quite unlike the brown, spiritless pies made from the can. Her recipe, which we have followed ever since, is in the *Pumpkin* section in the *Vegetable* chapter of this book.

Fall (September to December)

Before the rains come and while the sun still encourages growth, Fall is the time to plant cover crops in emptied beds. We plant a mix of winter peas, clover, and vetch, which restore nitrogen to the soil, and winter rye which replenishes the organic matter. The plants will be dug into the soil in the spring.

Fall is also the time to dig and fertilize beds for asparagus, artichokes and herbs, and plant garlic and shallots.

November through December is the big holiday that stretches on until after New Year's. Our biggest achievement in the last few years has been to simplify, simplify, simplify. Elizabeth grew up in a culture where holiday tables were supposed to be groaning with food, but we were the ones groaning after consuming it — or consigning way too many leftovers to the refrigerator. So we made it a practice to use only the foods we had raised ourselves, and keep the meal simple. Now, a typical Thanksgiving meal consists of baked ham or roasted turkey, mashed potatoes, Delicata squash, green peas from the freezer, and pumpkin pie. We do not spend all day cooking, there are not endless dishes to wash, and everyone rises from the table satisfied.

And that satisfaction, in working outdoors, being intimately involved with the life cycles and needs of soil, plants, and animals, having control over your own food for maximum health, is one reason to eat locally and seasonally. Another is knowing you are helping to mitigate climate change by avoiding being part of industrial agriculture, the machines, toxins, packaging, shipment, and waste. You can grow your own or purchase local foods, and support a local economy, while eating like royalty. Enjoy your meals, and enjoy this book!

Notes:

Recipe List

This *Recipe List* is a cross reference to the individual chapters outlined in the *Table of Contents*. It lists recipes alphabetically and by page number under the following groups: *Main Dishes; Side Dishes; Broths, Soups & Stews; Salads; Desserts; Dressings, Juices, Sauces, Tea & Condiments.*

Part 1. Main Dishes

Part II. Side Dishes

Part III. Broths, Soups & Stews

Vegetables

In Barbara Kingsolver's *Animal, Vegetable, Miracle: A Year of Food Life,* her daughter Camille notes that, since vegetables are stationary and can't avoid predators by running away, they have developed their own disease and pest-fighting compounds, such as antioxidants and phyto-chemicals. Because human beings evolved with these plants, those compounds benefit us, too, retarding cell aging and tumor growth. According to Harvard School of Public Health, eating vegetables helps prevent cardiovascular disease, such as heart attack and stroke; lowers blood pressure; fights cancer, diabetes and unwanted weight gain; aids vision; and improves gastrointestinal health. What's not to like?

Moreover, vegetables add potassium, fiber, folic acid, vitamins and minerals to a meal. While vegetables are best eaten fresh, they can be preserved by canning, fermenting, freezing, and other methods.

Two notes about nutritional information included in these entries:
~Some vitamins go by two different names: the common name, and the name of the vitamin subtype. Vitamin B complex is composed of several B vitamin subtypes: B-1 (thiamin), B-2 (riboflavin), B-3 (niacin), B-5 (pantothenic acid), B-6 (pyridoxine), B-7 (biotin), B-8 (inositol), B-9 (folic acid), and B-12 (cobalamin). Here we use the common name, listing other vitamins, such as A, C, E, and K, first and separately.
~There are many health claims for various vitamins and minerals. We recommend that you do research for your own needs.

Artichokes

Artichokes were cultivated in the Mediterranean area and spread to Europe from there. Artichokes contain vitamins A, C, E, K, pyridoxine, thiamin, riboflavin, niacin, pantothenic acid, folate, calcium, iron, magnesium, manganese, phosphorus, potassium, sodium, and zinc.

There is one kind of artichoke, called Green Globe, available in markets. These are grown year round in California, and are the big fat artichokes of which Lord Chesterfield said, "The artichoke is the only vegetable known of which there is more left when one has finished eating than when he began." This is because only the fleshy bottom of the leaves is edible. Elizabeth's mother used to serve these as a special treat. She would boil them until they were tender, about twenty minutes. We would strip the leaves and dip the fleshy ends into a sauce made of mayonnaise, milk, sugar and vinegar. We felt like kings. But there was a lot of inedible waste. We like Violeta artichokes. These are slender, and do not have the fleshy ends which make dipping or stuffing possible. We cut them from the plant when they are about the size of a lemon, eat the whole vegetable, and prepare it in a number of ways.

Tips for Artichokes

~Artichokes oxidize quickly. You can save their fresh color by immersing and cooking them in water acidified with lemon juice.

Marinated Artichokes

This is the way we mostly use artichokes. Cut them from the plant when they are small. Parboil until barely tender (a knife will pass through the stem), strip outer leaves, and place the artichokes in a vinaigrette of olive oil, white balsamic or herb vinegar, garlic granules, sugar, salt, pepper, dried basil and prepared mustard.

Marinate the parboiled artichokes in the dressing for twenty-four hours. Then drain and freeze them and serve them all winter in pasta dishes, on pizza, in quiches, tucked into focaccia, and on salads. Use the remaining marinade as salad dressing.

Pasta with Artichokes & Lemon

2 T olive oil
3 cloves garlic, minced
12 oz small, marinated artichokes, sliced (ideally, those you have processed and frozen)
1 t capers
Salt and pepper to taste
2 T lemon juice
1/2 C parsley, minced
Pasta of choice (we make linguini or spaghetti from scratch. See *Bread & Grains*)

Sauté the garlic in the olive oil, add the sliced artichokes to the pan and sauté until they are heated through and a little browned. Add capers, salt and pepper. Cook the pasta in boiling salted water with a little olive oil. Rinse with hot water and drain.

Add the artichoke mixture to the pasta and toss, then add the lemon and chopped parsley and toss again. Serve at once.

Sautéed Artichokes

You can use either Green Globe or Violeta artichokes for this recipe, as long as the fruit is small. Snip off the thorny tips and peel away the tough outer leaves. Parboil until tender, and slice them into thin, vertical slices. Sauté in olive oil, fresh lemon juice, diced garlic, and fresh ground pepper.

Spicy Pasta Sauce

2 T butter
2 T olive oil
1 medium onion, minced
3 cloves garlic, minced
1 T each minced fresh rosemary and fresh thyme
8 oz prepared marinated artichokes (see above)
2 t capers
Several Kalamata olives, halved
Parmesan or other hard cheese, grated
Salt and pepper to taste
9 oz linguini or other thin pasta (preferably home made. See *Bread & Grains*)

In a saucepan, sauté the onion in the butter and olive oil. When onion is just tender, add the garlic and sauté briefly. Add the herbs, the artichokes with their marinade, the capers, and the halved olives, and heat briefly. Add salt and pepper, toss together and set aside. Cook the pasta in boiling salted water with a little olive oil. Rinse with hot water and drain. Spoon warmed vegetables over cooked pasta. Top with cheese.

Stuffed Baked Artichokes

Prepare this elegant dish with Green Globe artichokes.

4 large artichokes, trimmed (pull off the tough outer leaves and cut away the thorny tips)
Juice of 2 fresh lemons
1/2 C olive oil, divided
1 large onion, finely chopped
4 cloves garlic, finely chopped
1/4 C parsley, finely chopped
1/2 lb pork sausage
1 C dry bread crumbs
1 C homemade chicken broth
1/2 t each oregano and pepper
Salt to taste
1/4 C grated Parmesan or other hard cheese
2 eggs

Trim the bottom ends of the artichokes so that they will sit upright. Bring a large pot of salted water to a boil. Add the lemon juice, and cook the artichokes in the acidified water until just tender — outer leaves should pull away fairly easily. (Do not overcook — the artichokes will continue to cook during the baking process.) Drain and cool.

Heat half the oil in a skillet. Add onion, garlic and

parsley, and cook until just tender. Add pork sausage and cook until nearly done. Transfer mixture to a bowl and add the bread crumbs, chicken broth, oregano, salt, pepper, and Parmesan. Mix gently and cool. Beat the eggs lightly and stir into the meat mixture. With a spoon, remove the "choke" from the vegetable (the fine fibers at the base). Fill this cavity with the meat mixture; spread the leaves and pack more of the mixture between them.

Place the stuffed artichokes upright in a shallow baking dish; drizzle with remaining olive oil and pour 1 cup water into the dish. Cover and bake at 350 for 40 minutes. Serve at once.

Arugula

Arugula is an aromatic, peppery salad green. It is also known as roquette, or rocket, and is very popular in Italian cuisine. It grows wild in Asia, all over the Mediterranean, and is cultivated as far south as the Sudan. In Roman times, arugula was grown for both its leaves and its seed, which was used for flavoring oils.

Arugula is considered a cool-weather green in this climate, but we grow it year-round, using shade cloth in the summer and cold frames in the fall and winter. Arugula contains vitamins A, B, C, E, K, calcium, potassium, phosphorus, magnesium, sodium, and folic acid.

Tips for Arugula
~Arugula can be used raw or cooked, but needs only a bit of heat — add at the end of cooking a dish.
~Add to pizza or pasta just before serving.
~Arugula is usually used to flavor other greens; adding a handful to lettuce really spices up a salad. But it can be used in other ways, as well, such as:

Arugula Stuffed Calzones
This dish, like calzones stuffed with kale, comes from a tradition where shepherds would take a "pie" with them out to the field — a folded crust enclosing meat, potatoes and vegetables that they could carry and eat with their hands. This dish calls for:

2 T olive oil
2 green peppers, diced

2 cloves shallots or garlic, minced
1 large bunch arugula, stemmed and chopped
2 C ricotta cheese
1 C mozzarella, shredded
1/2 C chopped fresh basil
A pinch of red pepper flakes
French bread dough
Cornmeal

In a large frying pan, warm the oil over medium heat. Add the green peppers and shallots or garlic. Sauté, stirring frequently, until the peppers are just tender. Add the arugula and cook until it is barely wilted. Stir in the ricotta, mozzarella, basil, and red pepper flakes.

Make French bread dough (see *Bread & Grains*) and allow it to rise. Divide it into eight equal pieces. On a floured surface, use a rolling pin to roll each piece into a 6-inch circle. Divide the filling among the pieces, mounding it on half of the dough, leaving a two inch edge. Fold the dough over the filling and crimp the edges well to seal them. Prick tops with fork. Brush the tops with a mix of egg white and water to make a golden, crunchy crust.

Sprinkle a large baking sheet with the cornmeal. Place the calzones on it and put in a cold oven. Turn the oven to 400 and bake until the calzones are golden.

Roasted Beet & Arugula Salad
2 lb beets
1 lb small red potatoes
1/3 C white balsamic vinegar
1 T olive oil
2 T prepared horseradish sauce
3/4 t salt
1 bulb fennel, trimmed, quartered, thinly sliced
2 scallions, thinly sliced
3 C fresh arugula, stems removed
6 oz feta cheese, crumbled

To roast the beets, preheat oven to 400. If beets are small, bundle two or three together in foil; if large, wrap each separately. Place on a baking sheet, and bake until tender (about one hour). When cool enough to handle, slip off the skins. Cut into 1/2-inch wedges. Meanwhile, cook potatoes until tender. In a large bowl, whisk together vinegar, oil, horseradish, and salt. Add fennel, scallions, arugula, beets, and potatoes. Toss to combine. Serve salad with feta crumbled over the top.

Beans, Dried

Beans were domesticated in Central and South America over 7000 years ago, moved northward through Mexico, and spread across the United States. In Central America, beans were part of the "Three Sisters:" corn, beans, and squash, often planted together. The pole beans were tied to the corn stalks, the squash planted below, each giving nutrients and shade to the other.

Beans contain vitamins A, C, pyridoxine, thiamin, iron, magnesium, zinc, potassium, folic acid, copper, phosphorus, calcium, and dietary fiber.

Tips for Dried Beans

~Be sure the beans are fresh (no more than a year from the vine) for best texture, flavor, and nutrition. Most natural food stores will have them in bulk, where they will be fresher than those in plastic bags.

~To remove the sugars from dried beans (the sugars cause gastric gas), cover them with plenty of water, boil one minute, let sit for an hour, drain and rinse before cooking.

~You can soak beans overnight to remove sugars, but the method above works better.

~Different sizes of beans require different cooking times. Scarlet Runner or kidney beans take longer than Snowcap or black beans, for example. If you want a medley of beans in your dish, cook them separately.

~During the second cooking, add minced onion, minced garlic, salt, pepper, basil, thyme, oregano, and a dried hot pepper or red pepper flakes. The hot pepper is optional, but it will produce a lovely warmth in the finished beans. Remove pepper before serving.

~Beans can be cooked and pressure canned, so you can just pull a jar off the shelf when in a hurry. Canned beans are wonderful for Chili con Carne. See *Keeping the Harvest* for instructions on drying, canning, and fermenting beans.

There are many kinds of beans available, each with its own flavor and uses. We grow three kinds of beans: Scarlet Runner, Snowcap — a pinto bean we got from Christine Langley years ago — and black beans. We eat beans most weeks.

Baked Runner Beans with Lemon & Rosemary

This recipe is much lighter than traditional baked beans, which use molasses and brown sugar.

1 C dried runner beans (makes 2 1/2 C cooked)
1 large garlic clove, minced
2 T olive oil plus more for serving
2 sprigs rosemary
Juice of one small lemon
Salt and freshly ground pepper

Boil the beans for one minute; remove from heat and let stand for an hour. Pour off cooking water and reserve.

Place the drained beans in a one-quart baking dish. Stir in the garlic, rosemary, and olive oil. Squeeze the lemon over the top.

Add enough of the reserved cooking water to cover the beans and bake them, partially covered, at 325 for 2 hours, or until tender. Check the water after 1 1/2 hours; add more if necessary so that the beans stay barely covered.

To serve, remove the sprigs of rosemary, season with salt and pepper, and drizzle a little olive oil over the top to add some gloss. Serve warm.

Beans in Wraps

2 C cooked beans
1 onion, diced
2 cloves garlic, diced
Olive oil for sautéing
1 lb ground beef or lamb
Grated cheese
Large flour tortillas
Leaves of lettuce, arugula, mustard, or spinach
1 avocado, sliced (optional)
Sour cream
Chili sauce or salsa

Sauté the onion and garlic in the olive oil. Add meat, cook until done, breaking it up into small pieces as you cook.

Place large flour tortillas on a baking sheet and wrap with a towel. Warm in the oven. When warm and still soft, place on plates, and fill each with beans, meat mixture, cheese, greens, and avocado. Fold into a wrap, seam-side down, and spread sour cream and chili sauce or salsa over the top.

Beans with Attitude

This is a great dish to serve a crowd, take to a potluck, or for leftovers; it keeps well in the refrigerator.

1 C each dried Scarlet Runner, black, and Snowcap beans
4 strips thick-sliced bacon, chunked
1 C diced onions
1 T minced garlic
1 quart home-canned tomatoes
1/2 C each brown sugar and chili sauce
1/4 C yellow mustard
3 T Worcestershire sauce
Salt to taste

In the morning, cook the beans according to the directions above — the first cooking to remove sugars, the second to add ingredients and flavors. Drain.

Cook bacon in a large pot until crisp; transfer to paper towel-lined plate. Add onions and garlic to pot, cook in bacon fat until tender. Stir in beans, canned tomatoes, brown sugar, chili sauce, mustard, Worcestershire sauce, and bacon. Season with salt. Transfer to a large baking dish and bake at 350 until bubbly, about 30 minutes.

Black Bean Salsa
1 lb ripe tomatoes, diced
1/2 C minced red onion
1/4 C cilantro, finely chopped
1 jalapeño pepper, seeded and diced
1 1/2 C cooked black beans
1 C corn, fresh or thawed
2 T lime juice
1/2 t salt

Cook the beans, according to directions in *Tips for Beans*. Gently stir all ingredients together, and serve with chips, tortillas, nachos, tacos, or as a side dish.

Beef, Bean & Barley Soup
For the Beans:
2 C dried Scarlet Runner beans
1 diced onion
2 cloves garlic, chopped
1 dried hot pepper or red pepper flakes
Dried basil and oregano
Salt to taste
For the Broth:
1 lb beef stew meat, or chuck roast cut into cubes
Olive oil or bacon fat for browning
1 onion, chopped
2 cloves garlic, minced

2 quarts homemade beef broth
1 C pearl barley

Cook the beans according to instructions in *Tips for Dried Beans*, adding onion, garlic, herbs, salt and dried hot pepper or red pepper flakes for the second cooking.

In a heavy pot (we use a cast-iron Dutch oven) slowly brown the beef in olive oil or fat. Add chopped onion and garlic. Cover with water, and cook slowly for 1-2 hours until meat is tender.

Cook the barley according to directions on the package. When all three ingredients are done, blend in the pot and add the beef broth. Season to taste.

You can make this soup the day before, but do not add the cooked barley until just before serving. It will absorb the liquid and swell up.

Chili con Carne
Bacon fat or olive oil
1 lb hamburger
1 onion, diced
2 cloves garlic, diced
1 quart home-canned tomatoes
3 C cooked Scarlet Runner beans
Salt, pepper, garlic granules and chili powder, to taste

Sauté onion and garlic in a large pot, until both are tender. Add hamburger and cook until browned, breaking it up into small pieces. Add tomatoes, beans and spices, heat through.

Beans, Fresh

Fresh beans are one of the most common vegetables grown in North America. They were formerly called "string beans" but the "string," which had to be stripped, has been eliminated from most varieties.

Like dried beans, fresh beans originated in South America (specifically today's Peru), and were brought to Central America by migrating peoples. The Spanish introduced them to Europe in the 16th century and they spread by trade through all parts of the world. Over 130 varieties of edible pod beans are known. "Snap beans" include pod colors of green, purple, red, or streaked. They vary in thickness (filet beans are thin, Romano beans wide).

Yellow beans are also known as "wax beans." All are easy to grow in the home garden and will produce prodigiously. Stagger planting unless you want a huge harvest all at once. Some are bush beans, some pole beans; we like both, though pole beans, like climbing peas, are easier to harvest.

Fresh beans contain vitamins A, C, E, K, thiamin, niacin, pyridoxine, calcium, iron, magnesium, manganese, phosphorus, potassium, and zinc.

Tips for Fresh Beans

~Best if boiled or steamed intact, rather than cut or snapped — they retain more nutrients.

~Before sautéing them, blanch briefly first; place in boiling water, then plunge into cold water to stop the cooking process.

~Purple beans will turn green during blanching.

~Fresh beans are wonderful simply sautéed with any combination of butter, garlic, onions, shallots, sliced mushrooms, fresh herbs, bread crumbs.

~Summer savory is a good herb to compliment beans.

~Freezing beans requires brief blanching first. They are a bit limp after freezing, but a nice addition to soups and stews.

~See *Keeping the Harvest* for instructions on making dilled green beans.

Salad Niçoise

There are many variations of this salad. We like to keep ours simple.

In the center of a large platter, place chunks of smoked fish, such as trout or salmon. Ringing the fish, place quarters or slices of hard-boiled eggs, or pickled eggs (see *Keeping the Harvest* for pickling eggs). Tucked between the eggs, place pitted Greek olives. Surround the eggs with fresh green beans that have been briefly parboiled. They should be tender, but still crisp. A good alternative is dilled green beans. Put lettuce leaves around the outside of the platter. Drizzle the salad with a light vinaigrette, made with minced garlic, olive oil, white balsamic or tarragon vinegar, sugar, salt, pepper, basil and prepared mustard. Ideally, each serving of the salad should have a little of each of these foods.

Green Beans & Tomatoes

This is a special way to prepare green beans.
1/3 C olive oil

1 1/2 lb fresh green beans (If you don't have small ones, parboil beans briefly and plunge into cold water, drain.)
2 garlic cloves, diced
1 medium onion, sliced into thin rings
4 small ripe tomatoes, chopped
5 T herb or red wine vinegar
1 1/2 t dried oregano
1/2 t each salt and pepper

Heat the olive oil in a heavy skillet, add the beans, and cook, tossing constantly, until beans are bright green and about half done.

Reduce heat and add garlic and onion. Cook, stirring, for about 1 minute. Add the rest of the ingredients and cook for about 5 minutes, tossing occasionally, until beans are tender and sauce is slightly reduced.

Green Bean & Nasturtium Salad

We grow nasturtiums because we love their saucy little faces, and cultivate them next to tomato and cucumber plants because they draw aphids and other critters away from the vegetables. But these flowers are also food, adding peppery zest to salads and dishes like this one.

1/3 C diced shallots
2 T tarragon or white balsamic vinegar
2 fresh tarragon leaves, coarsely chopped
Salt and pepper
1 lb small green beans
3 T olive oil
Nasturtium flowers

Toss the sliced shallots, vinegar, tarragon, and 1/4 teaspoon salt together in a large mixing bowl. Let sit for half an hour, uncovered.

Cut the beans diagonally into two-inch pieces. Blanch the pieces briefly, then plunge into cold water to stop the cooking process. Drain and dry them.

Stir the olive oil into the shallot mixture. Add the beans and toss. Season to taste with salt and pepper. Place nasturtiums decoratively on top of the beans.

Beans au Gratin

4 C green beans, cut in half, briefly parboiled
1/4 t salt
Dash cayenne pepper
3/4 C grated Parmesan or other hard cheese

2 T butter
1/3 C cream

Mix together the beans, seasonings, 1/4 cup of the cheese, 1 tablespoon of the butter, and the cream. Place the mixture in a buttered baking dish. Sprinkle with remaining cheese and dot with remaining butter. Bake at 425 for about 20 minutes.

Marinated Green (or Purple!) Bean Salad
Since purple or striped beans turn green when cooked, using them in this salad is a good way to preserve their color.

1 lb fresh beans
1/2 C minced onions
2 T olive oil
1 T herb or white balsamic vinegar
Chopped fresh herbs — thyme, dill, or summer savory
1/4 t salt
2 cloves garlic, chopped
Pepper to taste

Combine all ingredients except the beans to make a dressing. Marinate the raw beans for 24 hours before serving.

Beets

Beets originally grew wild in Western Europe and North Africa. We grow Cylindra, which has a long root, Early Wonder, which is round and whose greens are especially tender, golden beets, which are pretty and flavorful, and Winter Keeper, which lives up to its name.

Beet roots contain vitamins A, C, K, thiamin, riboflavin, niacin, pyridoxine, calcium, folate, magnesium, manganese, phosphorus, iron, sodium, and potassium. The greens contain the same nutrients, in larger quantity.

Tips for Beets
~When cooking whole beets, don't cut into the root itself, which will cause some of the nutrients to bleed out. Leave an inch of the stalks to boil, steam, or roast the beets.
~You can cut beets prior to cooking when no liquid is used, such as in roasted vegetables.
~To skin beets for cooking or canning, put them in boiling water for about ten minutes. Then put them in cold water, and the skins will slip off.
~Young beet greens can be torn into fresh salads.
~Treat beet greens like spinach. Steam them, and serve with vinegar and/or sour cream, or use in quiches.
~You can freeze beet greens. Parboil them briefly, plunge into cold water, pat dry, and place into freezer bags. As with spinach, when you thaw the beet greens, squeeze out residual moisture and dry on paper towels before adding them to dishes.
~Red beets will turn your body wastes red.

Beets & Greens
6 medium beets
Beet greens
1/2 C sliced red onion
1/4 C chopped chives
5 T olive oil
1 T red wine vinegar
Salt and pepper to taste

Roast the beets in foil at 400 until tender, 40-50 minutes. Cool, slip off the skins, and cut into wedges. Steam the beet greens until just tender — do not overcook. Drain, cool, and press out moisture. Chop. Toss beets and greens with the rest of the ingredients.

Beet Salad
2 lb beets, with 1 inch green and root left on.
2 T red wine vinegar
Salt, pepper, and sugar to taste
2 T olive oil
1 T sugar, or to taste
1/3 C fresh mint leaves, for garnish (optional)

Scrub beets and wrap them in aluminum foil, singly if they are large, in packets of two or three if small. Place packets on baking sheet and bake until beets are tender, at 400 for 30-45 minutes (depending on size). Test with fork for doneness. Open packets and let beets cool.

Combine vinegar, salt, pepper and sugar in a small bowl. Whisking constantly, drizzle in olive oil. When beets are cool enough to handle, slip off the skins. Cut beets into bite-sized pieces, and toss them in the dressing. Sprinkle with mint leaves before serving.

Casseroled Beets
2 lb beets

3/4 t salt
1/4 t paprika
3 T butter
Fresh lemon juice
1/3 C water
2 T minced onion

Peel and slice raw beets. Grease an oven-proof dish and layer the beets in it. Sprinkle with salt and paprika, and dot with butter. Add the lemon juice, water, and onion. Cover, and bake at 400 for 30 minutes or until beets are tender. Stir twice during baking.

Ginger Beets

2 lb beets
1 1/2 T each olive oil and grated fresh ginger root
2 T dark balsamic vinegar
Salt and pepper to taste

Scrub and wrap beets in aluminum foil (singly if they are large, 2-3 in a package if small). Roast at 400 for 40 minutes or so (depending on size) until the beets are tender. Cool, and slip off skins. Cut into chunks.

Heat oil on medium-low heat in a frying pan, and add ginger, simmering until flavor is released, but ginger has not browned. Add the beets and cook 2-3 minutes. Add vinegar and cook another minute or so. The oil, vinegar, and ginger create a nice glaze for the beets.

Borsch

There are at least as many recipes for this hearty soup as there are families who eat it. This is our favorite.

1/2 C chopped carrots
1 C diced onion
2 C peeled, diced raw beets
1 T butter
2 C homemade beef or other broth
1 C finely shredded cabbage
1 T dark balsamic vinegar
Sour cream

Barely cover the chopped carrots, onions, and beets with boiling water. Simmer, covered, for 20 minutes. Add the butter, broth, cabbage, and vinegar, and simmer for 15 minutes more. Ladle the soup into bowls, and garnish with sour cream. Serve with a crusty bread (see *Bread & Grains*).

Roasted Beets

Scrub and peel raw beets, and cut into bite-size pieces. Place in a baking dish, and toss with olive oil and herbs of your choice. Bake at 350 until tender, 30-45 minutes. This lovely solo can become a symphony: include other root crops, such as garlic, onion, turnips, parsnips, potatoes, and carrots, toss with dried herbs of your choice, and you have a colorful, tasty dish. Stir at least once during baking.

Bok Choi

In Eastern Asia, farmers cultivate hundreds of varieties of brassicas, some of which are called Bok Choi. In the United States, people sometimes refer to all of these as Chinese cabbage.

Bok Choi, which we distinguish from Napa cabbage because of their different growing habits and culinary uses, has thick, white, crunchy stalks, a little like celery, but less fibrous. The fleshy leaves are dark green.

Bok Choi contains protein, vitamins A, C, pyridoxine, pantothenic acid, thiamin, riboflavin, niacin, calcium, phosphorus, iron, sodium, and potassium.

Tips for Bok Choi

~Bok Choi is the classic green used in won ton soup.

~Remove stalks, wash and dry, and stuff them with cream cheese mixed with diced onion and a dash of salt. If the mix is stiff, soften with a bit of milk. Sprinkle with paprika, and serve as an hors d'oeuvre. Take to a potluck.

~Unlike other greens, Bok Choi should not be steamed; it gets mushy. Stir fry or sauté it alone or in combination with other vegetables.

~Bok Choi is versatile, and can be eaten as part of a salad, served as a main dish, or on the side as a vegetable.

Bok Choi Salad

1 1/2 lb Bok Choi, stalks and leaves chopped
1/4 C Tamari sauce
1 T fresh ginger, peeled and minced
2 T honey
2 cloves garlic, minced
1/4 C white balsamic vinegar

Red pepper flakes
Salt and pepper, to taste
1/4 cup toasted sesame seeds or slivered almonds

In a large bowl, combine Tamari sauce, ginger, honey, garlic, vinegar, and red pepper flakes. Toss Bok Choi with the dressing. Add salt and pepper to taste. Refrigerate at least one hour, until well chilled. Sprinkle with sesame seeds and serve.

Bok Choi Stir Fry
1 bunch Bok Choi (one plant)
1 medium onion or three large shallots
2 cloves garlic
1 inch peeled ginger root
3 T olive or sesame oil
A splash of Tamari sauce
1 T honey

Cut leaves and stalks of the Bok Choi on the diagonal into 2-inch pieces. Dice onion or shallots, garlic, and ginger.

Sauté the onion, garlic and ginger in oil until tender. Add Bok Choi and toss until just tender. Add Tamari sauce and honey, stir, and serve over rice.

This is a dish to which you can add leftover meat, such as diced chicken, pork, or beef. Add and heat just before serving.

Broccoli

Like other cruciferous (cabbage-related) vegetables, broccoli descends from plants that grow wild along the coasts of Europe. We grow broccoli in nearly every season, partly because it is a delicious vegetable (America's favorite, according to a poll taken at the EPCOT Center) and partly because it is a nearly perfect food.

Broccoli has 125% as much vitamin C as orange juice (two and one-half times the recommended dietary allowance) and as much calcium as milk. It also contains vitamins A, K, thiamin, riboflavin, niacin, ascorbic acid, phosphorus, iron, and potassium. (All cruciferous vegetables contain sulforaphane, a sulfur rich compound with many health claims on its behalf.)

Tips for Broccoli
~Organic vegetables may come with hangers-on, most of them not harmful to the plants (not counting slugs!). To avoid serving bugs to your family and friends, soak broccoli (and other cruciferous vegetables) in cold salted water for a few minutes before preparing.
~Don't throw away the stalk! Peel off the tough outer skin, chop, and cook with the florets in any dish you make.
~Broccoli can be steamed (which saves nutrients) or boiled, but do not overcook, which can happen quickly. Our practice is to get the water boiling, put in the broccoli florets and stalks, and turn the water off.
~Add lemon juice or vinegar at the table if you are going to use them. Applied earlier, they turn broccoli an unappealing dark color.
~Broccoli can be blanched and frozen, and used in soups, stews, or quiches.

Broccoli, Garlic, & Ginger Stir Fry
2 T olive oil
2 garlic cloves, minced
2 t minced ginger root
5 C broccoli florets and peeled, thinly sliced stalks
2 T water
1 T Tamari sauce

Sauté garlic and ginger briefly in oil. Add broccoli and stir to coat. Add water and Tamari sauce. Stir fry until the broccoli is bright green and tender.

Broccoli & Tomato Soup
2 cloves garlic, minced
2 T olive oil
1 C home-canned tomatoes
2 C chopped fresh broccoli
1/2 t nutmeg
4 C homemade meat or vegetable broth
1/2 C uncooked spiral noodles
Salt and pepper to taste
Grated Parmesan or other hard cheese.

In a large pot, sauté the garlic in the oil until soft. Add the tomatoes, broccoli, nutmeg and broth; simmer for 20 minutes. While the soup is simmering, cook the noodles, drain and rinse. Add to soup, along with salt and pepper. Top with grated cheese and serve.

Cream of Broccoli Soup
1 lb broccoli
1 carrot, scrubbed and chopped
1 medium onion, chopped
4 C homemade chicken or vegetable broth

3 T butter
2 cloves garlic, minced
3 T flour
1 C half-and-half
Salt and pepper to taste
A dash of nutmeg
Yogurt or sour cream for topping
Minced chives or scallions for topping

Cut the florets from the broccoli, trim, peel, and dice the stems.

In a large pot, bring the broth to a boil and add prepared broccoli, onion, and carrot. Lower heat and simmer until the vegetables are just tender. Cool slightly. Use a slotted spoon to lift out half the broccoli florets, and reserve. Puree the remaining vegetables, using a food processor or immersion blender.

Melt butter in a large saucepan. Add garlic, stir in flour, and sauté 2 minutes, whisking constantly. Add half-and-half, salt, pepper, and nutmeg. Cook until thickened, whisking constantly. Combine with the other ingredients, stirring until heated through. Do not boil. Ladle into bowls, and top each serving with yogurt or sour cream and chives or scallions.

Italian Style Broccoli

1/4 C homemade tomato sauce
1/4 t dried oregano
1 T white balsamic vinegar
2 T butter or olive oil
2 lb gently cooked fresh broccoli
1/2 C grated Parmesan or other hard cheese

Heat tomato sauce, oregano, vinegar, and butter until sauce bubbles. Pour over drained broccoli in a serving dish. Sprinkle with cheese.

Roasted Broccoli

Toss broccoli in a bowl with olive oil, chopped garlic, salt and pepper, and spread in an oven-proof dish. Roast in a 400 degree oven for 10-15 minutes, stirring frequently. It is done when a fork slips easily into a stalk. If you include the leaves, they will turn crisp and nutty tasting.

Brussels Sprouts

Brussels sprouts come from the same family as broccoli, but their breeding was refined in Brussels to produce the small, cabbage-like heads on a long stalk. They can be grown year-round, but are best in winter, after frosts make them sweet and firm.

Like liver, Brussels sprouts had a bad reputation in Elizabeth's generation. Her family did not grow them, and the ones her mother bought at the store were tough and had an old-cabbage flavor. But today's fresh, organic Brussels sprouts taste like butter (even when not covered by it), and are a wonderful source of nutrients.

Brussels sprouts contain vitamins A, C, K, pyridoxine, potassium, iron, thiamin, folate, manganese, magnesium, and phosphorus.

Tips for Brussels Sprouts

~Peel off the dark, loose, outer leaves and trim the tough bottom of the stalk to leave a firm, light-green bud.

~Briefly soak the sprouts in cold salted water. Cook them gently by either steaming or boiling — you want them tender, not mushy. Remove them from the heat before they are done: their internal heat will continue the cooking process. Overcooking causes them to lose nutrients and flavor.

~The easiest way to prepare Brussels sprouts is to cook them until they are barely tender, and then toss with butter, a little lemon juice, salt, and pepper.

~See *Onion* section for a recipe for *Brussels Sprouts and Glazed Onions.*

Brussels Sprouts with Bacon

1 lb Brussels sprouts, steamed until tender
1/4 lb bacon, chopped and cooked (remove bacon and set aside)
1/2 C finely chopped onions
Salt and pepper
Sauté onions in the bacon fat until just tender. Gently toss all ingredients together, season with salt and pepper.

Creamed Brussels Sprouts

4 C Brussels sprouts, trimmed and left whole
Fresh cream
Salt and pepper
Place Brussels sprouts in a baking dish, and cover the bottom of the dish with one-half inch of cream. Sprinkle with salt and pepper. Cover and bake at 350 for about 20 minutes. Gently toss before serving.

Marinated Brussels Sprouts

4 C whole or halved Brussels sprouts, trimmed
2 T tarragon or white balsamic vinegar
6 T olive oil
1 T minced fresh dill
1 clove garlic, minced
1 T lemon juice
1/4 t salt

Steam Brussels sprouts for 3 minutes or so, until tender but still firm. Plunge into cold water to stop the cooking process. Drain. Mix the remaining ingredients and pour over the Brussels sprouts. Marinate overnight.

Roasted Brussels Sprouts

1 1/2 lb Brussels sprouts, trimmed and halved
Olive oil, to coat
1/2 t each salt and pepper
Dried herbs, such as basil, oregano, and thyme

In a large bowl, toss Brussels sprouts with olive oil, salt pepper, and herbs. Place in a casserole, and roast at 425 until tender and slightly browned, about 20 minutes, tossing in the pan once during the baking.

Cabbage

Wild cabbages are native to Northern Europe, domesticated in Germany. Fermented cabbage, as in sauerkraut, nourished Northern Europeans through cold winters and helped save Captain Cook's crew from scurvy because of its high vitamin C content.

Cabbage contains vitamins A, C, E, K, thiamin, niacin, pyridoxine, folate, pantothenic acid, choline, calcium, iron, magnesium, phosphorus, potassium, sodium, zinc, and selenium.

Tips for Cabbage

~There are many types of cabbage to grow — firm white heads for making coleslaw and sauerkraut, red for braising, winter savoy for salads and wraps.
~Stored in a cool place, cabbage will retain its vitamin C for up to six months.
~Fresh cabbage should be quartered and soaked in cold salted water to expel dirt and bugs.
~Overcooked cabbage will give you a mushy vegetable and fewer vitamins.

~See *Keeping the Harvest* for fermenting, storing, and preparing sauerkraut and Kimchi.

Baked Cabbage

3 C shredded cabbage
3/4 C cream
2 well-beaten eggs
1 T sugar
1/2 t each salt and paprika
A handful of breadcrumbs
Grated cheese

Place the cabbage in a buttered baking dish. Blend cream, eggs, sugar, salt, and paprika, and pour over the top. Top with breadcrumbs and a little grated cheese, and bake about at 325 for 40 minutes.

Stuffed Baked Cabbage

As an unreconstructed European, Henning loves stuffed vegetables — especially cucumbers, bell peppers, and cabbage.

8 whole large cabbage leaves, briefly parboiled, drained. To keep the cabbage leaves from tearing, soak the cabbage until the leaves loosen, cut the bottom of the cabbage closely, and pull leaves off from the bottom of the cabbage head.

1 lb ground beef or mixed ground beef and lamb
1 medium finely chopped onion
4 T finely chopped fresh parsley
3/4 t salt
1/2 t dried thyme
4 cloves garlic, minced
A few grains cayenne pepper
2 T white balsamic vinegar
3 T brown sugar
1 t capers
Sour cream
Paprika

Mix all the above ingredients, reserving the sour cream and paprika. Divide the meat mixture into eight parts. Put one on each flattened leaf, and fold the leaf around it. Place in a baking dish, seam side down. Spoon sour cream on top, and sprinkle with paprika. Bake, covered, at 375 for 50 minutes.

Cabbage Soup

4 C homemade beef stock
1 large onion, minced

1 1/2 T butter
1 small head white cabbage. Quarter, soak in cold salted water, remove core. Use about 3/4 pound, thinly sliced.

Sauté the onion in the butter. Add the beef stock and bring to a boil. Add cabbage, cook until just tender. Season with salt and pepper.

Cole Slaw
Quarter, core, soak and slice a white cabbage.

For a creamy dressing, mix mayonnaise (preferably home made), milk or cream, tarragon or white balsamic vinegar, sugar, sour cream, salt, and caraway seed, amounts to taste.

For a spicier dressing, mix 1/3 cup pickled ginger (minced, including juice), 3 tablespoons rice wine vinegar, 3 tablespoons toasted sesame oil, 1/4 teaspoon salt. You can add toasted sesame seeds and thinly sliced scallions.

Mayonnaise
It is easy to make your own mayonnaise for this and other dressings and dishes. We use an immersion blender to combine the ingredients. It is possible to make mayonnaise with a wire whisk, but we find this easier and faster. Use a container that is just larger than the blender, such as a pint canning jar.

1 whole egg
3/4 cup oil; we use grape seed oil because it is flavorless; you can also use olive oil for a more pronounced flavor, or any other oil you choose.
1 t white balsamic vinegar
1/4 t salt
1/4 t prepared mustard; we use honey mustard, but you can use any other according to taste.

Put egg into jar. Add all other ingredients. Place blender in the bottom of the jar and activate to emulsify. As soon as ingredients are blended, raise blender very slowly to complete emulsion. Add more salt and some pepper, to taste. Mayonnaise will keep in the refrigerator for several days.

Red Cabbage, Carrot, & Kohlrabi Slaw
3 C shredded red cabbage
1 medium kohlrabi, shredded
2 carrots, shredded
1 small red onion, halved and thinly sliced
6 T olive oil

1 T white wine vinegar or apple cider vinegar
1 T fresh lemon juice
1 t Dijon mustard
1 T honey
Salt and pepper to taste

In a large bowl, toss prepared cabbage, carrots and kohlrabi to mix.

In a small bowl, whisk together all the other ingredients until blended and smooth. Pour dressing over vegetables and toss to mix. Cover and chill for at least an hour before serving.

Sweet-Sour Braised Red Cabbage
This a favorite side dish during the winter months, and often appears on our table for Christmas dinner.

A head of red cabbage, about 2 lbs
4 slices thick cut bacon, chopped
2 thinly sliced apples
1/4 t salt
1/2 medium onion, diced
1/2 C red wine or 2 T honey and 2 T red wine vinegar
1 t caraway seed

Cut the cabbage into quarters, remove core, slice thinly, and soak in cold salted water. Brown the bacon, remove from pan, and sauté the onion in the fat.

Remove the sliced cabbage from the water, leaving it moist. Place in a large, heavy pot, cover, and let it simmer 10 minutes. Then add the sliced apples, caraway seed, red wine or honey and vinegar. Adjust to taste.

Add the sautéed onion and stir. Cover the pot and simmer the vegetables until tender. This could take up to an hour, but do not let the cabbage get too soft — it should have some bite to it. If liquid is left at the end, uncover the pot and cook gently until it is absorbed. Add browned bacon and serve warm.

Carrots

Carrots probably developed from Queen Anne's lace, and originated in Afghanistan. Carrots contain Beta-carotene (converted to vitamin A) and vitamins C, D, E, K1, biotin, pyridoxine, calcium, phosphorus, and potassium. We grow several varieties for a year-round harvest.

Tips for Carrots

~Since most of the carotene is in the outer layer, you should scrub, rather than peel carrots.

~Root vegetables that are raised non-organically take chemicals and heavy metals into the roots. You cannot get rid of the toxins by scrubbing or peeling the vegetables.

~Cooking carrots allows carotene and vitamins to be more readily absorbed by the body.

~Carotene requires animal fats to convert to vitamin A. So it is healthy — as well as toothsome — to serve cooked carrots with butter.

~The "baby carrots" sold in stores are usually either carrots harvested while they are small, or chunks of large carrots shaved down to size. They are slightly less nutritious than mature, unprocessed carrots, but still good for you.

~Remove tops from carrots to keep water and nutrients in the root. Store in the refrigerator.

Carrot Cake

Henning, European born, did not believe that vegetables could be made into cakes and breads until Elizabeth served him carrot cake and zucchini bread. He has since become a convert. The following recipe makes a rich, moist cake.

1 C sugar
1 C wheat bran
4 eggs
1 C vegetable oil (we use organic grapeseed oil)
2 C flour
2 t each baking soda and cinnamon
1 t salt
2 t vanilla
3 C grated carrots
1/2 C chopped walnuts
1/2 C raisins

Mix together the sugar, bran, and eggs; add the oil and vanilla and mix well. In a separate bowl, sift together flour, soda, cinnamon and salt, then stir into the sugar mix. Add carrots, walnuts and raisins, and mix well. Pour the batter into three greased loaf pans, spreading the sides higher than the center. Bake at 350 about 30 minutes, or until a knife inserted into the center comes out clean.

If you use powdered sugar to frost this cake,

sprinkle it on while the cake is still warm. For a traditional frosting, use:

18-oz package of cream cheese, softened
1/2 C butter, melted
2 C powdered sugar
Fresh lemon juice, as needed
1 C finely chopped walnuts

Mix together the cream cheese, butter, and powdered sugar. Add lemon juice until the frosting can be easily spread. Stir in nuts and frost the cake.

Curried Carrot Soup

3/4 C chopped leeks, shallots or onion
2 T butter or olive oil
2 t curry powder (Zanzibar or another sweet curry powder is especially good for this soup)
1/4 t pepper
1 1/2 lb carrots, scrubbed and chopped
2 C homemade chicken or vegetable broth

In a large pan, sauté leeks, shallots or onions in butter or oil until tender. Stir in curry powder and pepper and cook a few minutes longer. Add carrots and broth, cover and simmer until carrots are tender. Process some or all of the soup, using a food processor or immersion blender. We like chunky soup, so we leave most of it unprocessed.

Glazed Carrots

2 lb carrots, scrubbed and sliced
2 T butter
Salt and pepper
2 T brown sugar
2 T chopped parsley

Cook the carrots until just tender. Drain, and then return them to the pan with the butter, salt and pepper, stirring or shaking until the butter has melted and coated the carrots. Sprinkle on the sugar, mixing gently until the carrots are glazed. Sprinkle the parsley over the top and serve at once.

Italian Marinated Carrots

1 lb carrots, scrubbed and cut into 1/2-inch slices
2 T minced garlic
1/2 t salt
1/2 C olive oil
1/4 C red wine vinegar
1 T dried oregano
1/2 t black pepper
In a medium saucepan, bring 1/2 cup salted water

to a boil. Add carrots, and cook until they are just tender. Drain off liquid. In a quart jar, combine garlic, salt, oil, vinegar, oregano, and pepper. Add drained carrots, and mix well. Cover and refrigerate 24 hours, shaking occasionally.

Roasted Carrots

Any amount of carrots, depending on desired number of servings. Wash and cut them in 1-inch pieces. Toss with olive oil, a little salt and pepper, and favorite dried herbs, such as tarragon, thyme, basil, oregano. Place in roasting pan and roast at 350 for an hour, stirring once.

Cauliflower

Cauliflower originated on the island of Cyprus from where it moved to Syria, Turkey, Egypt, Italy, Spain and northwestern Europe. All cruciferous vegetables descended from a common kale-like ancestor.

Cauliflower contains vitamins C, K, protein, riboflavin, niacin, magnesium, phosphorus, pyridoxine, folate, pantothenic acid, potassium, and manganese.

Mark Twain, possibly reflecting on its elegant appearance, called it "A cabbage with a college education." A glance at a seed catalog will show you white, orange, purple and green cauliflower, some varieties with tight, closed heads, some less dense, some with crown-like florets.

Tips for Cauliflower

~Soak cauliflower in cold salted water before preparing, in order to remove dirt and critters.

~If lightly cooked, cauliflower will lose small amounts of the vitamins but retain the minerals.

~If you live in an area with hard water, you can add a dash of lemon juice to the cooking water to prevent white curds from yellowing.

Cauliflower Soup

1 large head cauliflower
1/4 C butter
1 medium onion, chopped
3 ribs celery, chopped
1/4 C flour
4 C homemade chicken broth
2 C milk or cream
Nutmeg, salt and pepper
Separate florets and chop the stalk; steam the

cauliflower and reserve the water. Sauté onion and celery in the butter until tender. Stir in flour gradually and then add broth and enough of the reserved cooking water to make a thin broth. Add milk or cream; heat but do not boil. Add the florets and season with nutmeg, salt and pepper, to taste. Partially puree the steamed stalks using a food processor or immersion blender, to make a creamy soup that still has some solids remaining.

Cauliflower with Cheese Sauce

1 head cauliflower
3 T butter
3 T or less of flour
2 C milk
1 t dill weed, dried basil, or dried thyme
1/2 C grated Parmesan or other hard cheese
1/4 t salt
Pepper to taste

Divide the cauliflower into florets and steam until barely tender; do not overcook. Set aside. Melt the butter, gradually whisk in flour, then slowly add milk and seasonings. Add cheese and whisk over low heat until cheese is softened. Place steamed cauliflower in a baking dish, cover with sauce, and bake at 350 until lightly browned. Serve at once.

Marinated Cauliflower

1 large cauliflower
1/2 C olive oil
2 T red wine vinegar
1 T lemon juice
2 garlic cloves, minced
2 t sugar
1 t each salt and basil
1/8 t pepper
1/2 C red onion, thinly sliced
1/2 red pepper, thinly sliced
2 T parsley, chopped

Divide cauliflower into florets; discard stems (compost or give to the chickens). Steam the cauliflower until barely tender. Do not overcook. Chill florets in cold water to stop cooking process. Drain and place in a bowl. In another bowl, whisk together olive oil, vinegar, lemon juice, garlic, sugar, salt, pepper and basil. Stir in onion, red pepper and parsley. Pour marinade over cauliflower. Cover and chill in refrigerator overnight. The salad will keep up to three days in the refrigerator. Before serving, bring to room temperature so that the olive oil will return to a liquid state. Stir before serving.

Roasted Cauliflower

1 head cauliflower
1/4 C olive oil
7 cloves garlic, chopped
1/4 t red pepper flakes
2 t salt
1 t dried thyme

Cut cauliflower into florets and short pieces of stalk (about 8 cups). In a bowl, toss cauliflower with other ingredients. Transfer to a large baking dish. Roast at 400 for 20 minutes, stirring once.

Steamed Cauliflower

Gently steam cauliflower florets and chopped stalk. Serve with grated cheese, paprika or your own vinaigrette.

Celeriac

Celeriac is derived from wild celery, and has been known since ancient times. It was used for medicinal and religious purposes in ancient Greece, Egypt, and Italy. It is mentioned in Homer's Odyssey as "selinon," but did not become an important vegetable in Europe until the Middle Ages, cultivated in most of Europe by the 17th century. Celeriac is also called "celery root"; just be aware that it is different from the root of the domesticated celery plant.

Celeriac contains vitamins C, K, thiamin, riboflavin, niacin, pantothenic acid, pyridoxine, potassium, manganese, and phosphorus.

Tips for Celeriac

~Celeriac has a mild, distinct flavor, a blend of celery and parsley.
~Choose firm, medium size celeriac, free of soft spots.
~Refrigerated and kept moist, celeriac can keep for 2-3 weeks.
~To prepare, trim off any leaves and the root end. Scrub well and cut away skin.
~Cut pieces can be kept from browning by placing in water with a little lemon juice.
~Cut matchstick pieces for serving raw.
~Cook cubes until tender before mashing with potatoes and garlic, or other root vegetables.
~Add celeriac to salads, soups and stews.
~See *Parsnips* for *Parsnip and Celeriac Soup*.

Celeriac & Carrot Soup

1/2 large celeriac, peeled and chopped
1/2 lb carrots, scrubbed and chopped
2 cloves garlic, chopped
1/4 C plain whole milk yogurt
2 T honey
1 t ground coriander
1 t finely grated peeled fresh ginger root (be sparing)
Salt and pepper
A topping for the soup, such as homemade croutons or pepitas (prepared pumpkin seeds)

Place celeriac, carrots and garlic in a large pot; add 6 cups of water. (For added nutrients and deeper flavor, use homemade vegetable or meat broth.) Bring to a simmer over medium heat; cook until tender, 30-45 minutes. Let cool slightly. Process in a food processor with yogurt, honey, coriander, and ginger until smooth; season with salt and pepper. Reheat, but do not boil. Garnish each bowl with preferred topping.

Celeriac Remoulade

This is a simpler version of the salad below, and a classic in French cooking.

1 lb celeriac, trimmed, peeled and julienned
Juice of one lemon
6 T mayonnaise (preferably homemade)
1 T Dijon or honey mustard
A pinch of sugar
Salt and pepper

Put julienned celeriac in a bowl and add lemon juice, tossing to coat. Mix the dressing, adding salt and pepper to taste. Drain the celeriac, toss in the dressing, and let it rest for thirty minutes before serving.

Celeriac Salad

2 medium celeriac, trimmed, peeled, julienned
Fresh lettuce greens
1/4 red onion, sliced
1/2 green pepper, sliced, seeds and membrane removed
3 T mayonnaise (preferably homemade)
1 T honey mustard
1 T chopped parsley
Salt and pepper

Put julienned celeriac in cold water with a little

lemon juice until ready to use. Then prepare other vegetables. Mix mayonnaise and mustard, season with salt and pepper, and toss with celeriac, red onion, and green pepper.

Place lettuce greens on a platter. Top with mixed vegetables and parsley.

Roasted Celeriac

1 celeriac, peeled
3 medium potatoes, scrubbed
Olive oil
Salt
Butter
Minced rosemary
Honey, to taste

Cut celeriac and potatoes into small chunks; toss with olive oil and salt. Roast at 400 until vegetables are tender, 30-40 minutes. Toss with melted butter, rosemary leaves, and a little honey, to taste.

Celery

Wild celery grows in wet places all over Europe, the Mediterranean, Asia Minor, the Caucasus, and southwest toward the Himalayas. It is believed to have originated in the Mediterranean area. It was developed as a food plant in Europe, and brought to the Americas in the 1800s.

Celery has high levels of antioxidants and enzymes. It contains vitamins A, C, K, cobalamin, pyridoxine, folate, manganese, potassium, and fiber.

Tips for Celery

~Celery can be cultivated in the home garden, most toothsome when "blanched" — that is, having soil piled around the stalks so they stay tender and white. Planting in a trench makes this outcome easier.

~When harvesting, just cut or pull off the stalks you need. The celery plant will stay fresh in the ground, and grow up again from the center.

~Celery can be eaten raw or cooked. It's a great snack to put in children's lunches, with or without peanut butter.

~Add diced celery to green salads.

~Celery can be sautéed with onions, garlic, red bell pepper and zucchini or yellow summer squash to make a tasty side dish.

~Use the leaves as a flavoring for broth, soups, stews, or stir-fries. Leaves can also be used as a garnish.

Celery-Apple Salad

2 T each olive oil and fresh lemon juice
1/4 t each salt and pepper
2 C each thinly sliced apple and celery
Leaves from 3 stalks flat-leaf parsley (1/2 C)
1/3 C sliced red onion

Combine first four ingredients. Add remaining ingredients, toss to coat.

Cream of Celery Soup

3 T butter, divided
1 C chopped onion
1 1/2 C chopped leeks, white and light green parts
5 C chopped celery
1 1/2 C diced celery
4 cloves garlic, minced
2 bay leaves
4 C homemade chicken broth
Salt to taste
1/3 C cream
Pepper to taste
Red pepper flakes, to taste
Parsley or chives, chopped, for garnish

Melt 2 tablespoons butter in large heavy pan. Sauté onions, leeks, and chopped celery in the butter until vegetables are softened. Add minced garlic, and cook for 1 minute more. Add chicken broth and bay leaves. Salt to taste. Bring to a boil, then reduce heat to low; cover and simmer for 15 minutes.

While soup is simmering, melt 1 tablespoon butter in a sauté pan. Add diced celery. Ladle 1/2 cup of the simmering broth from the soup pot into the sauté pan. Simmer for 5 minutes to soften the celery. Set aside.

Process soup in a food processor or with an immersion blender. Stir the cream and the braised diced celery into the processed soup. Add salt, pepper, and red pepper flakes to taste. Heat, but do not boil. Serve in bowls, sprinkling each with chopped parsley or chives. Serve with a crusty bread.

Stuffed Celery

This is a holiday "must have" dish on our table.
8 stalks celery, using larger, outer stalks

1/2 lb cream cheese or homemade quark
Milk or cream for softening cream cheese or quark
1/4 medium onion, minced
Salt
Paprika

Trim, wash, and dry stalks. Cut into 3-inch pieces. Mix together cream cheese or quark, minced onion and salt, adding enough milk or cream to soften. Put celery on a cookie sheet and use a spoon to fill each piece with the cream cheese mix, mounding high. Sprinkle stuffed celery with paprika and place on a serving dish.

Chinese Cabbage

Although many vegetables, including Bok Choi, are commonly called "Chinese cabbage," in this section we refer to Napa Cabbage that has a long, tightly wrapped head, a mild flavor and crisp texture. These plants originated in China, near Beijing, and are widely used in Chinese cuisine. In the 20th century, they have become a common crop in Europe, the Americas, and Australia.

Napa cabbage contains vitamins A, C, K, folate, niacin, pantothenic acid, pyridoxine, riboflavin, thiamin, sodium, potassium, calcium, magnesium, manganese, phosphorus, and zinc.

Tips for Napa Cabbage
~Use Napa cabbage in a stir-fry, first adding the crisp stalks, then the tender leaves
~Napa cabbage can be stored in the refrigerator for several days without losing vitamins or crisp texture.
~Napa cabbage makes a good substitute for lettuce in a salad, or for white cabbage in a slaw.
~Add to soups with a beef or chicken base.

Kimchi
4 C chopped Napa cabbage
3 T rice wine vinegar
4 sliced garlic cloves
2 fresh or one dried hot red pepper, seeds removed
1 t salt

Combine all ingredients, stir well, chill overnight.

Napa Cabbage Salad
3 C shredded Napa cabbage
2 carrots, coarsely grated

1 T honey
3 T sesame oil
2 T Tamari
Pepper
1 inch fresh ginger root, grated

Combine honey, oil, Tamari and pepper in a large bowl. Add grated ginger root and mix well. Add shredded Napa cabbage and grated carrots and turn them into the dressing. Mix well.

Napa Cabbage Stir-Fry
1/2 lb Napa cabbage, thinly sliced
4 cloves garlic, minced
4 scallions, finely chopped
3 T Tamari
1 T sesame oil
1 t red pepper flakes
1/2 t sugar
1 T vegetable oil (we use grapeseed oil)
Salt
2 t toasted sesame seeds

Stir the garlic, scallions, Tamari, sesame oil, red pepper flakes and sugar together in a small bowl. Set aside.

Heat the oil in a large skillet. Add the cabbage, season with a pinch of salt, and stir and toss until the cabbage is just wilted. Remove from heat and pour dressing over the cabbage, tossing gently to combine. Before serving, sprinkle with toasted sesame seeds.

Napa Wraps
Outer leaves of a Napa cabbage, steamed or blanched until they are tender but still firm enough to handle without tearing.

Prepare your favorite wrap filling: ground meat, onion, cooked rice, for example.

Place cooked filling(s) into a large cooked Napa leaf, fold leaf firmly, and place seam side down in a baking dish. Top with cheese or tomato sauce and bake at 350 until hot and bubbly.

Corn

Corn was cultivated in Central Mexico over 7000 years ago, started from a wild grass. People in

Central America came to rely on corn as a major source of food, called maize. From Mexico, corn spread north into the Southwestern United States, and down the coast to Peru. About 1000 years ago, as people migrated north to the eastern woodlands of present day North America, they brought corn with them.

Corn grown in the United States today has been cultivated for animal feed, oils, alcohol, flour, sugar, and as an ingredient in processed foods, fiber, household cleaners, and paper products.

Cornfields take up more than 90 million acres of agricultural land in the U.S., but only 1.5% of corn is consumed as food we recognize — corn on the cob, or popcorn, for example. Most of the corn we eat we are not aware of — for example, in corn-fed meat, eggs and dairy products, or as high fructose corn syrup, other sweeteners, and additives in processed food. In fact, we ingest so much corn that nutritionists consider the American diet basically corn-based.

Corn is a fine food, if organically raised, but it is a grain, not a grass, and so contains more Omega-6 fatty acids than Omega-3s.

According to the National Institute of Health, both Omega 6 and 3 are essential acids the body does not produce, and must be obtained through diet. Both play a crucial role in brain function, and in normal growth and development. Omega 6 helps stimulate hair and skin growth, maintain bone health, regulate metabolism, and maintain the reproductive system. Excessive consumption, however, can cause inflammatory disease, raise blood pressure, and can be a factor in the development of dementia. Omega 6 is found in soy products, walnuts, corn, vegetable oils — used in cooking or as ingredients in snacks, sodas, and other processed foods — and in commercial salad dressing.

Omega 3 aids brain growth and development in infants, prevents inflammatory diseases and depression in adults, lowers blood pressure, aids eye health, slows the development of plaque in the arteries, reduces the likelihood of heart attack, stroke, and autoimmune diseases. Excessive consumption can cause blood thinning. It is found in fatty fish, shellfish, flaxseed oil, walnuts, avocados, and Brussels sprouts.

The ideal ratio of Omega 6 to Omega 3 fatty acids in the diet is 4:1. By contrast, the American diet has a ratio between 10:1-50:1. Consider the balance in your own diet when choosing the foods you eat. Consider, for instance, that grass-fed meat and dairy products have a naturally balanced ratio of Omega 6 and 3. Vegetables other than corn have a preponderance of Omega 3.

High fructose corn syrup is particularly pernicious. A common sweetener in processed foods, especially in soda and commercial fruit juices, it is processed by the body differently from other sugars; it is quickly absorbed, and has been linked to insulin spikes, obesity, diabetes, and high blood pressure.

A change in labeling laws has allowed manufacturers to list this ingredient simply as "fructose" or "corn syrup." Read labels carefully and avoid all processed foods containing corn syrup in any form. This includes syrup for pancakes which is mostly made from corn syrup. Use organic maple syrup instead; while more costly, it promotes good health.

Tips for Corn

~We put the water on to boil before we pick corn from the stalk and shuck it, tossing the greens on the compost pile before heading to the house. The sugars in corn turn to starch very quickly once the corn is off the stalk.

~Cooking time should be only long enough to make the corn tender. Pierce a few kernels with a sharp knife to determine when it is done to your satisfaction. We usually put the corn into boiling water and then turn the burner off to achieve tenderness in about 5 minutes. Overcooked corn will be starchy, flavorless and tough.

~Young corn on the cob can be eaten without cooking, or used in salads.

~To remove kernels from cob, hold cleaned cob (greens and silk removed) over a bowl, and use a sharp knife to scrape the kernels from the cob. See *Keeping the Harvest* for tips on freezing corn.

Corn Salad

4 C fresh or defrosted corn
1 C cherry tomatoes, halved
1/3 C crumbled feta or other cheese
1/4 red onion, finely chopped
1/4 C fresh basil, thinly sliced

3 T olive oil
Juice of one lime
Salt and pepper, to taste

Toss all ingredients together in a large bowl, season with salt and pepper.

Southwest Corn Salad

1 C black beans, cooked the day before with onion, garlic, and 1 dried hot pepper. (See instructions in *Dried Beans*)
3 C fresh corn kernels (about 6 ears)
2 red bell peppers, chopped, minus seeds and membrane
1 avocado, chopped
1/2 red onion, finely chopped
2 T olive oil
Juice of 2 limes
1/2 t ground cumin
2 T minced scallions

In a large bowl, toss ingredients together.

Sautéed Fresh Corn

6 ears fresh corn, kernels cut from cob
2 T butter
A sprinkling of fresh herbs: cilantro, parsley, or chives
Salt and pepper to taste

In a large sauté pan, melt butter. Add corn, salt and pepper. Cook briefly until corn is tender. Place in serving dish, and sprinkle herbs on top.

Corn Chowder

This is a great winter soup, worth freezing corn for. The recipe is easy to double.

1/2 C chopped bacon
3 T chopped onion
1/2 C chopped celery
3 T chopped green paper, minus seeds and membrane
1 C diced raw, peeled potatoes
2 C water
1/2 t salt
1/4 t paprika
1/2 bay leaf
3 T flour
2 C milk, divided
2 C corn
Chopped fresh parsley, for garnish

In a large pot, sauté the bacon until lightly browned. Add onion, celery and green pepper and sauté until vegetables are tender. Add water, potatoes, salt, paprika, and bay leaf and simmer until potatoes are tender. Bring to a near boil and gradually whisk in flour and 1/2 cup of the milk.

In a separate pot, heat the corn in the rest of the milk and add to soup. Heat, but do not boil. Garnish with parsley.

Corn Cakes

This is a recipe Henning created. Our annual crop began with a small jar of flint corn, also called Painted Corn or Indian corn, that Cedar Charnley gave us. We grew it out, and have had a fine harvest every year. Flint corn differs from sweet corn in that it is dried and shelled and stored in glass jars, and has to be cooked much longer.

1 C kernels of dried painted corn
1 T soda
5 t flour
2 eggs
3 strips bacon, diced
1/2 onion, diced
2 cloves garlic, chopped
Red pepper flakes, salt and pepper, to taste

Soak corn in water and soda for twenty-four hours. Drain, rinse, add more water and cook corn on low heat for several hours, until tender. Drain and rinse. Briefly sauté bacon, onions, and garlic and process all ingredients in a food processor until they are smooth, but still retain some texture.

Make the resulting batter into flat cakes and fry in a non-stick pan in olive oil until brown and crispy on the edges. We use an ice cream scoop to get the right amount of batter in the pan, then flatten with a spatula. Delicious served with anything. Apple sauce makes a great companion to the savory cakes.

Cucumbers

India is probably the original home of the cucumber, where it has been cultivated for over 3000 years, introduced to other parts of Europe by the Romans or Greeks. It is a member of the squash family.

Cucumbers contain vitamins A, C, K and E,

magnesium, potassium, phosphorus, calcium, folate, and manganese.

In a seed catalog, you will find many kinds of cucumbers, but we just divide them into slicers for fresh eating and picklers for preserving.

Tips for Cucumbers

~Pick cucumbers early in the morning when sugars are high and the cucumbers are crisp.

~Cucumbers store well in the refrigerator.

~Salting cucumber slices before using them in salads will release their water. Peel, slice, place in a colander, salt the slices, toss, let drain for about an hour, then rinse and pat dry.

~Cucumbers produce chemicals called cucurbitacins that can make them bitter to the taste. Irregular watering or temperature fluctuations in the garden can exacerbate this problem. A simple way to remove the bitterness is to cut off the tip of the cucumber and with that piece rub the cut in a circular motion. A white foamy substance will emerge. Repeat on the other end and wash the cucumber to remove the bitter flavor.

~See *Keeping the Harvest* for making cucumber pickles.

~See *Basil* in *Herbs* for a cucumber, basil and tomato salad.

Simple Cucumber Salad

2 cucumbers, peeled, sliced, salted, rinsed, drained
3 T olive oil
2 T red wine or white balsamic vinegar
1/2 t salt
1 small onion or 2 shallots, minced
Pepper, to taste
Fresh dill or parsley, minced, to taste

Mix ingredients for dressing, then toss prepared cucumber slices in it.

Creamy Cucumber Salad

1 large cucumber, peeled, halved lengthwise, seeded, and sliced into thick half moons.
1 t salt (for dressing — use 2 t additional salt to prepare cucumbers)
3 T each mayonnaise (preferably homemade) and sour cream
3 T minced red onion
2 T white balsamic vinegar
1 T each sugar and chopped fresh dill
Place cucumber slices in a colander; sprinkle with

salt, toss to coat, and let drain 15 minutes. Rinse and pat dry.

Combine all other ingredients in a bowl. Add cucumber slices and toss to coat. Chill before serving.

Sautéed Sliced Cucumbers & Onion

1 lb cucumbers
1 clove garlic, minced
1 C finely sliced onion
2 T butter
3 minced chives
2 T chopped parsley
Salt and pepper

Peel, seed, and slice cucumbers. Salt, let stand, rinse, and drain. Sauté onions and garlic in butter until tender. Add the cucumber and sauté briefly. Toss in herbs, and season to taste with pepper and salt.

Gazpacho

This cold summer soup has as many variations as there are regions in Spain, its country of origin. This is our favorite. It can serve as a first course, or, with a good French bread (see *Bread & Grains*), as a meal in itself. Use a food processor for ease of preparation.

2 peeled cloves garlic, quartered
1 fresh jalapeño pepper
4 scallions
1 celery stalk
1/2 medium green bell pepper
2 tomatoes
2 C tomato juice, preferably homemade
1 medium cucumber
2 T lemon juice
1 t salt
1/4 t black pepper

Halve jalapeño and remove seeds. (Use gloves to avoid burning skin from the pepper's natural oils.)

Trim scallions and celery and cut into 1-inch pieces. Quarter and seed tomatoes and bell pepper. Peel cucumber, cut in half lengthwise, remove seeds and cut cucumber to fit the feeding tube of a food processor.

Use the metal blade of the food processor to chop garlic and jalapeño. Add scallions, celery, and green pepper and pulse to a medium chop. Put in large mixing bowl. Pulse one half the tomato chunks until coarsely chopped. Add to mixing bowl.

Puree the remaining tomato until smooth, about one minute. With machine running, pour in 1/2 cup of tomato juice through the feeding tube. Add to mixing bowl with remaining tomato juice and stir.

Insert slicing disc, stand cucumber slices upright in the feeding tube and slice, using light pressure. Add to mixing bowl with remaining ingredients and stir. Cover and chill before serving.

Note: This recipe can easily be doubled; it helps to have a food processor that holds 14 cups.

Sweet-Sour Stuffed Cucumbers

This traditional German recipe is a seasonal pleasure.

4 cucumbers
1/2 lb hamburger
1 onion, diced
1 garlic clove, minced
1/3 C parsley, minced
Butter for sautéing
Bacon fat or olive oil for browning
1 egg, beaten
Salt and pepper, to taste
1 slice of bread, soaked in water, milk, or broth, and then squeezed and crumbled
1 t capers, if desired
Juice of one lemon
1 tomato, skinned
Cotton string
Sugar and cream, to taste

Place hamburger in a bowl. Sauté onion, parsley, and garlic in butter. Add salt and pepper, and mix together. Add to hamburger. To those ingredients, add softened bread and beaten egg, and capers, if used, and mix well.

Peel the cucumbers. Cut them in half lengthwise, and remove seeds. Salt the cavities and drip with lemon juice. Fill the hollows of one half of each cucumber with the meat mixture, mounding it high. Top with the other half of the cucumber, and tie the halves together with string.

In a heavy frying pan, brown the cucumbers on all

sides in bacon fat or olive oil. Add a little water to the pan. Add the skinned tomato, cover, and braise on low heat for 30 minutes, until the meat mixture is cooked through.

Remove cucumbers and keep warm. Season the sauce with a little sugar and cream; thicken with flour, if desired. Pour sauce over meat. Serve at once.

Fennel

Fennel is a member of the carrot family, grown for its edible stems, leaves, and seeds. Fennel originated in Southern Europe and the Mediterranean. It was used by the ancient Egyptians as food and medicine, and considered a snake bite remedy in ancient China. Pliny (23-79 AD), the Roman author of *Naturalis Historie,* used the aromatic herb to treat twenty-two different ailments. During the Middle Ages, it was hung over doorways to drive away evil spirits.

Fennel contains vitamins A, C, pyridoxine, niacin, pantothenic acid, potassium, calcium, phosphorus, iron, magnesium, zinc, copper, manganese, selenium, and folate. There are many health claims for fennel teas and oils.

Tips for Fennel

~All parts of the fennel plant are useful: the seeds as flavoring, the leaves as an herb or tea, stems for flavoring, and the bulb as a vegetable. Fennel has a mild anise flavor.

~You can chop up the bulb or leaves in green salads.

~The leaves are good on fish, particularly with lemon and butter.

~Keep raw slices of fennel from discoloring by placing in water with a little lemon juice.

~Fennel can be eaten raw; brush slices with olive oil and lemon juice, sprinkle with salt and pepper.

~The stems can be used in soup stocks in place of celery.

Roasted Fennel

4 T olive oil
4 fennel bulbs, cut into thin slices, fronds reserved
Salt and pepper, to taste
1/3 C shredded Parmesan or other hard cheese
Lightly oil the bottom of a 9x13-inch glass baking

dish. Add the sliced fennel. Sprinkle with salt and pepper, then with the cheese. Drizzle with the oil. Bake at 375 until the fennel is fork tender and the top is golden brown, about 45 minutes. Chop fennel fronds to make about two teaspoons. Sprinkle over the roasted fennel and serve.

Fennel & Broccoli Sauté

8 T water
3 C sliced fresh fennel bulb
2 T olive oil
2 garlic cloves, minced
4 C broccoli florets and pieces of peeled stalk
3 T white wine
2 T fresh lemon juice
Salt and pepper

In a large pan, heat the water. Simmer the fennel in the water until it is just tender. Add the oil, garlic, and broccoli and sauté for one minute. Add the wine and sauté the vegetables until the wine evaporates and the broccoli is tender but still firm. Sprinkle the lemon juice over the vegetables. Season with salt and pepper. Serve at once.

Fennel in White Wine with Tarragon

2 C thinly sliced fennel bulb
1 C homemade chicken broth
1 t dried tarragon, tied in cheesecloth
1/4 C dry white wine
1 T butter
1 T flour
1/4 t salt
1/4 t pepper
Chopped fresh parsley

In a large saucepan, combine fennel, broth, and tarragon. Simmer until fennel is tender. Drain, saving cooking liquid. Discard tarragon. Set fennel aside. Add enough white wine to cooking liquid to make one cup. Bring to a boil.

In a second saucepan, melt butter and add flour, whisking constantly. Gradually add the liquid from the first saucepan to the roux, stirring constantly. When sauce begins to thicken, add salt and pepper. Add fennel and reheat, but do not boil. Sprinkle with chopped parsley. Serve at once.

Fennel & Mushrooms

3 C sliced fennel bulb
1/4 C fennel leaves, minced
1/2 lb button mushrooms, sliced
3 T butter
1 T olive oil

Sauté mushrooms in oil and butter until tender; remove mushrooms and set aside. Place sliced fennel in pan and cook until just tender — it should be crunchy. Mix in mushrooms, fennel leaves, salt and pepper. Blend and serve.

Cream of Fennel Soup

2 T butter or more, for sautéing
1 1/2 C diced onion
4 1/2 C chopped fennel bulb
3 C homemade chicken broth
1/2 C half-and-half
1/2 C milk
Salt and pepper

In a large soup pot, sauté the onion in butter until tender. Add the fennel and chicken broth; simmer until fennel is tender.

With an immersion blender or in a food processor, puree half the soup, return to the pot, add the half-and-half and milk and heat through. Do not boil. Season with salt and pepper to taste.

Garlic

Garlic is an ancient food, and so rich in health benefits that it can be regarded as medicine. Elizabeth once saw a friend with a garlic clove protruding from her ear — she explained that she had an earache, and the garlic would cure it. She was relying on folk knowledge — garlic has been used medicinally for over 3000 years — but the healing powers of garlic have now been established in over 1000 medical studies. Garlic is a plant in the allium family, closely related to shallots, onions, and leeks. Originally cultivated in central Asia, garlic is now grown all over the world. The Chinese, Egyptians, and Greeks mention garlic in their earliest writings; in fact, the first recorded labor strike was over garlic: Egyptian slaves building the pyramids refused to work until they were given their daily garlic ration. The Egyptians took oaths in the name of garlic, and the Greeks gave it as an offering to their gods.

Garlic contains vitamins A, C, E, K, folate, niacin, pantothenic acid, pyridoxine, riboflavin, thiamin, manganese, selenium, calcium, copper, potassium, iron, phosphorus, magnesium, and zinc. There are many health claims for garlic for its anti-microbial, anti-cancer, anti-diabetic, immune-boosting and cholesterol-lowering properties.

We have grown garlic on S&S Homestead Farm for over forty years. We received our first heads from a neighbor, Lori Ann Cotton, and by now, we call it S&S garlic because it has naturalized to our soil. We like the flavor and the fact that it has never developed any fungus. It is juicy, mild but tasty, and it keeps so well, in bundles or braids that decorate the house and barn kitchens, that we always have a year-round supply.

The cloves of garlic we eat are also cloves that are planted in the fall, each of which will make a sturdy head by spring. We grow about 750 heads per year, mulching them well and watering them during the dry months with a trickle hose. After harvesting in August, we dry them briefly on the warm soil and then bundle or braid them. Garlic in some form is part of our daily diet. We also grow Elephant garlic. It is not a true garlic, closer to leeks in its genetics, and its flavor is mild. The cloves are large, easily peeled, and can be used as you would use garlic, onion, shallots, or leeks in a recipe. It does not keep as long as true garlic, but is excellent while it lasts.

Tips for Garlic

~Peel garlic quickly by pressing on the clove with the blade of a knife, which loosens the skin. Garlic "peelers," which resemble a piece of rubber, will loosen the skin of several cloves at a time.

~To release its biological (and therefore medicinal) properties, garlic must be cut or crushed. To add flavor to broth, soups, or stews, add chopped cloves to the dish as it cooks.

~Cook garlic in olive oil to produce flavored oil for frying or sautéing, but remove it before adding other food. Browned, it can become bitter.

~Do not store garlic in olive oil without an acidifier such as lemon juice or vinegar to prevent botulism, which can result from the oil's providing a medium for the bacterial activity of the garlic.

~For beef and lamb cuts, pierce the meat and push in slivers of garlic. To lamb, add rosemary leaves to the garlic slivers.

~Cook scrambled or fried eggs with sautéed or fresh garlic. If you like, add sautéed onion and minced dried tomatoes.

~We always slice or dice garlic, but we leave you to judge the following note from Anthony

Bourdain, chef and author: "Smash it with the flat blade of your knife if you like, but *don't* put it through a press. I don't know what that junk is that squeezes out of the end of those things, but it ain't garlic."

~Bourdain also recommends roasting garlic for a subtle flavor, and using both fresh and roasted garlic in salad dressing. Roast the garlic in its skin, and squeeze it out to add to dressings, soups, and sauces.

~See *Keeping the Harvest* for preparing roasted garlic cubes.

Garlic Dressing

Mince 2 cloves of garlic. Add olive oil, some prepared mustard, dried basil or a mince of fresh herbs, salt, pepper, sugar, herb vinegar. Mix and let stand. Add a few flakes of red pepper, and you have a wonderful dip for French bread. You can also use this as a dressing for rice, pasta, potatoes, or vegetables.

Baked Garlic

After an hour in the oven, this delicious appetizer is soft, sweet, and mellow. Use new garlic; the skins are white and soft, even edible.

6 whole heads garlic
4 T unsalted butter
1/3 C homemade chicken broth
Salt and pepper to taste

Remove papery outer skin of garlic, leaving heads whole. Arrange heads in a baking dish just large enough to hold them comfortably. Add butter and broth and set dish on the middle rack of the oven. Bake at 350 for 1 hour, basting occasionally, until garlic heads are golden brown and tender. Season with salt and pepper to taste; serve immediately. There will still be the inner skin on the garlic cloves; squeeze the garlic out with a fork. In a pinch, you can skip the broth and simply drizzle some olive oil on the garlic before baking.

Creamy Garlic Salad Dressing

1 C sour cream
1/2 C mayonnaise (preferably homemade)
1/3 C milk
2 t sugar
2 T finely chopped green onions, shallots, or chives
3 garlic cloves, minced
Fresh herbs of your choice, minced

1/2 t salt
1/8 t pepper

In a small bowl, whisk the sour cream, mayonnaise, milk, and sugar. Stir in onions, garlic, salt and pepper, and fresh herbs of your choice. Cover and refrigerate at least 1 hour before serving.

Garlic Sauce for Pasta

3 T olive oil
8 cloves garlic, minced
1 C chopped scallions
4 C chopped fresh tomatoes, drained
2 T minced fresh basil
2 t fresh thyme or 1 t dried thyme
1/4 C white wine
Salt and pepper, to taste
Parmesan or other hard cheese, grated

Sauté the garlic and scallions in oil until just tender. Add the chopped tomatoes, herbs, and wine. Simmer for 10-15 minutes. Season to taste, and serve over cooked pasta. Top with cheese.

Roasted Garlic Herb Butter

A good spread for French bread, chicken, or fish

1 whole garlic bulb with cloves or 1 large clove Elephant garlic
Olive oil
1 T each minced fresh rosemary and thyme
1/2 C butter, softened
1/2 t each salt and pepper

To Roast the Garlic:
Peel and discard the outer layers of the whole garlic bulb, leaving intact the skins of the individual cloves of garlic, or use a whole, peeled head of Elephant garlic. If using a garlic bulb with individual cloves, cut 1/4-1/2 inch from the top of the bulb, exposing the individual cloves of garlic.

Place the garlic in a baking pan or muffin tin, cut side up. Drizzle a couple of teaspoons of olive oil over each exposed head, using your fingers to rub the oil over all the cut cloves. Bake at 350 for 1 hour, until the cloves are lightly browned and soft. Allow to cool, then press the cloves from their skins with a knife or your fingers.
For the Butter:
Mix herbs, garlic, butter, salt and pepper. Spread on bread or over fish or fowl.

Kale

Kale originated in the eastern Mediterranean and Asia Minor, where it was cultivated for food by 2000 BC. Kale was introduced into Canada and the U. S. by Russian traders in the 19th century.

There are many kinds of edible kale — we grow Russian, Curly, Redbor, Winterbor, and Nero di Toscana. There are also ornamental kales, better known for their beauty than for their tenderness.

Kale is a brassica (a relative of cabbage) and therefore hardy, with leaves constantly regrowing on stalks, and readily available in the garden during the winter. Kale is also full of nutrients, providing 25% more absorbable calcium than milk, containing vitamins A, C, E, and K, thiamine, riboflavin, niacin, folate, iron, magnesium, manganese, potassium, selenium, sodium, and zinc.

Tips for Kale
~When storing kale in the refrigerator, keep the stalks on, and the kale dry.
~Remove stalks before sautéing or steaming kale.
~Blanch a bundle of kale (1-2 minutes in boiling water) and then plunge it into ice water to stop the cooking. You can use it for several days, adding it to eggs, sautéed with garlic as a side dish, or serving it as a part of topping for pasta.
~Add raw, chopped kale to soups and casseroles.
~Kale takes a bit longer to cook than spinach or chard. Boil or steam it until just tender, but still bright green.

Caldo Verde (Portuguese Soup with Kale)
2 1/2 lb potatoes, peeled and thinly sliced
2 T olive oil
2 C diced onion
2 T minced garlic
6 C homemade chicken broth
1/2 lb sliced pepperoni, sautéed and drained
4 C kale, stemmed and chopped
1 T fresh lemon juice

Sauté potatoes in olive oil. Add onion and garlic and cook until they are just tender. Add broth and simmer. Add prepared pepperoni. Add kale and simmer until tender. Salt to taste. Add lemon juice before serving.

Potatoes & Kale à la Grecque

3 large potatoes, scrubbed and cut into 1 inch chunks
10 large leaves of kale, stemmed and chopped
2 C water
1/2 t each basil and dill seed
1/4 t oregano

For Topping:
2 tomatoes, chopped
1 C Feta cheese crumbled, or 1 C grated Parmesan
1 medium red onion, diced, sautéed in olive oil
A few Kalamata olives, halved

Place potatoes, kale, water, and herbs in a large pot. Cover and bring to a boil. Reduce heat and simmer until potatoes are tender. Drain. Place tomatoes, onion, cheese, and olives on the table for topping.

Jan's Kale Dip

(Courtesy of Jan Sundquist. This is an incredibly good dip. She serves it with white corn chips, but it is good with raw or steamed vegetables, too.)

1 C kale leaves
1 C mayonnaise (preferably homemade)
1 C plain yogurt
Fresh lemon juice
1/2 C diced scallions
1 C parsley
Salt, pepper, and hot sauce to taste

In a food processor, process kale, mayonnaise, and yogurt. Add lemon juice, scallions, salt, pepper, and hot sauce, and process again. Add parsley, and process.

Sautéed Kale

1 1/2 lb tender kale leaves, washed and torn into small pieces
3 T olive oil
5 cloves garlic, thinly sliced
A pinch of red pepper flakes
Juice of a small lemon

In a large pot, sauté the garlic in the olive oil. Add red pepper flakes. A handful at a time, add the kale and let it wilt, stirring frequently. (The water on the washed kale will be enough liquid.) Be sure the kale is thoroughly cooked. Just before serving, add lemon juice, or let people add it on their own.

Kale Salad

8-10 large kale leaves, stemmed
2 T olive oil
1/4 t salt, pepper to taste
3 T minced fresh dill or mint, or a mix of the two
1 T apple cider vinegar
1 t prepared mustard
Pinch of red pepper flakes
3 oz Feta cheese
1 C cherry tomatoes, halved
1/3 C chopped Kalamata olives
1/4 red onion, minced

Cut the kale into ribbons, and place in a large salad bowl. Add 1 tablespoon of the oil, salt, pepper, and dill and/or mint. With your hands, massage the ingredients until the kale is soft and glistening. In a small bowl, mix the remaining oil, vinegar, mustard and red pepper flakes. Pour it over the kale and toss to coat. Crumble in the feta, add the tomatoes, olives and red onion and toss again.

Henning's Puréed Kale

Henning created this recipe; it is flavorful and versatile.

12 large leaves of kale, washed, stemmed, and torn into medium pieces.
4 strips thick cut bacon, chopped
1/2 red onion, minced, or a mix of onion and shallots, minced
5 cloves garlic, minced
1/2 t each salt and pepper
A shake of red pepper flakes
1 egg

In a large pot with a steamer basket, steam kale leaves until they are soft. In a frying pan, cook bacon until browned. Remove. Sauté onion/shallots and garlic in bacon fat until soft.

Cool kale slightly, then put all ingredients (including bacon fat) into a food processor. Pulse until blended, but not mushy — it should have some texture. If made ahead, place in a casserole dish in the oven to keep warm before serving.

Kohlrabi

The name comes from the German *kohl,* which means "cabbage" and *rabi,* which means "turnip." It is a plump, charming vegetable, ranging in color from white to purple. The edible bulb sits on top of the ground. It is a brassica, related to cabbage, broccoli, cauliflower, kale, and Brussels sprouts.

Kohlrabi and Brussels sprouts are the only commonly known vegetables of Northern European origin. Domesticated from a wild cabbage, kohlrabi made its way to Southern Europe and the Mediterranean, and, in the 17th century, to the Americas.

Kohlrabi contains vitamin C, pyridoxine, riboflavin, niacin, pantothenic acid, folate, potassium, copper, manganese, phosphorus, calcium, and iron.

Tips for Kohlrabi

~Most sources tell you to harvest kohlrabi when it is young, 2-3 inches in diameter. But the kohlrabi we grow can swell to the size of baseballs and still remain sweet and tender. Humus-rich soil and consistent watering are key.

~Kohlrabi can be eaten raw or cooked.

~Kohlrabi keeps for up to two months packed in moist sand or in the refrigerator. Cut off the leaves and store the bulb.

~Kohlrabi is great fresh. Peel the bulb, sprinkle with salt or paprika, or dip it in a vegetable dip.

~The greens are edible, and can be steamed or sautéed by themselves or with other greens. Sautéed with garlic or gently cooked in water and salt, they are delicious.

~We like to add slivered raw kohlrabi to coleslaw.

~You can steam, boil, roast, bake or grill kohlrabi, or cook and mash it with potatoes.

Steamed Kohlrabi

Peel, slice, and steam lightly to preserve the vitamins and the crunch. Serve with butter, salt, and pepper.

Casseroled Kohlrabi

2 large or 4 small kohlrabi, peeled and sliced
1 large potato, peeled and sliced
2 cloves garlic, minced
1 onion, minced
1 T each butter and flour
1 pint homemade chicken broth
Salt, paprika, dried thyme, dried basil, to taste
1 pint frozen peas, thawed

Cook the kohlrabi and potato until both are tender but still firm. Drain and set aside, reserving cooking water.

In a frying pan, melt the butter and sauté the garlic and onion in it, and then stir in the flour until you have a paste. Slowly add the broth and the cooking water, and whisk until you have a medium thick sauce. Stir in salt, paprika, thyme, and basil, and keep cooking gently, adjusting, until herbs are softened.

Layer potatoes and kohlrabi in a casserole dish. Add peas. Pour sauce over the top, and warm in the oven until sauce is bubbly.

Kohlrabi & Carrot Sauté

4 C peeled and sliced kohlrabi
2 C sliced carrots
4 T minced garlic
2 t each minced fresh parsley and tarragon
2 T butter
2 T olive oil
2 T fresh lemon juice
Salt and pepper

In a frying pan, melt butter, add oil, and sauté the garlic, carrots and kohlrabi until tender but still firm. Mix in the herbs and lemon juice, season with salt and pepper. Serve at once.

Henning's Norwegian Vegetable Chowder

Cut any root crops, such as potatoes, turnips, kohlrabis, rutabagas, onions, carrots, beets, or parsnips, into large pieces. Place in a crockpot, cover with whole milk (preferably raw milk from a grass-fed cow). Add any herbs and spices you like, such as minced garlic, rosemary, basil, oregano, or thyme. Set the crockpot on high, and let the vegetables simmer until they are tender. Note: You can do this on the stove, but in a crockpot the milk will not boil or scald. Another alternative is to place milk, herbs and vegetables in a Dutch oven and bake until vegetables are done. The milk will take on a rich flavor. This is a tasty one-dish meal, served with sourdough rye bread or focaccia and (preferably homemade) butter. (See *Bread & Grains*).

Kohlrabi & Carrot Slaw

It is helpful to have a food processor with a slicing blade, or a salad shooter, to aid preparation.

1 large kohlrabi, peeled, trimmed and grated
1/4 head red cabbage, shredded
2 medium carrots, scrubbed and grated
1/2 red onion, grated

4 T chopped cilantro
1/4 C mayonnaise (preferably homemade)
1 T each cider vinegar and sugar
1 t salt

Combine the prepared vegetables in a large bowl. In a smaller bowl, whisk together the mayonnaise, cider vinegar, sugar, and salt. Pour the dressing over the slaw, and mix until fully coated. Chill for several hours before serving.

Leeks

Leeks were cultivated by the Egyptians and by the Romans, who introduced them to Europe. The Welsh adopted leeks as their national plant. According to tradition, they wore leeks in their helmets to distinguish themselves from the Saxons they were battling and so defeated their enemy in 640 A.D.

Leeks, like garlic, onions, shallots and chives, are a member of the allium family. They contain vitamins A, C, E, and K, folate, niacin, pantothenic acid, riboflavin, thiamin, calcium, copper, iron, magnesium, manganese, phosphorus, selenium, and zinc.

Tips for Leeks
~Leeks are easily grown in the home garden from spring through winter. They have a delicate flavor and are particularly tasty after a frost. Unlike garlic and onions, which must be harvested and dried during the summer for winter consumption, leeks can remain in the ground most of the year.
~Fresh leeks can be eaten raw or cooked.
~Leeks can be cut, briefly blanched and frozen(see *Keeping the Harvest*). They should be thawed and sautéed before using for soups or pasta.
~Recipes may stipulate "white part only," but the tender green stalk can be used, as well.
~When leeks develop a bulb and flower at the top, chances are they are tough at the base. Cut off the root and slide a knife into the base of the leek. If it is not tender, cut it into pieces and put into the compost pile.
~Leeks will store well in the refrigerator.
~You can use leeks in recipes in place of onions, garlic, or shallots.

Leek & Potato Soup
6 leeks, carefully cleaned, thinly sliced
1 T olive oil or butter

4 medium potatoes, thinly sliced
4-5 C homemade chicken, pork, beef, or vegetable broth
1 t dried thyme
1 C milk or cream
2 T sour cream or yogurt
Pepper, to taste
1 T parsley or chives, chopped

Sauté the leeks in olive oil or butter until tender. Simmer the potatoes and thyme in the broth for 15 minutes. Add the leeks and simmer for another 10 minutes. At this point, you can process all or part of the soup in a food processor or with an immersion blender — we like ours chunky, and so process only part of it.

Add the milk or cream to the soup and heat, but do not boil. Season to taste with pepper, serve in bowls, and garnish with sour cream or yogurt and fresh herbs. Frozen leeks work well for this soup.

Pasta with Leeks & Scallions
6 medium leeks, thinly sliced
2 T butter
10 scallions, thinly sliced
8 shallots, finely chopped
Pepper and salt, to taste
2 C homemade vegetable broth (see below for ingredients and instructions)
1 C half-and-half
Fettuccini
Grated Parmesan or other hard cheese

For the Broth:
Early in the day, put diced carrots, onion, potatoes, celery, garlic, and greens from the garden (chard, spinach, kale, or beet greens, for example) and a mix of fresh or dried herbs in a pot with 4 cups of water. Cook the vegetables down slowly, until 2 cups of broth remain. Drain, set aside vegetables for the chickens or compost pile, and set broth aside.
For the Solids:
In a large skillet, melt butter. Add prepared leeks, scallions, shallots, garlic, pepper, and salt. Cook until vegetables are tender, stirring often. Add broth and half-and-half, cook until reduced. Set aside and keep warm.

Cook fettuccini and drain. Toss with vegetables and broth. Serve warm. Add cheese at the table.

Baked Leeks

2 T butter
1/4 C flour
1 1/2 C milk
1/2 C shredded cheddar or other hard cheese
1/2 t garlic granules
Salt and pepper, to taste
4 medium leeks, sliced in rounds
Bread crumbs for topping

Melt butter over low heat. Whisk in flour until smooth. Gradually stir in milk and cheese until cheese is softened. Season with garlic granules, salt and pepper. Remove from heat. Arrange the leeks in a single layer in a greased 9x13-inch baking pan and cover with the cheese sauce and bread crumbs. Bake at 400 for 30 minutes until leeks are tender and sauce is bubbly. (Note: this is a versatile dish, and can be spiced up with hot sauce or made more substantial by paving the casserole with with thinly sliced potatoes.)

Lettuce

Lettuce was first cultivated by the ancient Egyptians who turned it from a wild plant whose seeds were used to produce oil into a food plant grown for its succulent leaves. It traveled from there to Greece and to Rome, and was brought by the Romans into Europe and from there to America.

Lettuce contains vitamins A, C, D, E, K, cobalamin, pyridoxine, calcium, magnesium, phosphorus, potassium, sodium, and zinc.

Tips for Lettuce

~We grow several different kinds of lettuce, starting the seedlings in the greenhouse and setting them in hardening-off boxes to grow sturdy before transplanting into the garden. Because lettuce is a cool-weather crop, we plant it in the shade of other plants, such as climbing peas, when the weather gets warm. Succession planting assures us of lettuce until frost gets serious. In winter, we grow lettuce and other succulent greens in the greenhouse.

~A friend of ours, a homeopathic physician, has a list of ten things you can do to improve your health immediately. The first item on the list is to make your own salad dressing. Read the labels on commercial salad dressings: many contain trans fats, stabilizers, sodium, sugar, high fructose corn syrup, and other chemicals you probably don't want to eat.

Below, find some recipes for vinaigrette and milk-based dressings.

~Lettuce purchased at the store, unless it was locally grown, has probably traveled a long way, and had its vitamins depleted by frequent washing or misting. Grow your own.

~Lettuce is a "cut and come again" plant, so you can get many servings from a single plant. Just take off the outer leaves or cut the whole head leaving two inches above ground — the plant will regrow. You can also buy your lettuce at a local farmers market or food stand.

~To store lettuce, put washed and dried leaves in a damp paper towel in your refrigerator.

Caesar Salad

1/2 C olive oil
4 cloves garlic, peeled, minced, and smashed
1/2 loaf French bread, preferably a day old (see *Bread & Grains*)
Dried herbs of your choice
1/4 C fresh lemon juice
4 oz Parmesan cheese, grated
1 t anchovy paste or 1-2 anchovies, minced
2 fresh eggs
1/4 t freshly ground pepper
1/2 t salt
4-6 small heads of Romaine lettuce, inner leaves only, rinsed, patted dry

In a large bowl, whisk together the olive oil and garlic. Let sit for half an hour. Meanwhile, make the croutons. Cut the French bread into small cubes, and toss with olive oil, garlic granules, and dried herbs of your choice. Place on a baking sheet lined with parchment paper. Broil until brown and crunchy, tossing at least once. Watch them carefully — they will burn quickly. Remove from oven and set aside. Add prepared anchovies and eggs to the oil and garlic mixture, and whisk until creamy. Add salt, pepper, and 1/4 cup of lemon juice. Whisk in half of the Parmesan cheese. Add more lemon juice, to taste.

Tear off bite-sized chunks of the Romaine lettuce. Add to the oil mixture and toss until coated. Add the rest of the Parmesan, toss. Add the croutons to the salad, toss, serve immediately.

The raw eggs add creaminess to the dressing, but if you don't have a trustworthy source for eggs, omit them. Commercial eggs may contain salmonella bacteria. Eggs from your own chickens should be washed just before using.

Daily Salad With Vinaigrette

Comb your garden, choosing lettuce, arugula, mustard greens, cucumbers, tomatoes, sugar peas, scallions, and herbs in season such as parsley, chives, marjoram, or basil. Prepare the vegetables, add a few edible flowers, such as nasturtiums, for beauty and flavor.

Dress with a mix of:
Olive oil
White balsamic vinegar
Minced fresh garlic or garlic granules
Salt, pepper, to taste
Dried or minced fresh basil
Prepared honey mustard
Sugar or honey to taste

You can make enough dressing at one time to refrigerate and have on hand for the next day. Be sure that you do *not* store fresh garlic in olive oil without an acidifier, such as lemon juice or vinegar. Botulism can result.

Greek Salad

8 C Romaine lettuce, torn into bite-size pieces
2 cucumbers, seeded and chopped
3 large tomatoes, seeded and chopped
3 scallions, sliced
16 pitted Kalamata olives, halved
1/2 C diced red onion
1 1/2 C crumbled feta cheese
2 T chopped fresh mint
Salt and pepper, to taste

Mix all ingredients, dress with vinaigrette below:

Lemon Vinaigrette:

1 clove garlic, minced
1/4 t salt
2 T fresh lemon juice
1/4 t Dijon mustard
9 T olive oil
4 T red wine vinegar
1/2 t dried oregano
Pepper

If you choose to use only olive oil and vinegar, use a 2:1 ratio. Mix before tossing with the salad. Traditional Greek salad does not call for lettuce of any kind: this is our preferred version.

Wilted Lettuce Salad

For the Salad:
1 head leaf lettuce, washed and torn into pieces
5 scallions, diced
3 slices thick-cut bacon
Salt and pepper, to taste
For the Dressing:
1/2 C bacon grease
1/2 C white balsamic vinegar
1/4 C water
1 T sugar

Cook the bacon and crumble. Reserve the grease for the dressing. Cut the scallions into the lettuce, and add crumbled bacon. Sprinkle with salt and pepper to taste. Heat dressing ingredients to boiling, and pour over the salad. You may add sliced hard boiled eggs to make this salad a complete meal.

See *Dill* entry in *Herbs* for a dill and yogurt dressing. See *Garlic* entry above for a creamy garlic dressing.

Blue Cheese Dressing

This salad dressing can also be used as a dip for vegetables or chips. It will keep in a glass jar in the refrigerator for up to two weeks. Best if made the day before using.

2 1/2 oz blue cheese
3 T milk
3 T sour cream or yogurt
2 T mayonnaise (preferably homemade)
2 t white balsamic or white wine vinegar
1/4 t sugar
1 finely minced clove garlic
2 T finely snipped chives
Salt and freshly ground black pepper, to taste

Place milk and vinegar in a small bowl, let set for five minutes. Then mash in blue cheese with a fork until mixture resembles large-curd cottage cheese. Stir in sour cream or yogurt, mayonnaise, vinegar, sugar, and minced garlic until well blended. Season to taste with salt and pepper. Chill before using.

Green Goddess Dressing

This dressing can be used on salads, as a dip, as a spread for sandwiches, or as a topping for baked potatoes or salmon. Will keep for a week in the refrigerator.

2 t anchovy paste or 2-4 canned anchovies

1 garlic clove, minced
3/4 C mayonnaise (preferably home made)
3/4 C sour cream
1/2 C chopped parsley
1/4 C chopped tarragon
3 T chopped chives
2 T fresh lemon juice
Salt and pepper, to taste

Put all of the ingredients in the bowl of a food processor and process until you get a smooth dressing, about 30-45 seconds. (You can vary the herbs as you like, using basil instead of tarragon, for example.)

Mustard

The mustard plant is a brassica, like cabbage, and was first cultivated in Sumer, Greece and Italy. The plant is known all over the world, and its seeds are used to produce the processed or dried mustard we use at our tables and in cooking.

Mustard leaves contain vitamins A, C, E, K, folate, niacin, pantothenic acid, riboflavin, thiamin, calcium, copper, iron, manganese, selenium, and zinc.

Tips for Mustard
~Mustard greens are best harvested in the morning, and used fresh.
~Use mustard greens in wraps, and on hamburgers and sandwiches for their spice, crunch, and nutritional value.
~Mustard will last a long time in the garden, resisting frost, but will get hotter in taste with warmer weather.
~For salads, choose the small, tender leaves.
~Mustard greens will keep a few days in the refrigerator, wrapped in a damp paper towel, but fade quickly.

Braised Mustard Greens
4 slices bacon, diced
1/2 C thinly sliced onions
2 cloves garlic, minced
1 lb mustard greens, stemmed and torn into pieces
1 C homemade chicken or vegetable broth
2 T white balsamic vinegar
2 t sugar
1/4 t each salt and pepper
A sprinkle of sesame seed (optional)

In a large frying pan, cook bacon. Remove to paper towels. In remaining bacon fat, sauté onions over medium heat until they begin to caramelize. Add the minced garlic and cook a minute more, until fragrant. Add the mustard greens and broth and cook until the greens are just wilted. Toss with vinegar and sugar. Season with salt and pepper. Sprinkle with sesame seeds, if desired.

Mustard Salad with Roasted Potatoes & Tomatoes
For the Salad:
4 C chopped unpeeled potatoes
1 T olive oil
1 t salt
1/2 t pepper
5 C mustard greens, stems removed, chopped
4 tomatoes, quartered
1/4 red onion, sliced thin
For the Dressing:
1/4 C red wine vinegar
1/2 T minced shallot
1 clove garlic, minced
1 T maple syrup
1 t Dijon mustard
1 T finely chopped fresh parsley
1/3 C olive oil
2 T water
1/2 t salt
1/2 t pepper

Toss chopped potatoes with olive oil, salt and pepper in a roasting pan and cook at 375 until golden brown, about 20 minutes. Stir at least once during roasting.

While potatoes are roasting, chop vegetables. Prepare dressing by blending all ingredients in a food processor. When potatoes are done, remove from oven and let them cool for 10 minutes.

Place mustard greens in a large salad bowl, top with potatoes, tomatoes and onions, and pour 1/2 cup of dressing over salad. Toss to combine. Season with salt and pepper to taste.

Simple Mustard Greens Salad
Like raw kale, mustards become more tender and palatable if massaged by hand.

2 bunches mustard greens
1/2 C grated Parmesan or other hard cheese

1/3 C olive oil
1/4 C lemon juice
3 large cloves garlic, minced
1 T Tamari sauce
1 minced anchovy fillet or 1/2 t anchovy paste
1/2 t pepper, 1/4 t salt

Strip leaves from the stems, wash and dry. Tear into small pieces and place in a large bowl. Add the rest of the ingredients. With your hands, massage the greens to work in the flavoring. The volume of greens will be reduced by half, look darker and a little shiny. Adjust seasonings. Serve at once.

Onions

Onions are native to Western Asia, grown in Chinese gardens as early as 5000 years ago, and are referenced in the oldest Vedic writings of India. In Egypt and Sumer, onions have been traced back to 3500 and 2500 BC, respectively. Because onions were originally a wild crop, fresh or dried, they were probably a staple in the diet of prehistoric peoples.

Onions are a member of the allium family, which include shallots, scallions, leeks, garlic, and chives. There are many kinds of onions grown now, generally divided into yellow, red, and white. Subsets include Vidalia, Walla Walla Sweets, and Spanish Red, for example.

Onions contain vitamins A, C, pyridoxine, folate, calcium, iron, manganese, magnesium, phosphorus, potassium, zinc, copper, and selenium.

Tips for Onions
~Different onions serve different purposes: know what you want before you plant or buy. For example, yellow and red onions will overwinter in a cool, dark place; Walla Walla Sweets should be used upon purchase or harvest.
~The substance that brings tears to your eyes when you cut an onion is sulfuric fumes. To lessen the effect, chill the onion and cut into its root last; you can also rinse the onion and the knife under cold running water.
~Onions are powerful antioxidants, and have anti-inflammatory, antibacterial, and anti-fungal properties.
~See *Thyme* entry in *Herbs* for a recipe for French onion soup.

Pico de Gallo
This condiment can be used on tacos, as a dip, or as an addition to wraps with beef and beans. Fresh or thawed corn can be added, as well.

6 Roma tomatoes, diced
1/2 red onion, diced
1/2 jalapeño, seeded and diced, membrane removed
3 T cilantro, stemmed and chopped
1 scallion, minced
Juice of 1/2 lime
Salt to taste

Mix the first 5 ingredients in a bowl. Squeeze the lime juice over. Sprinkle with salt, mix, and adjust for flavor.

Brussels Sprouts with Glazed Onions
1 lb Brussels sprouts
Salt and pepper
1 T butter, divided
1 T olive oil, divided
1 red onion, thinly sliced
2 T dark balsamic vinegar

Soak Brussels sprouts in cold, salted water for a few minutes to release dirt and critters. Pull off outer leaves and trim the stems. Cook Brussels sprouts briefly in boiling water, until just tender, then plunge into cold water to stop the cooking process. Drain well, then cut in half.

Heat 1/2 tablespoon butter and 1/2 tablespoon olive oil in a large skillet over medium heat. Add Brussels sprouts and cook, tossing occasionally, until they are brown and crisp on the edges, about 3 minutes. Season to taste with salt and pepper, transfer to a large bowl, and cover to keep warm.

Add remaining butter and oil to the pan over medium-low heat. Add onions and cook until soft, 3-4 minutes. Add vinegar and stir to deglaze. Cook until vinegar is reduced and onions are glazed. Add to Brussels sprouts, toss well, serve immediately.

Onion Frittata
This is an easy way to make a meal from eggs. The key is to have all the ingredients ready before you begin sautéing the onions. You can use fresh vegetables, such as chopped broccoli or sliced mushrooms, and try different cheeses.

8 large eggs
1/2 C finely grated Parmesan or other hard cheese
6 large fresh basil leaves, chopped
6 large sage leaves, minced

2 t fresh minced rosemary
1/2 t each salt and pepper
3 T olive oil
1 C thinly sliced onion
1/3 C ricotta or feta cheese

Whisk first seven ingredients in a medium bowl and set aside. Heat oil in an ovenproof skillet over medium heat. Add onion, sauté until soft, or continue cooking until onions are caramelized. Reduce heat to low. Stir in egg mixture. Spoon dollops of cheese over the top. Cook until cheese begins to set, lifting the edges so the egg can flow to the bottom. Place in oven, and bake at 400 until just set, 7-10 minutes. Cut into wedges, serve at once or at room temperature.

You can use other vegetables, such as chopped broccoli or sliced mushrooms, for this dish.

Parsnips

The parsnip, a root vegetable closely related to carrots and parsley, has a long, cream-colored tuberous root. Native to Eurasia, it has been widely used since antiquity, cultivated, for example, by the Romans. It was used as a sweetener in Europe before cane sugar was adopted. Parsnips were well known by the first English colonists in America, who grew them in Virginia in 1609.

Parsnips contain vitamins C, E, K, folate, magnesium, calcium, iron, potassium, and choline.

Tips for Parsnips
~Parsnips are easily grown in the home garden, preferring rich clay soil, but any well-drained soil will produce a good crop.
~Parsnips overwinter well, and are sweeter after a frost.
~You can dig parsnips in the fall and store them in the refrigerator or in a cool, dry, well-ventilated place.
~Small parsnips, like carrots, can be scrubbed; larger, older parsnips should be peeled.

Roasted Parsnips
Like other root crops, parsnips are delicious roasted. They need to be peeled; the peel is tougher than that of potatoes or carrots. Cut them on the bias to get similar sized pieces and provide more surface for crisping.

After peeling, cut parsnips to cover the bottom of a 9x13-inch glass pan. Toss with olive oil and dried herbs of your choice: oregano, basil, thyme, and tarragon, for example, and a little salt and pepper.

Roast at 400 until parsnips are tender on the inside, crispy on the outside, about 25 minutes; stir when halfway done.

You can roast parsnips with carrots, and the results are colorful and delicious.

Herbed Butter Parsnips
Peel desired number of parsnips, and cut into rounds. Sauté in 1 tablespoon butter and 1 tablespoon olive oil, then season with salt and pepper. Add enough water to cover, and bring to a boil. Lower heat and simmer until parsnips are tender. Soften 1/2 C butter (more or less, depending on number of parsnips) and mix with 1/2 C chopped fresh herbs, such as parsley, chives, oregano, or thyme. Season with a little salt and pepper.

Spread some butter in the bottom of a serving bowl. Top with hot, cooked parsnips, dot with more of the butter. Add a little of the cooking liquid to moisten the dish. Serve warm.

Parsnip & Celeriac Soup
4 bacon strips, chopped
1 large onion, chopped
4 cloves garlic, minced
4 C cubed celeriac
4 C cubed parsnips (peel before cutting)
2 C cut carrots
4 C homemade chicken or other broth
2 cubes frozen garlic (see *Keeping the Harvest*) or garlic granules, to taste
1 bay leaf
2/3 C cream
2 t minced fresh thyme, or 1 t dried thyme
2 t salt
1 t pepper
1/4 t nutmeg

In a Dutch oven, cook bacon over medium heat until crisp. Remove with slotted spoon; drain on paper towels. Sauté onion and garlic in bacon fat.

Add celeriac, parsnips, broth and bay leaf, and cook briefly in fat with the onions and garlic. Add enough water to cover the vegetables. Bring to a boil. Reduce heat and cook, stirring occasionally, until vegetables are tender, about 20 minutes.

Remove bay leaf. Puree soup with an immersion blender, or cool soup and puree in batches in a food processor. Return to pot. Stir in cream, thyme, salt, pepper and nutmeg. Heat, do not boil. Top servings with bacon.

Potato, Carrot, & Parsnip Soup
1/4 C butter plus 2 t olive oil
5 C sliced onion
2 C carrots cut in 1/2 inch pieces
1 C parsnips, peeled and cut in 1/2 inch pieces
1 quart homemade chicken, pork, or beef broth
2 cubes frozen garlic (see *Keeping the Harvest*)
2 1/2 C potatoes, cut in 1/2 inch pieces
1/4 C chopped parsley
1 t fresh thyme, minced
1 1/4 C half-and-half
1/4 C sherry
Salt, pepper, and garlic granules, to taste

Sauté onions in melted butter and oil until golden. Add carrots and parsnips and cook 10 minutes. Add broth, garlic, potatoes, parsley, and thyme. Cover and simmer until potatoes are tender, stirring occasionally.

Puree half the soup; return puree to remaining soup in the pot. Stir in half-and-half and sherry. Season with salt and pepper. Heat, do not boil.

Peas

Peas, members of the legume family, date from the late Neolithic period of Egypt, Greece, Syria, Turkey, and Jordan. They were well known in Medieval Europe. Split peas, a branch of the pea family, were developed in the late 19th Century.

The most common peas in the home garden are sugar peas — also known as snap peas or snow peas, eaten in the shell — and shelling peas. Sugar peas are commonly trellised; shelling peas may be bush peas or climbing peas.

Nothing says "summer" like fresh peas out of the garden. Among gardeners, the fiercest competitions are about whose tomatoes ripen first, and whose peas emerge first. We know a local gardener who planted peas in the fall and mulched the seedlings to protect them in winter, just to be the first to say,

"My peas are up!"

We grow sugar peas and Alderman climbing peas, both of which are easy to harvest. They need to be in separate beds in order to avoid cross-pollination. Sugar peas, right off the vine, can be used in various dishes and fresh salads or just put out on the counter for a snack. They will disappear faster than potato chips.

Peas contain vitamins A, C, E, and K, thiamin, riboflavin, niacin, folate, calcium, iron, magnesium, manganese, phosphorus, potassium, sodium, and zinc.

Tips for Peas
~Pick sugar peas every morning for daily consumption or for storage in the refrigerator.
~Pick shelling peas daily in the morning when the sugars are high. You will get plenty of peas of a nice small size that way. They will keep for several days on the kitchen counter, shelled or unshelled.
~Shelling peas becomes a late-afternoon-on-the-porch activity, shared by the whole family. Shells can be composted or fed to sheep, cows, or chickens.
~Shelled peas will hold for a long time, so that you can freeze a large batch all at once — they don't have to be processed right after picking.
~For information about freezing peas and other vegetables, see *Keeping the Harvest*.

Mediterranean Sugar Peas
The peas should be harvested early in the morning, stems and strings removed, and then parboiled very briefly to retain their crunch. You can use frozen sugar peas for this dish.

1 1/2 t butter
1 clove garlic, minced
1/4 each t dried basil, oregano, and thyme
1/2 lb fresh sugar peas, trimmed
1 T or more water
1 T olive oil
1 t fresh lemon juice
Salt and pepper, to taste

Melt butter in a skillet over medium heat; cook and stir garlic until fragrant, about 30 seconds. Stir in herbs and sugar peas. Add water. Cook and stir until peas are bright green and tender, about 2 minutes. Stir in olive oil and lemon juice. Season with salt and pepper. Serve at once.

Peas with Onion & Garlic

2 T olive oil
1 onion, chopped
2 cloves garlic, minced
16 oz frozen peas, partially thawed (do not drain)
1 T homemade chicken stock
Salt and pepper, to taste

Heat olive oil in a skillet over medium heat. Stir in onion; cook until softened. Stir in garlic; cook until fragrant. Break up peas in their package, add to skillet; cover and cook until the peas are tender but still firm. Season with salt and pepper.

Creamy Mushroom Peas

2 C frozen peas
2 T butter
1 C sliced fresh mushrooms
1 small onion, chopped
1 T flour
1 C half-and-half
1/4 t each salt and pepper
1 pinch ground nutmeg

Fill a medium saucepan about half full with salted water. Bring to a boil, add peas, and cook just until peas pop to the surface, drain. Melt butter in a medium saucepan over medium heat. Add mushrooms and onions and cook until tender.

Sprinkle flour over the mushrooms, and cook for 1 minute, stirring constantly. Gradually stir in half-and-half, season with salt, pepper, and nutmeg. Cook and stir until smooth and thick. Stir in peas, and remove from heat. Let stand for 5 minutes before serving.

Split Pea Soup

This is a great way to use a leftover ham bone. Simmer bone in 4 quarts of water for several hours until you have a hearty broth and any remaining meat can be pulled off and set aside. (You can do this the day before you prepare the soup.)

3 C dried split peas
4 carrots, scrubbed and chunked
1 large onion, chopped
1 peeled potato, diced
Salt, pepper, and garlic powder, to taste

Get the broth to a boil, then add split peas. Cook gently for about an hour until split peas are mushy. Add carrots, potato, onion, salt, pepper and garlic granules (you can use minced fresh garlic or frozen garlic cubes instead). Simmer until carrots are tender. Adjust seasonings. Add cooked bits of ham. Serve with French bread (see *Bread & Grains*).

Peppers

Peppers originated in the Western Hemisphere, and have been used as a culinary staple since 7500 B.C. Spanish explorers carried peppers back to Europe, from where they spread to Africa and Asia. Peppers are now part of cooking in most places in the world.

Peppers contain vitamins A, C, E, and K, folate, niacin, pyridoxine, riboflavin, thiamin, sodium, potassium, calcium, copper, iron, magnesium, manganese, phosphorus, selenium, and zinc.

Tips for Peppers

~Seed catalogs will tempt the gardener with dozens of different kinds of peppers, but they are easily divided into "sweet" and "hot," the hot peppers ranging from warm to blistering. Generally, intensity of heat in the pepper decreases as the size increases.

~Peppers are easily grown in the home garden, but to thrive they need a strong start and a warm environment, such as a greenhouse.

~When seeding or cutting hot peppers, wear latex gloves, and do not touch your eyes, nose or mouth. The oils will burn your skin. Water will not wash the oils away, but vinegar or rubbing alcohol will remove them from your hands.

~Seed and remove membrane from hot peppers before cooking. They contain the phytochemical capsaicin that produces heat. If you want a hotter taste, leave seeds and membrane in the pepper.

~Hot peppers can be frozen trimmed or whole. The latter will result in a hotter pepper.

~Hot peppers can be air dried or dried in a dehydrator, and strung in your kitchen or kept on a platter. We use these whole, to cook in beans, soups, or stews, where they provide a warm flavor. Remove pepper from the dish before serving.

~Sweet peppers vary. Green peppers are the brightest in flavor, and will become mellower as they turn yellow or red.

~Sweet peppers can be frozen. Remove membrane and seeds and chop (no need to blanch).

Freeze pieces on cookie sheets, put into freezer bags and use in winter casseroles, soups or stews.

~To roast peppers, halve them lengthwise, remove seeds and membranes. Place pepper halves, cut side down, on a foil-lined baking sheet. Bake in 425 oven for 20 minutes or until skins are blistered and dark, or broil for 8-10 minutes. Bring foil up to enclose and steam peppers. Let stand until cool enough to handle. Gently remove skin before slicing.

Stuffed Green Peppers

Like stuffed cabbage leaves and cucumbers, stuffed green peppers make an excellent one-dish meal.

4 pepper casings (to prepare, carefully remove the cap of the pepper and use a spoon to remove seeds and membrane)
2 T olive oil
1/2 lb ground beef
3 T minced onions
1 C cooked rice
2 well-beaten eggs
1/2 t salt
1/4 t paprika
1/3 t curry powder

Parboil pepper casings until nearly tender, about 8 minutes. Do not overcook — the casings should be firm. Drain and reserve.

Sauté the onions and hamburger in olive oil, breaking up the hamburger to a mince. Remove the pan from heat, and add the rest of the ingredients, mixing well. Place the pepper casings in a baking dish that will keep them upright, stuff with filling and bake at 350 for about 10 minutes.

Red Pepper & Zucchini Sauté

A good vegetable dish for summer, when zucchini and peppers are fresh off the vine.

1 medium zucchini, thinly sliced
4 cloves garlic, minced
1/4 red onion, diced
1 roasted red bell pepper, thinly sliced (See *Tips* above for roasting peppers)
1 t paprika
1/2 t salt

Heat oil in a large skillet over medium heat. Add garlic and onion and sauté until tender. Add zucchini slices and sauté until slightly softened. Add bell pepper slices and sauté briefly until warmed. Stir in paprika and salt and toss to coat. Serve at once.

Stuffed Poblano Peppers

This recipe can come together quickly if you cook the beans and rice the day before. We add salt, pepper, diced garlic, onion, and herbs to the beans as they simmer.

4 large Poblano peppers
1 C cooked black or other small beans
1 C cooked brown rice
1/3 C salsa (preferably home made)
1/3 C shredded cheddar or other hard cheese, divided
1/3 C mozzarella or other soft cheese, divided

Roast the whole peppers under the broiler, about 5 minutes per side, until the skin blisters. Place peppers in a bowl and cover until steam softens them and they are cool enough to handle. Rub off the papery skin with your fingers. Cut the pepper in half, remove seeds and membrane.

Stir together beans, rice, salsa and half the cheese. Spoon into prepared peppers, mounding the mixture. Place peppers in a lightly greased shallow baking pan. Cover with foil. Bake at 375 for 15 minutes. Sprinkle with remaining cheese. Broil until cheese melts.

Potatoes

Potatoes were first cultivated in the Andes, where they grew in every color and size. The Spanish took them to Europe, including them in the crews' diet to prevent scurvy. Potatoes came to North America in the 1700s, and have been an important part of the diet ever since. Potatoes have a dramatic history in every country in Europe, including their role in Ireland, culminating in the Irish Potato Famine (a tragic lesson about mono-cropping) which brought many Irish to America.

Potatoes contain vitamin C, thiamin, niacin, riboflavin, pyridoxine, folate, iron, calcium, phosphorus, magnesium, and potassium.

Tips for Potatoes

~Potatoes are part of our weekly diet, and we grow several varieties from our own seed: Red Norlands, sold as "new" potatoes in grocery stores, are small when harvested, low in starch, and should be cooked in their skins; Fingerlings, which are small and tender, can be scrubbed and sliced for frying; Russets are for baking. Yukon Golds can be used in any recipe as can California Whites, which are larger and just as versatile. Potatoes are also part of the diets of our cows, pigs, and chickens.

~Uses of potatoes include boiling, baking, stuffing, frying, mashing, roasting, and as a base for salads. Be aware of what you want: blue and purple potatoes, for example, cook much more quickly than white or yellow potatoes, so you don't want to cook them together.

~Remove the eyes and green sections from potatoes. These contain a toxic substance (solanine), created when potatoes are exposed to light.

~If possible, scrub, rather than peel, potatoes. Most of the nutrients are in the peel and right below its surface.

~Boiling potatoes will destroy some of the nutrients. Baking and roasting preserves them.

~Prepare potatoes just before using. Busy cooks often wash, peel, and cut potatoes early and keep them in water to prevent their oxidizing. It's convenient, but the water removes nutrients.

~See *Keeping the Harvest* for storing potatoes and other root crops.

Mashed Potatoes
1-2 large potatoes per person
Cream
Butter
Salt, pepper, and garlic granules
Fresh chives, snipped into small pieces

Peel desired number of potatoes and cut them into large chunks. Cook gently in salted water until potatoes come apart when pierced with a fork; do not let them become mushy. Drain, and begin mashing with a potato masher. Add butter, cream, salt, pepper, and garlic granules, to taste. When potatoes are mashed, stir in snipped chives.

Home Fries
French fries available in fast food restaurants may taste good, but their flavor comes from oils that have been used a number of times — and thus transformed into trans fats — and adulterated with various chemicals, including silicone, to prevent the oil from foaming. Make your own fries at home. Scrub unpeeled potatoes and cut into elongated wedges. Heat olive oil in a cast-iron frying pan, and

add prepared potatoes. Add paprika, salt, garlic granules and pepper, to taste. Fry over medium heat, tossing until tender and browned.

Oven French Fries
An alternative to Home Fries is to roast the potatoes.

2 large scrubbed, unpeeled baking potatoes or unpeeled fingerling potatoes
1 T olive oil
Salt, to taste

Cut potatoes into elongated wedges. Mix olive oil and salt, coat potato wedges with the mix and place them on a lightly oiled baking pan. Bake at 350, turning occasionally, until golden brown and crispy, about 40 minutes. (We prefer simple fries, with just oil and salt. If you want something jazzier, use other spices, such as garlic granules, paprika, or chili powder, as well.)

Roasted Garlic Potatoes with Rosemary
This is a basic side dish that you can make into a main meal by adding other root vegetables such as beets, kohlrabi, turnips, parsnips, onions, and carrots.

3 medium potatoes per person
5 cloves garlic, peeled and chopped
Leaves from 3 sprigs of rosemary
Olive oil
Salt, to taste

Peel or scrub and cut the potatoes into bite-sized chunks. Do the same with other root vegetables you want to add. Place in a large bowl, and toss with oil, garlic and rosemary, adding other herbs, such as basil and thyme, if other vegetables are used. Brush a large baking pan with olive oil, and spread potatoes, vegetables and herbs. Don't crowd the potatoes or vegetables too much — they need room to brown. Bake at 400 for 45 minutes or so until vegetables are tender on the inside, crisp on the outside. Stir once or twice during baking.

German Potato Salad
This recipe can be halved to feed a family, or doubled to feed a crowd, and can be made a day ahead.

8 medium potatoes
1/4 C white balsamic vinegar
1/2 C water, divided

1/4 C sugar
1/2 t salt
2 T flour
8 slices bacon, chopped
3/4 C diced onion
Diced dill pickles to taste

Scrub potatoes and cut into bite-sized chunks. Cook until barely tender — they must be firm enough to slice — drain and place in large bowl. While potatoes are cooking, combine vinegar, 1/4 C water, sugar, and salt, and bring to a boil in a small saucepan. Mix flour with 1/4 C water in a small bowl, then stir the blend into the vinegar mixture and simmer while stirring, until the sauce is clear and thickened. Set aside.

Fry bacon pieces in a skillet until nearly cooked, add onions and continue cooking until the bacon is crisp and the onions are tender. Add, including the bacon fat, to the vinegar mixture and stir. Remove bacon and onions from the sauce with a slotted spoon and add to the potatoes. Spoon about half the remaining sauce over the potatoes and mix. Be judicious — you don't want the potatoes to be soggy. The remaining sauce can be stored in the refrigerator.

Fold chopped dill pickles into the dressed potatoes. Let stand at room temperature, stirring every half hour or so. Serve, or refrigerate and serve later, but salad should be at room temperature.

You can also use a vinaigrette as a dressing.

Scalloped Potatoes
This is a wonderful way to use leftover ham.

8 C peeled and thinly sliced potatoes
1 t salt
2 T flour
6 T butter
Pieces of cooked ham
1 medium onion, diced
2 C milk or cream
Paprika
Dried mustard

Parboil potato slices briefly, until barely tender. Drain. Place in a greased 9x13-inch baking pan in two layers, sprinkling each layer with flour, diced onion, pieces of ham, and dots of butter. Heat milk or cream, mix in salt, paprika, and mustard. Pour the mixture over the potatoes, sprinkle the top with

paprika, and bake at 350 for 35 minutes.

Potato Pancakes
Russet potatoes are the best to use for this recipe because of their firmness.

4 C (about 2 lb) whole potatoes
1/2 C grated Parmesan or other hard cheese
1/2 C diced scallions (white parts for potato mix — reserve diced green parts for garnish)
2 eggs
1 T flour
1 t each salt and pepper
1/4 t baking powder
1/4 C olive oil

Early in the day, peel and simmer whole potatoes in salted water until they are about half cooked — if overdone, they will not shred properly. Refrigerate. When potatoes are thoroughly chilled, shred them. You can use a salad shooter, the coarse shredding disk on a food processor, or a food grater.

An alternative to cooking and chilling the potatoes is to shred them raw, and then let the shreds drain in a colander to remove moisture.

In a large bowl, gently toss the shredded potatoes with the cheese and the diced scallions. Use your hands — a spoon will break up the potato shreds.

In a small bowl, whisk together eggs, flour, salt, pepper, and baking powder. Pour over the potato mixture and gently toss to combine, using your hands to keep the potato shreds intact.

Heat a non-stick skillet over medium heat, and add some oil to prevent potatoes from sticking. The heat must be carefully monitored: too cool, and the potatoes will soak up the oil; too hot, and they'll brown without cooking properly.

Gently form pancakes with your hands — you can use an ice cream scoop to measure quantity. Place flattened potato pancakes in the heated, oiled pan, leaving plenty of room between them. Cook 3-5 minutes per side, until deep golden brown. Transfer to a warm platter in the oven. Garnish with scallion greens and serve at once. Applesauce makes a great condiment to the savory pancakes.

Jansons Frestelse (Janson's Temptation)
This is a special-occasions dish we learned from

one of Henning's colleagues from Sweden. We serve it with homemade sausages, leg of lamb, pork, ham, or beef roast. It can easily be doubled for a company meal.

4 large potatoes, peeled and cut into elongated wedges (about 1/2 inch thick)
1 large onion, sliced thinly
2 T butter
1 tin anchovy fillets, including oil
1 pint heavy cream

Sauté onion in butter until golden. Drain potato wedges and place half of them in the bottom of a lightly greased 9x13-inch baking dish. Distribute sautéed onion over the potatoes.

Cut the anchovy fillets in half, retaining the oil, and place over the onions. Cover with remaining potato wedges and sprinkle with the oil from anchovies.

Bake, uncovered, at 450 for 20 minutes. Remove from oven and lower temperature to 350. Pour cream over the potatoes until almost level, but not covering, the top layer. Bake for 60 minutes.

Kartoffelklösse (Potato Dumplings)

German potato dumplings can be made from raw or boiled potatoes. The following recipe for dumplings made from boiled potatoes is adapted from *Lüchow's German Cookbook*.

3 lb medium-sized potatoes, preferably baking potatoes
3 egg yolks, beaten
3 T each cornstarch and Cream of Wheat®
1/2 t pepper
1 1/2 t salt
1/4 t each nutmeg and garlic granules
1 C toasted white bread cubes
Organic flour, as needed
1 1/2 qt boiling salted water

Peel the potatoes, cut into chunks and cook in salted water until soft enough to pass through a potato ricer. Add egg yolks, cornstarch, cereal, salt and spices, and mix with your hands. Shape into 2-inch dumplings and place a bread cube in the center of each. It is a good idea to shape one dumpling first, and if it does not hold together while cooking, beat a little flour into the dumpling mixture before shaping the remainder.

Roll each dumpling lightly in flour. Cook in rapidly boiling salted water 15-20 minutes. Remove dumplings from water, serve hot. Makes 12 or more dumplings.

Leftover dumplings may be cut in half and sautéed in butter.

Dumplings are a good accompaniment to roast beef or *sauerbraten*.
If you leave out the pepper and garlic, the dumplings are excellent in combination with stewed plums or other fruit.

Pumpkins

Pumpkins originated in Central America over 7500 years ago, and moved north, gaining sweetness and size as they migrated. They were a mainstay for European settlers.

Pumpkins contain vitamins A, C, E, K, thiamin, folate, pantothenic acid, niacin, iron, magnesium, phosphorus, riboflavin, potassium, copper, and manganese.

Tips For Pumpkins

~There are many kinds of pumpkins available in a range of colors, some developed for carving at Halloween, some for their tasty flesh. We grow pumpkins for consumption — ours and the animals' — and store them in bins in the barn where they stay cool and protected.
~As an alternative, bake and process the flesh right away, and freeze it for soups or pies.
~To prepare seeds for salads, soups, or snacking, cut the pumpkin in halves or quarters, scrape out the pulp and seeds, and rub the pulp off the seeds. Wash and dry seeds, coat them with oil, sprinkle with a little salt, and toss them in a cast-iron pan until they begin to pop. Let most of them pop. Cool. They can be used right away, or stored in a glass jar.

Pumpkin Pie

Preparation is easy. Cut the pumpkin in halves or quarters, scoop out the seeds and save for processing. Wet the cut sides of the pumpkin, and place the pieces, skin sides up, on a baking sheet lined with parchment paper or aluminum foil. Bake at 400 until the flesh is very soft — about an hour. Let the pieces cool a bit, peel off the skin, and process the flesh in a food processor until it is creamy. Put the creamed pumpkin by 1 cup measures in freezer bags and freeze until ready to use.

For the Pie Filling:
1 C cooked pumpkin
1 T flour
1/2 C sugar
3/4 C milk
1/4 t each of ginger, nutmeg and cinnamon
2 eggs

Mix pumpkin, flour, and sugar together, and beat in milk, spices and eggs. Pour into a prepared 9-inch pie crust (see *Tree Fruits and Berries*) and bake at 425 for 15 minutes. Reduce heat to 350 and bake 45 minutes, until knife blade comes out clean.

Simple Pumpkin Soup

This is a cozy soup for winter evenings.

2 lb cooked pumpkin
3 C scalded milk or chicken broth
1 T each butter and flour
2 T brown sugar
Salt, pepper, ginger, and cinnamon, to taste
3/4 C light cream if you have used the chicken broth

Place the cooked pumpkin in the milk or broth. Knead together the butter and flour and add it to the liquid. Add sugar, spices and cream, if used. Heat, but do not boil. Serve at once.

Company Pumpkin Soup

This soup requires more preparation than the simple soup above, but the resulting dish has a subtle and elegant flavor, worthy of a main dish to serve to guests.

1/3 C prepared pumpkin seeds (see above)
6 strips thick-sliced bacon, diced
1 C diced onions
1/2 C chopped celery
1/2 C diced carrots
2 bay leaves
2 T minced fresh rosemary
1 T minced fresh garlic
1/2 C dry sherry, divided
5 C homemade beef or vegetable broth
4 C processed pumpkin
1 C half-and-half
1/4 C honey
1 T apple cider vinegar

Salt, pepper, and nutmeg, to taste

Cook bacon in a pot until crisp. Transfer solids to a paper-towel-lined plate. In the bacon grease, cook onions, celery, carrots, bay leaves, rosemary, and garlic over medium heat until vegetables begin to brown and soften, about seven minutes.

Deglaze pot with sherry, reserving 2 tablespoons. Scrape up any brown bits, and cook until sherry is evaporated. Stir in broth and pumpkin; heat to a boil. Reduce heat and simmer soup, partly covered, until vegetables are fork-tender, 10-15 minutes. Discard bay leaves. Puree soup in a food processor or with an immersion blender.

Return soup to pot, and stir in half-and-half, honey, cider vinegar, two tablespoons sherry; heat until warmed through. Season soup with salt, pepper and nutmeg, to taste. Top servings with pumpkin seeds and bacon.

Rutabaga

Rutabagas, also called "Swedes," were developed from a hybrid between the turnip and wild cabbage, probably in Scandinavia or Russia, as recently as the 17th century. They are grown for human and animal consumption.

Rutabagas contain vitamins C, E, K, thiamin, riboflavin, niacin, pantothenic acid, folate, pyridoxine, phosphorus, potassium, sodium, manganese, calcium, iron, and zinc.

Tips for Rutabaga

~Like carrots and beets, rutabagas are good both raw and cooked, and lend a distinctive flavor to soups, roasted vegetables, and salads.

~Rutabagas should be peeled if they are mature; if they are young, you can cook them without peeling.

~Add cooked rutabagas to mashed potatoes to add a rich flavor.

~Cook rutabagas while fresh, or wash, dry, and store in the refrigerator after harvesting. They will keep well in a root cellar or sand box.

Roasted Rutabagas

Roast rutabagas by themselves or with turnips, beets, onions, carrots, and potatoes to make a full meal or as a side dish for a roast. Prepare vegetables, toss with olive oil and desired herbs, such as fresh thyme, rosemary, dried basil and oregano, salt and pepper, and roast at 400 for an hour, tossing occasionally, until fork tender.

Root Vegetable Gratin

2 potatoes, scrubbed and thinly sliced
1 each rutabaga, turnip, parsnip, and small celeriac, peeled and thinly sliced
Salt, to taste
3 cloves garlic, minced
2 T butter
1 1/4 C homemade chicken broth
1 C heavy cream
1 T chopped fresh thyme
1 pinch each nutmeg and cayenne pepper
Olive oil
1/2 C finely grated Parmesan or other hard cheese

Bring pot of salted water to a boil. Add prepared vegetables, and cook uncovered for three minutes. Immerse in cold water to stop the cooking process. Drain and set aside.

Cook garlic in butter in a large skillet over medium heat until garlic starts to sizzle. Stir in chicken broth, cream, thyme, nutmeg, and cayenne pepper. Cook until mixture simmers.

Coat a 9x13-inch baking dish with olive oil and spread vegetables evenly in dish. Pour broth and cream mixture over vegetables and top with half the cheese. Cover baking dish loosely with aluminum foil, and bake in preheated oven at 375 for 40 minutes.

Remove baking dish from the oven and top with remaining cheese. Bake uncovered until vegetables are browned, bubbling, and tender, about 30 minutes. Let settle for 15 minutes before serving.

Rutabaga & Parsnip Soup

2 T butter or olive oil
1/2 C chopped onion
2 large rutabagas and 1 parsnip, peeled and cut into one-inch pieces
1 t dried sage
1 T honey
1/2 C cream
A topping, such as pepitas, croutons, chopped parsley or minced scallions

Sauté onions in butter until tender. Add prepared

rutabagas and parsnips and stir, then pour in broth, bring to a boil, lower heat and simmer until vegetables are tender. Puree all or part of soup in a food processor or with an immersion blender, adding the sage and honey. Return to pot, add cream and heat but do not boil. Serve, sprinkling topping of choice over bowls of soup.

Spinach

Spinach originated about 2000 years ago in Persia, from where it traveled to China, and from there to Sicily, and northern Europe via Spain. It gained popularity in England and France because it appeared early in spring before other vegetables were available.

Spinach contains vitamins A, C, K, E, folate, iron, calcium, phosphorus, sodium, zinc, copper, manganese, niacin, thiamin, riboflavin, pantothenic acid, potassium, and magnesium.

Tips for Spinach

~Spinach is versatile, eaten raw or cooked.
~In the home garden, it rivals lettuce for first appearance in spring, and, like lettuce, is a "cut and come again" crop: you can harvest the outer leaves, or cut the whole plant two inches from the soil, and it will regrow.
~Spinach will "bolt" (develop seed and stop producing leaves) with heat, so should be planted in a cool, shady area.
~There are many kinds of spinach; we like savoy spinach, with firm, crinkly leaves.
~Spinach is easily frozen — blanch, squeeze out water, place into freezer bags in desired amounts — and then it is available for quiches, casseroles, and soups throughout the winter.
~When using frozen or freshly cooked spinach, be sure to squeeze out residual moisture.
~Use spinach as a topping for pizza — add fresh leaves after pizza comes out of the oven so leaves do not burn.
~Use spinach, freshly cooked or frozen, with sautéed onion, garlic, ricotta and homemade basil and tomato sauce as a filling for lasagne, in place of meat.

Spinach Salad
For the Salad:
Our favorite spinach salad makes a complete meal. Combine fresh leaves of spinach, chopped hard

boiled eggs, crisp bacon, minced sautéed onion. You can fancy it up with water chestnuts, chopped apples, roasted pumpkin seeds, chopped avocado, bean sprouts, sautéed mushrooms or shredded cheese, if you like. We like to let the spinach dominate the salad, so we keep it simple.
For the Dressing:
Diced garlic, olive oil, prepared mustard, dried basil, sugar, salt, pepper, a little white balsamic vinegar or lemon juice. Serve with a good crusty bread.

Spinach Omelet

5-6 large fresh spinach leaves, roughly cut
6 eggs, scrambled with a little cold water or milk
Salt and pepper, to taste
Minced clove of garlic, or garlic granules

Pour eggs, mixed with salt, pepper, and garlic, into a buttered nonstick pan and cook, lifting the edges to let the liquid run to the bottom and cook. When the eggs are set, put the chopped spinach on one side of the omelette and turn the other side over the spinach. Cook another two to three minutes, just enough to tenderize the spinach. To the spinach, you can add cooked bacon, sautéed mushrooms, sautéed onion, or shredded cheese.

Creamed Spinach Crepes

For the Crepes:
2 C flour
2 T granulated sugar
6 eggs
2 C milk
4 T melted butter

Combine all ingredients and beat well. Spread crepe batter thinly in a heated non stick pan. Cook until golden on both sides. Set aside. (Recipe makes ten large crepes.)
For the Filling:
3 medium onions, diced
6 cloves garlic, diced
A generous amount of fresh spinach, stemmed and sliced
Cream, as needed
Salt, pepper and nutmeg, to taste
Butter and olive oil
Basil and tomato sauce, preferably home made (See *Keeping the Harvest* for recipe)

Sauté the onions and garlic in the olive oil until just tender. Add the spinach and stir until it has broken down. Add just enough cream to coat the spinach

and create a bit of sauce. Add salt, pepper and nutmeg to taste.

Place a large spoonful of the spinach mixture down the middle of each crepe, roll up crepe and place seam side down in a baking dish. Cover each crepe with tomato and basil sauce. Bake at 300 until heated through, about 20 minutes. Place a little sauce from the baking dish over each crepe before serving.

We serve this dish with green salad with vinaigrette dressing. The brightness of the vinaigrette complements the creamy taste of the crepes.

Summer Squash

Summer squashes were a regular part of the diet of indigenous peoples in North, Central, and South America.

We grow patty pan, crookneck, and yellow straight summer squash; all provide prodigious harvests, and can grow large without losing tenderness or flavor.

Squashes contain vitamins A, C, D, E, and K, cobalamin, pyridoxine, thiamin, riboflavin, niacin, folate, pantothenic acid, calcium, magnesium, iron, phosphorus, sodium, zinc, copper, and manganese.

Tips for Summer Squash

~Summer squash should be harvested before the shells harden.
~Squash can be stored in a cool dark place; check regularly for mold.
~Summer squash can be pickled along with other vegetables. (See *Keeping the Harvest.*)
~Summer squashes have very short cooking times, and are best sautéed, steamed, roasted, or stir-fried. Boiling makes them mushy.
~Summer squash, sautéed by itself or with zucchini, is easy and quick. We like to begin with sautéed onion and garlic; you could also add mushrooms and herbs. Grated cheese is a good topping.

Summer Squash Frittata

3 T butter
2 C each zucchini and summer squash, chopped into 1/2 inch cubes
1 small onion, coarsely chopped

12 eggs, lightly beaten
1/2 C sour cream
1 t salt
3/4 t pepper
1/3 C chopped fresh basil leaves

Melt butter in ovenproof skillet over medium heat; add zucchini, squash and onion, and sauté 10 minutes or until onion is tender. Remove from heat. Whisk together eggs, salt, pepper, and sour cream. Pour over vegetable mixture in skillet. Bake at 350 for thirty minutes, until edges are browned and center is set. Sprinkle with chopped basil.

Summer Squash Enchiladas

2 T each butter and flour
1 t chili powder
1 C milk
1 C grated cheddar cheese
Salt and pepper, to taste
3 C diced summer squash
2 T olive oil, divided
1 C diced onion
3 garlic cloves, minced
1/2 t minced fresh hot peppers
4 large flour tortillas
3 1/2 C diced tomatoes

In a small saucepan, melt the butter and stir in the flour and chili powder to make a thick paste. Add the milk a little at a time, whisking after each addition to prevent lumps. Add the cheese and heat gently, stirring constantly, until the cheese has softened. Season to taste with salt and pepper.

Steam the squash until it is barely tender. In a frying pan, heat the oil and sauté the onion, garlic, and hot peppers until tender. Add the squash and two-thirds of the sauce. Toss to coat.

Brush a 9x13-inch baking dish with olive oil. Spoon some filling into each tortilla and roll like a crepe. Place seam side down in the baking dish, making sure there is enough olive oil under the tortilla to prevent it from sticking during baking. Spoon the extra sauce on top. Sprinkle with diced tomatoes. Bake the enchiladas, at 350 uncovered, for 30 minutes or until heated through. Serve at once.

Summer Squash Gratin

2 T butter
2 each medium zucchini and summer squash, thinly sliced
2 shallots, minced
1/2 t salt
1/4 t pepper
4 garlic cloves, minced
1/2 C cream
1 C bread crumbs, divided
1/2 C hard cheese, grated and divided

In a large skillet, sauté zucchini, summer squash and shallots. Sprinkle with salt and pepper. Cook, stirring occasionally, until squashes are barely tender. Add garlic, and cook until garlic is fragrant. Add cream. Cook until thickened. Remove from heat.

Stir in 1/2 cup bread crumbs and one-quarter cup cheese. Spoon mixture into greased 9x13-inch baking dish. Sprinkle with remaining bread crumbs and cheese. Bake uncovered at 450 for 8-10 minutes, until golden brown.

Summer Squash with Pasta

2 T olive oil
1 small red onion, diced
2 cloves garlic, minced
2 medium tomatoes, chopped
1 t salt
1/4 t pepper
2 each small zucchini and yellow squash, sliced thinly
Linguini or other thin pasta
3 fresh basil leaves, chopped
Shredded hard cheese

Heat the oil; stir in onion and garlic and sauté until tender. Mix in tomatoes, season with salt and pepper. Cook until tomato breaks down. Mix in zucchini and squash. Cover, reduce heat, and simmer until ingredients are tender. Meanwhile, cook pasta. Drain, rinse with hot water. Place in serving bowls and top with cooked vegetables, fresh basil leaves, and shredded cheese.

Swiss Chard

Swiss chard was developed from wild beets in the Mediterranean. It was eaten by the early Greeks and Romans, but cannot easily be recognized in their literature because it went by more than ten different names. Swiss chard spread into Europe and the Americas in the 1830s. The "Swiss" part of the name honors the nationality of the botanist who described the plant. There are now multiple colors of chard to choose from.

Swiss chard contains vitamins A, C, E, K, thiamin, riboflavin, niacin, pantothenic acid, pyridoxine, phosphorus, selenium, zinc, folate, calcium, copper, magnesium, manganese, iron, and potassium.

Tips for Swiss Chard

~Chard is easily grown in the home garden, and is winter hardy. Like kale, it will withstand cold and frost, and is a good vegetable to harvest during the winter months.

~Chard is "cut and come again." Harvest the outer leaves, and more will grow from the center.

~The stalks are tender enough to cook with the leaves. Start them cooking before you add leaves.

~Young chard can be used raw in salads, and can substitute for spinach in many recipes.

~Tear a few leaves of chard into bite-sized pieces, and add to soups at the end of cooking.

~Chard can be frozen for use in winter quiches, soups and casseroles. Chop, blanch briefly, chill in cold water, let it drain, squeeze out the moisture, and put in freezer bags. Squeeze out residual moisture before cooking.

Simple Swiss Chard

2 T olive oil
4 cloves garlic, minced
1 bunch Swiss chard, stalks removed, leaves sliced
2 T dark balsamic vinegar
Salt and pepper to taste
Grated cheese for topping

Heat the olive oil in a large skillet over medium heat. Cook garlic until tender. Add chard and vinegar, and cook until chard is wilted. Season with salt and pepper, top with cheese. You can dress this dish up a bit by sautéing the stalk with some onion, and adding it to the dish.

Swiss Chard with Tomatoes and Pasta

3 T olive oil
4 cloves garlic, minced
1 medium onion, chopped
6-8 plum tomatoes, chopped
1 bundle Swiss chard, finely chopped, stalks removed
Pasta, such as penne, that will hold the sauce
Grated Parmesan or other hard cheese

Sauté garlic and onion in heated olive oil in large skillet until tender. Add tomatoes and cook until they break down.

Steam chard until it is just tender, then plunge into cold water to stop cooking process. Remove chard from cold water, squeeze out residual moisture, and mix with the tomato mixture. Add salt and pepper to taste.Cook pasta, drain, and add to vegetable mixture, adding cooking water as needed for a moist sauce. Heat briefly, and serve with cheese added at the table.

Roasted Swiss Chard with Feta

1 bunch chard, leaves and stalks separated and chopped
1 large onion, chopped
2 T olive oil, divided
Salt and pepper to taste
1 C feta or other cheese, crumbled or grated

Toss the chopped chard stalks and onion in a bowl with one tablespoon olive oil. Season with salt and pepper, and spread into a lightly oiled 9x13-inch baking dish. Bake at 350 until the chard stalks have begun to soften and the onion is beginning to brown.

Toss the chard leaves with one tablespoon olive oil, a little more salt and pepper. Sprinkle the greens over the stalk and onion mixture, then scatter the feta or other cheese over the top.

Return to oven and bake until stalks are tender and the cheese is melted, about 20 minutes.

Steamed Chard

Chop and steam fresh chard lightly, and serve with a dash of vinegar, or vinegar and butter, or a mixture of sour cream and garlic that has been sautéed in butter.

Tomatoes

Is there anything to compare with the first tomatoes of summer, picked right off the vine? Just maybe the tomato sauce you make and preserve yourself, or the dried tomatoes you soak in olive oil and add to casseroles or omelettes. Or the homemade salsa that sings with cilantro and chili peppers.

The tomato is native to Western South America, taken back to Europe by the Spanish. They were planted as ornamentals at first, because they belong to the nightshade family and were thought to be poisonous (the leaves are). The French called them "pommes d'amour" or "love apples", presuming them to be a mild aphrodisiac. Now they are an essential ingredient in most national cuisines.

Tomatoes contain vitamins A, C, E, K, pyridoxine, thiamin, riboflavin, folate, pantothenic acid, potassium, phosphorus, magnesium, calcium, sodium, iron, manganese, copper, and zinc.

Tips for Tomatoes

~Seed catalogs offer dozens of kinds of tomatoes in all sizes and colors, ranging from nearly black to light yellow, for slicing, cooking, saucing, or drying. We grow a variety of tomatoes for all those purposes, including cherry tomatoes right next to the kitchen to pop into a salad. Tomatoes require heat to develop, so we raise most of our plants in a high tunnel hoop house.

~Tomatoes that are not fully ripe when picked will continue to ripen off the vine.

~Fresh tomatoes taste best at room temperature.

~Do not use aluminum pans or utensils when cooking tomatoes. The high acid in the tomatoes will create a chemical reaction that turns the tomatoes bitter.

~The high acid content of tomatoes will naturally slow down the cooking process of some other foods. For example, beans cooked with tomatoes will take up to 20% more cooking time.

~See *Keeping the Harvest* for tips on drying, freezing, and canning tomatoes, and making various sauces.

~Find a recipe for *Pico de Gallo* in the *Onion* section.

Crostini

2 C chopped fresh Roma or other paste tomatoes
2 T chopped shallots or 1/4 chopped onion
1/4 C chopped fresh basil
3 T olive oil
3 T white balsamic or herb vinegar
1/2 t pepper
1 t salt
Sliced French bread (see *Bread & Grains*)

In a bowl, combine the tomatoes, shallots or onion, and basil. Add all the other ingredients except the bread, and mix well. Toast the bread under the broiler until golden brown. Using a slotted spoon,

top the bread with the tomato mixture, and feast!

Fresh Tomato Soup

4 C chopped fresh tomatoes
1 small onion, diced
4 garlic cloves, diced
4 whole cloves (the spice) placed in a spice bag or wrapped in a little cheesecloth and tied with cotton string)
2 C homemade chicken broth
1 T dried oregano
1 t dried thyme
2 T each butter and flour
1 t salt
2 t sugar or to taste

In a stock pot, over medium heat, combine the tomatoes, onion, garlic, cloves (in spice bag), chicken broth, oregano, and thyme. Bring to a boil, and cook gently for 20 minutes to blend the flavors. Remove from heat, let mixture cool, remove spice bag, and process in a food processor or with an immersion blender. Place in a large bowl.

In the now empty stock pot, melt the butter over medium heat. Stir in the flour to make a roux, cooking until it is a medium brown. Gradually whisk in a bit of the tomato mixture, so that no lumps form, then stir in the rest. Season with sugar and salt, adjusting to taste.

Marinated Tomato, Cucumber & Onion Salad

1 C water
1/2 C white balsamic or herb vinegar
3 T olive oil
1/4 C sugar
1 t each salt and pepper
3 cucumbers, peeled and thinly sliced
5 Roma or other paste tomatoes, cut into wedges
1 small red onion, thinly sliced
1 clove garlic, thinly sliced
Whisk water, vinegar, oil, sugar, salt, and pepper together in a large bowl until blended. Add cucumbers, tomatoes, onion and garlic, and stir to coat. Cover and marinate in refrigerator for 2 hours.

Tomatoes & Swiss Chard

1 bunch Swiss chard
1 medium onion, diced
2 cloves garlic, minced
1/4 C olive oil
2 T fresh lemon juice

1/3 C butter
2 medium tomatoes, chopped
Salt and pepper

Separate chard leaves from stalks, and roughly chop both. Steam stalks until tender. In a small skillet, cook onion and garlic in oil and lemon juice until tender. In large skillet, heat butter, add chard leaves and tomatoes, and sauté about four minutes. Mix with chard stalks, onion, and garlic, and season to taste.

Turnips

Turnips grow in temperate climates, and have a long history of domestication and use, dating back at least to Greek and Roman times. The wild ancestors of the turnip range from Europe through Southwest Asia. It was originally grown for the oil from its seed. Noted in Greek and Roman times as good for human consumption, it became important fodder for livestock in Northern Europe in the 18th century, feeding animals in the winter after the hay ran out.

Turnip roots contain vitamins C, E, K, calcium, iron, manganese, and zinc. The greens contain a lot of vitamin A, and more of the other nutrients than the roots do.

Tips for Turnips

~Turnips will hold well in the soil throughout the winter; if you have problems with critters invading your harvest, store the turnips in a sand box, or in your refrigerator where they will keep a month or longer.

~Small to medium-sized turnips are sweet, with firm flesh; older, larger ones may turn fibrous and woody, but are good in soup.

~Non-organic turnips may be waxed, and should be peeled.

~Turnips can be eaten raw, flavored with lemon juice or an oil-and-vinegar dressing. They have great flavor and crunch!

~Turnips are an excellent addition to soups, stews, and roasted vegetables.

~Try boiling and mashing turnips with potatoes. They add a mild, sweet flavor.

~Do use the greens, especially when young. Light steaming reduces the sharp flavor; boiling or overcooking strips them of their vitamins. Serve steamed greens with butter and a dash of vinegar. Turnip greens can be added to fresh salads.

Cream of Turnip Soup

2 T butter
2 C diced onions
6 C diced turnips
4 C homemade chicken broth
2 bay leaves
1 C diced kale
1 C milk or cream
Salt and pepper

In a large pot, sauté the onions in the butter until just tender. Add turnips, chicken broth, and bay leaves. Simmer until turnips are tender. Remove the bay leaves, and cool the soup slightly. Puree half the soup in a food processor, or use an immersion blender. Add the kale and milk or cream. Simmer gently until kale is limp; do not boil. Season with salt and pepper to taste. Serve hot.

Fresh Turnip Salad

3 C grated turnips
2 C grated carrots
1/2 C each minced red onion and minced parsley
1 C raw or prepared pumpkin seeds (salt, toss in a frying pan with a little oil until they begin to pop).

Toss all ingredients together and mix with a vinaigrette made of 1/4 C olive oil, 3 T lemon juice, 1/2 t sugar, salt and pepper to taste.

(Once grated, the turnip will begin to oxidize. Make just before serving to preserve the color.)

Turnip Casserole

1 each turnip and medium potato, peeled and sliced
1 onion, sliced
1 medium zucchini, sliced
1 large tomato, sliced
2 slices cooked bacon (optional)
Grated Parmesan or other hard cheese
Dried basil, thyme, oregano, salt and pepper

Place sliced vegetables in layers in a casserole dish, lightly sprinkling with herbs, salt and pepper. Be sparing with these, especially salt and pepper.

Begin layering with turnips, then add potatoes, onion, bacon, if used, zucchini, and top with tomatoes and cheese. Bake, uncovered, at 350 for about an hour until vegetables are cooked through and cheese is bubbly. Check halfway through; if vegetables are dry, add a little water or broth.

Turnip Greens

You can add any greens to this recipe — mustard, beet, collard, spinach, or Swiss chard, for example.

1/4 C olive oil
6 large garlic cloves, minced
1 lb turnip greens, thinly sliced
Salt to taste
Grated cheese (optional)

Heat the oil in a heavy skillet. Sauté garlic until golden, remove with slotted spoon and reserve. Add greens and sauté until tender. Add salt to taste. Just before serving, sprinkle reserved garlic over greens. Top with grated cheese.

Turnip Greens with Pork

Turnip greens are often cooked with prepared bacon or ham, which sweetens the dish. Turnip greens can be boiled, but we prefer the lighter touch of sautéing.

1 C chopped bacon or small chunks of cooked ham
8 C turnip greens, washed, stemmed, and chopped
2 T fresh lemon juice
1 T olive oil or residual bacon grease
1 medium onion, chopped
Salt and pepper, to taste

Sprinkle turnip greens with lemon juice and set aside. In a large pan, cook bacon or brown pieces of cooked ham (for ham, use a little olive oil) Remove meat, and sauté onion in grease or oil.

Add greens to pan, and sauté until tender. Place greens in a large bowl, toss with salt and pepper to taste. Toss with vinaigrette, and sprinkle bacon or ham over the top. Serve warm.

Winter Squash

Winter squash, like summer squash, originated in the Americas. Native Americans cultivated the main varieties we grow today.

Winter squash contains vitamins A, C, K, niacin, pyridoxine, manganese, copper, potassium, and folate.

Tips for Winter Squash

~We grow Delicata, acorn, butternut, and Hubbard squash.

~We refer to these varieties as "winter keeper" squash, because, properly stored, they will keep for months. When they have reached maturity in color and size, (and in any case before the first frost), harvest, wash and dry them, and store them in a cool, dark place. (See *Keeping the Harvest*.)

~Some of the winter squashes have a tough skin, and need a sharp knife to open them up. Delicata and acorn have such tender skins you can eat them with the flesh after baking.

~Squash can be frozen. Cut it raw into cubes, or bake and process it in a food processor, bag and freeze it, and you have a ready-made base for soup or pies.

Baked Squash

This is our favorite way to prepare squash, particularly acorn and Delicata. Cut the squash in half lengthwise, scoop out the seeds and place the squash, cut side down on aluminum foil or parchment paper in a baking dish with a little water. Bake at 350 until a knife slides through easily. Serve with butter and salt.

Butternut Squash Soup

For the Soup:
1 C chopped onion
3/4 C each chopped celery and carrot
2 T butter
6-8 C chopped butternut squash
1 large tart green apple, cored, and chopped
3 C homemade chicken broth
1 C water
Nutmeg, cinnamon, cayenne, salt, pepper to taste
For Garnish:
Fresh parsley, chopped
Chives, chopped
Dash of paprika
Sour cream

Sauté onion, carrot, and celery in butter. Add squash, apple, broth and water, bring to a boil. Reduce to simmer, cover, and cook 30 minutes or so, until squash and carrots have softened. Cool. Puree the soup in batches in a food processor or with an immersion blender. Add pinches of nutmeg, cinnamon, and cayenne. Add salt and pepper to taste. Heat through. Top servings with fresh parsley, chives, and a dollop of sour cream.

Zucchini

Ancestors of zucchini came from the Americas. They were native to Mexico and the northern parts of South America more than 7000 years ago. Europeans took them home where their cultivation began; zucchini was developed in Italy in the 19th century, and brought to California by Italian immigrants in the 1920s.

Zucchini contains vitamins A, C, K, pyridoxine, riboflavin, folate, copper, phosphorus, thiamin, potassium, and manganese.

Tips for Zucchini

~One zucchini plant, properly tended, can feed an entire family for a season. When they get too large to use, give them to the chickens.

~Zucchini can be eaten raw in salads or cooked by steaming, grilling, stuffing, baking, as an ingredient in casseroles, frittata, or in breads.

Marinated Zucchini

Cut three small zucchini into thin slices and steam briefly until tender but still crunchy. Prepare marinade by shaking 2 t prepared mustard, 1/4 t salt, 1/4 t pepper, 2 t white balsamic vinegar, 1 clove minced garlic, and 1/2 C olive oil in a jar. When zucchini has cooled, toss with the marinade and refrigerate. Serve chilled.

Stuffed Baked Zucchini

4 small zucchini
2 T butter
1/2 C minced onions
1/2 t salt
1/4 t paprika
Dash of nutmeg
1 egg, beaten
1/2 C bread crumbs, divided
1/2 C grated cheese

Wash the zucchini and cut lengthwise, scooping out the pulp and leaving a half-inch shell. Reserve pulp. Sauté the onions in the butter. Add the reserved pulp, salt, paprika and nutmeg to the onions. Cook, stirring, until they are hot. Remove from heat and add the beaten egg, half the breadcrumbs, and half the cheese.

Rub the shells with butter, and fill with the stuffing. Place in a baking dish. Sprinkle the top with the remaining bread crumbs, cheese, and a bit more paprika. Bake at 350 until tender, about 20 minutes.

You can vary this recipe according to what you have on hand: Hot or sweet peppers, tomato sauce, or cooked meat, for example.

Zucchini & Apple Bread

The wonderful thing about zucchini is that when amounts become overwhelming, you can freeze it. Some people freeze it in chunks to use for winter soups and casseroles. We shred it, add shredded apples, pop it in a freezer bag and use it all winter for bread. (For each bag, use two cups of zucchini and one cup of apple.) Remove it from freezer and thaw before using. You will use the liquid, as well.

3 eggs
1 C vegetable oil (we use grape seed oil)
1 C sugar
1 C wheat bran flakes
2 t vanilla
2 C shredded zucchini
1 C shredded apple
3 C flour
2 t baking soda
1 t salt
1/2 t baking powder
1 1/2 t cinnamon
3/4 t nutmeg
1 C finely chopped walnuts

Cream together eggs, oil, sugar, bran, and vanilla. Stir in the zucchini and apple (using liquid, if zucchini and apple were frozen). In a separate bowl, combine the remaining ingredients. Stir the dry ingredients gently into the zucchini mixture until just blended. Divide the batter into two greased bread pans. Bake at 350 for 1 hour. Cool in pans and then turn onto a rack.

Zucchini Casserole

A simple version of the vegetable casserole described in the *Turnip* section. In a casserole dish, layer thick slices of zucchini, onions, and tomatoes. Top the zucchini layer with a sprinkle of dried thyme, and the tomato layer with dried basil, and cover with grated cheese. Bake, uncovered, at 350 for one hour. Makes its own, delicious sauce.

Zucchini Sautéed with Basil

2 T olive oil
1/2 small onion, cut in slices, rings separated
6 small zucchini, thinly sliced
1 C sliced mushrooms (optional)
2 t fresh minced basil, or 1/2 t dried basil
Salt and pepper to taste

Parmesan or other hard cheese, grated

In a large frying pan, heat olive oil and sauté onion until soft. Add zucchini rounds, mushrooms, and basil and sauté until lightly browned. Cover and cook until fork tender. Garnish with cheese before serving.

Zucchini Soup

This is an excellent use for zucchini that was shredded and frozen in the summer.

3/4 C chopped leeks, shallots, or onion
4 cloves garlic, chopped
2 T butter
1/4 t pepper
2 lb zucchini, chopped
2 C homemade chicken broth
Grated hard cheese, for garnish
Any of the following fresh herbs: 2 T minced dill, 1/4 C chopped basil, 1-2 sprigs chopped parsley
Thinly sliced summer sausage (optional)

In a large pot, sauté leeks, shallots or onions until tender. Add pepper and garlic and sauté 2 minutes longer (do not brown). Add zucchini and broth, cover and simmer until zucchini is tender. Cool briefly, remove about half the soup and puree it in a food processor, or use an immersion blender. Return to soup pot and heat through. Garnish bowls of soup with grated cheese and chopped herbs. This soup is very mild in flavor, and we have found that adding thin slices of summer sausage enhances the flavor and texture.

Zucchini with Garlic & Tomato

1 1/2 lb zucchini, thinly sliced
1 1/2 t olive oil
4 cloves garlic, minced
1 large tomato, seeded and chopped
3/4 t dried oregano
1/4 t salt
A pinch of pepper

In a large skillet, over medium heat, warm the oil. Add the garlic and cook for 30 seconds, until tender. Add the zucchini, toss to mix. Reduce heat. Cover and cook for 5 minutes, until zucchini softens. Add and warm chopped tomato. Add the salt and pepper and stir gently to mix. Sprinkle the zucchini with grated cheese before serving.

July 23, 2009
Garden Cress

Herbs

The benefits of herbs go beyond adding flavor to food. Wild plants, before they were domesticated and bred for size, appearance, keeping qualities, and surviving long distance transport, had more of the vitamins, minerals, antioxidants, and essential oils that keep us healthy. Herbs remain the closest to the wild plants humans evolved with, and are an ancient source of medication and aesthetic delight. A bundle of dried lavender next to a braid of garlic makes your kitchen look peaceful and bountiful. In the garden, herbs provide beauty and attract pollinators.

Herbs are easy to grow, and many of the most useful ones, such as rosemary, tarragon, sage, thyme, marjoram, and oregano, are perennial. We just have to whack them back from time to time to keep them from becoming trees. We renew our basil, chive, parsley, and cilantro plants as needed.

We have a perennial herb garden planted around a large rock that takes in heat during the day and releases it at night to benefit the herbs. Annual herbs are planted in beds. We have a small greenhouse just off the kitchen where we grow rosemary, thyme, and parsley, and as we are cooking, those herbs are just a step and a snip away. We grow a variety of herbs for daily tea: German camomile, nettle, catnip, calendula, marshmallow, mint, and sage. Some of these teas

we use fresh, some we prefer to dry. If you don't have space for a garden, plant herbs in containers on your deck or in a sunroom.

Tips for Herbs

~Drying herbs or flowers for tea is not difficult. Harvest young plants in the morning after the dew is off but before the sun has dried up the oils. Bind them by the stems, place them head down in a paper bag with holes punched in it, tie the bag closed, and suspend it from a rod in a place with air circulation and that is not exposed to sunlight.

~Herbs can also be placed in a dehydrator set at 125 and dried for several hours (from 12 to 24). Allow the leaves to cool and place in a jar.

~You can dry herbs in the oven by placing them on a baking sheet, setting the oven at the lowest temperature, and leaving the door open for air circulation. Check frequently so that the herbs do not burn. Let herbs cool and then store in jars.

~An easy way to dry herbs is to harvest them and place them on a fine mesh screen, and keep them in a warm, dry place until fully dried. Store in glass jars.

~In addition to what we grow ourselves, we also purchase dried culinary herbs from Blossom Grocery, which supplies them in bulk. We buy only what we need at a given time, and know that the herbs are fresh.

~Place a bowl of freshly cut herbs on your table as you would salt and pepper; sprinkle them over egg dishes, on soups or stews, potatoes, and salads. They are nature's greatest condiment.

Basil

Basil is a member of the mint family, along with other culinary herbs like rosemary, sage, and lavender. It is believed that basil originated in India, but it has been cultivated for over 5000 years all over the globe. It is easily adapted to different climates, because whole plants can be grown indoors away from cold and frost.

In Egypt, basil has been found in ancient tombs, and was likely used as an embalming agent. It was a symbol of mourning in ancient Greece, where it was known as the royal herb. It has a long history in traditional medicinal systems, as in India.

Basil contains vitamins A, C, K, manganese, copper, calcium, iron, folate, magnesium, and omega-3 fatty acids.

Tips for Basil

~Use one third the amount of dried basil when substituting it for fresh basil: 1 tablespoon of fresh chopped basil equals 1 teaspoon dried.

~Fresh basil should be rinsed under running water and patted dry.

~Chop leaves and add at the end of cooking a dish, such as a pasta sauce; heat will cause basil's volatile oils to dissipate.

~There are over 60 different varieties of basil, each with its own distinct flavor. These include hints of lemon, thyme, jasmine, clove, cinnamon, and anise.

~For best flavor, pick the leaves before the plant begins to flower.

~To store fresh basil, layer leaves between damp paper towels and keep in the refrigerator up to four days. You can keep whole stalks in a glass of water, store in the refrigerator, and use within a week. Do not wash leaves until you're ready to use them.

~Do not store basil in oil; it creates an environment for botulism.

~You can freeze basil, but we prefer to make pesto and freeze that.

Pesto

2 C basil leaves, compacted
1/2 C pine nuts or walnuts
4 cloves garlic
1/2 t salt
1/4 C olive oil
1/2 C grated Romano or Parmesan cheese

This is a traditional recipe; we prefer to make and freeze the pesto without the cheese and add homemade cheddar to the dish upon serving.

Use the metal blade of a food processor to chop cheese and garlic. Add remaining ingredients except oil and process until combined. With machine running, pour oil through the feeding tube, and process until combined. Scrape down bowl and process until smooth.

We make large quantities of pesto during basil season and freeze it. We do not recommend freezing it in ice cube trays because of freezer burn. Just place pesto in small jars or freezer bags and put them in the freezer. It keeps up to three years this way. You can put frozen pesto directly into a small saucepan, heat it slowly, and thin with a little white wine. Put it over pasta, add homemade French bread (see *Bread & Grains*) and a salad, and you have dinner. Pesto is also a great topping for pizza, sandwiches, potatoes, or soups.

Tomato & Basil Salad

This simple salad is wonderful in August when both tomatoes and basil are abundant.

6 ripe tomatoes, sliced
3 T olive oil
1 T white balsamic vinegar
Pepper, to taste
1/2 C finely chopped basil leaves

Lay tomato slices on a platter and sprinkle with basil leaves. Mix oil, vinegar and pepper together and pour over the top. Let salad sit for 30 minutes until the flavors are absorbed by the tomatoes.

Basil, Tomato, & Cucumber Salad

This salad, the heart of many a summer meal, is a variant of the salad above, adding slices of fresh cucumbers to the tomatoes, and 1/4 teaspoon of prepared mustard to the vinaigrette dressing. An alternative dressing is made from homemade mayonnaise, yogurt, and dill (see *Dill* section, below).

Chives

A member of the allium family (onions, garlic, scallions, leeks, and shallots, for example), chives have been used as a medicinal and culinary herb for 5000 years. They grow in the Americas, Europe, Africa, and Asia, and have been used in traditional Chinese medicine because of their stimulatory properties, and all over the world for their flavor.

Chives are a perennial plant, easily grown in the home garden, and available for most seasons of the year. We maintain a bed of chives that we access nearly every day. Their flavor is mild, but they will gently spice up any dish you add them to.

Chives contain vitamins A, C, E, K, folate, pantothenic acid, pyridoxine, riboflavin, thiamin, sodium, potassium, calcium, copper, iron, magnesium, manganese, phosphorus, selenium, and zinc.

Tips for Chives

~Chives are perennials, coming back every year. To start chives in your herb garden or in a large pot near your kitchen, plant them in the spring. They need sun and regular watering.

~Chives grow in clumps, and it is best to harvest the whole clump at a time, using scissors, leaving two inches at the bottom so the plant can grow again.

~Chives will produce a pretty purple flower, edible when young, very popular with pollinators, and nice in a bouquet on the table. However, the stems producing the flowers are tough and hollow, not usable in cooking.

~Cut a clump of chives and put it in a glass of water in the kitchen. Mince those chives to sprinkle over almost any dish you serve: eggs, potatoes, fish, salads, cooked vegetables, and soups, for example.

~To freeze chives, wash and dry them completely. Snip into small pieces. Freeze on a parchment lined baking sheet for 10 minutes. Put them into a freezer bag, remove air, and freeze. Be sure to use them still frozen — do not thaw.

~You can add chives to any other herb, such as basil, nettle, cilantro, or parsley, that you use to make pesto.

Cream Cheese & Chive Omelet

2 T butter
4 large eggs
2 T minced chives
2 T water
1/8 t salt
1/8 t pepper
2 oz cream cheese, cubed
Salsa (preferably homemade)

In a large nonstick skillet, melt butter. Whisk the eggs, chives, water, salt and pepper in a bowl and add to skillet over medium heat. As eggs begin to cook, lift edges, letting uncooked egg flow underneath until eggs are set. Place cubed cream cheese on one side, and fold the other side over the filling. Slide omelet onto a plate, cut in half. Serve with salsa.

Cilantro & Coriander

The herb cilantro and its seed, coriander, come from the same plant, but have very different tastes and culinary uses. Cilantro is an herb, coriander a spice. The plant is mentioned in the Bible, and the seeds have been found in ruins in the Middle East dating back to 5000 B.C. The herb is native to regions spanning from Southern Europe and Northern Africa to Southwestern Asia.

Cilantro and coriander contain vitamins A, C, E, K, thiamine, riboflavin, niacin, pantothenic acid, calcium, iron, magnesium, manganese, phosphorus, potassium, sodium, and zinc.

Tips for Cilantro & Coriander

~As with any fresh herb, add chopped cilantro at the end of cooking the dish, to preserve its flavor and texture.

~Cilantro is an essential ingredient in many Latin dishes, such as salsa, guacamole and ceviche, and can be used in salads, egg dishes, with shrimp or avocado.

~Pick cilantro while fresh in the morning, and store it in water in a jar on the counter or in the refrigerator.

~Add 1/4 C chopped cilantro to 1 cup homemade mayonnaise (see *Vegetables*) to serve on cold shrimp, crab, salmon, or tomatoes.

~Coriander seeds are usually toasted before being ground to bring out their full flavor. Our recommendation is to purchase the prepared spice in a natural foods store, but gathered at home they can be toasted in a dry skillet and ground in a food processor.

Carrot & Cilantro Soup

4 large carrots, scrubbed and cut into 1-inch pieces
1/4 large onion, chopped
1 quart homemade chicken broth
1/2 C chopped fresh cilantro

Place all ingredients in a large saucepan. Bring to a gentle boil and cook until the carrots are tender, about 10 minutes. Remove from heat and allow to cool slightly. Puree the soup until smooth in a food processor or with an immersion blender. Reheat before serving. Add a bit of sour cream to the soup, if desired.

Cilantro & Pumpkin Seed Pesto

Cilantro pesto is delicious on pasta, fish, pork, potatoes, bread, or vegetables. Like true nuts, pumpkin seeds have a rich oil content and give the pesto a warm, deep, slightly bitter flavor. If you don't grow them yourself, be sure to buy the dark-green hulled seeds, not the beige seeds that look like they came from a jack-o'-lantern.

1/3 cup pumpkin seeds
2 C gently packed cilantro leaves
3 cloves garlic, peeled
1 T fresh lemon juice
1 t seeded and chopped jalapeño
1/2 t salt
1/3 C olive oil

Toast the pumpkin seeds in a small dry skillet over medium heat. When you hear a seed pop, shake the pan continuously until most of the seeds are puffed instead of flat. Pour them onto a paper towel to cool.

Process the toasted pumpkin seeds with all ingredients except the oil in a food processor until finely ground. Stop the machine and scrape down the sides. With the machine running, pour the oil in a steady stream through the feeding tube and continue to process until the mixture is smooth. Taste and add additional salt and jalapeño if needed. Freeze in small jars or freezer bags.

Tomato Salad with Cilantro

4 ripe tomatoes, sliced
1/4 C finely chopped cilantro
1/2 C olive oil
1/4 C fresh lemon juice
Pepper, to taste

Lay tomato slices on a platter. Sprinkle chopped cilantro over the tomatoes. Mix oil, lemon juice and pepper together in a bowl, and drizzle over the tomatoes and cilantro.

Dill

Dill belongs to the same family as parsley and celery. It is native to the Mediterranean region and western Asia. In the southern Mediterranean region, as early as 3000 B.C, dill was popular for its magical and medicinal properties. It was cultivated by the ancient Babylonians and Assyrians. The ancient Romans revered dill and adorned themselves and their tables with it for special occasions. To the Greeks, dill signified wealth.

Our word "dill" comes from the Old Norse word "dylla," meaning "to soothe," because parents used it to ease the stomach pains of crying babies and lull them to sleep. Puritans and Quakers gave their children dill seed during long church services as an appetite suppressant.

Dill contains vitamins A, C, folic acid, riboflavin, niacin, Beta-carotene, pantothenic acid, pyridoxine, thiamine, calcium, iron, manganese, copper, magnesium, phosphorus, and zinc.

Tips for Dill

~To harvest the mature dill seed, cut the head of the plant and shake off the seed, or use the whole head when making pickles.
~Dill seed tastes like a mild version of caraway and can be used instead of caraway in rye bread.
~1 tablespoon chopped fresh dill weed is the equivalent of 1 teaspoon dried dill.
~If you buy dried dill weed, purchase it at a natural foods store, where the herb will be relatively fresh.
~If you gather dill from the garden, do it in the morning and store in water until using it.
~As with other herbs, the flavor will diminish with cooking, so add it to a dish at the last minute.
~To make a quick dill butter, add 1/4 cup minced fresh dill weed to 1/2 cup softened butter. Mix well, cover and refrigerate for 2 hours before using. Wonderful as a spread on bread or with seafood.
~See *Keeping the Harvest* about using dill seed and the head in dill pickles.

Dill Yogurt Dressing

This is our preferred salad dressing, which can also be used as a dip for fresh vegetables or on baked potatoes.

1 1/2 C plain whole milk yogurt
1/2 C mayonnaise (preferably homemade)
Minced fresh garlic to taste
2 t fresh lemon juice
1/2 C finely chopped dill weed
Pepper and sugar, to taste
Enough milk to create the desired consistency

Mix all ingredients together and chill before using. You may need to add more milk before serving a second time, because the dressing will thicken.

Garlic Dill Carrots

6 large carrots, scrubbed and cut into 1/2-inch pieces
2 t chopped dried tomatoes
1 T butter, melted
1 t dill weed
1 t garlic granules
1/2 t pepper
1/4 t salt

Cook carrots until tender, drain, place in medium bowl. Mix other ingredients in small bowl, pour over carrots and serve.

Shrimp Salad with Dill Dressing

1 lb medium fresh shrimp, peeled and deveined
Juice of 1 lemon (set 2 t of juice aside)
1/2 C celery, finely diced
3 T minced red onion
Salt and pepper, to taste
1/2 C homemade mayonnaise, *or* 1/4 C mayonnaise and 1/4 C sour cream, mixed
1 t Dijon mustard
1 1/2 T fresh dill, chopped, plus more for garnish

Bring a pot of salted water to a boil, and add the lemon juice. Add the fresh shrimp to the pot and cook gently for 2-3 minutes until pink and opaque. Transfer the shrimp to a bowl of ice water to stop the cooking process. Drain and pat dry. (An alternative is to use precooked, frozen shrimp. Defrost, rinse and pat dry before using.)

Place the shrimp, celery, red onion, lemon juice, salt, pepper, mayonnaise (or mixed mayonnaise and sour cream), mustard, and dill in a bowl. Toss gently to coat.

Garnish with additional fresh dill and serve, or refrigerate up to one day. Serve over greens or with fresh French bread (see *Bread & Grains*).

Smoked Salmon, Capers, & Dill Sauce

This recipe is a lighter alternative to the heavy cream used in most recipes for smoked salmon pasta sauce.

8 oz pasta
1/2 lb smoked salmon, broken into small pieces
1/4 C olive oil
1 large garlic clove, finely chopped
1 T capers, drained
1/4 C fresh dill weed, coarsely chopped
2 T finely diced red onion
1/4 t salt
Pepper, to taste
2 T grated hard cheese, plus extra for serving

Pull the smoked salmon into bite-sized pieces and place in a large bowl. Mix together olive oil, garlic, capers, dill, onion, salt, pepper, and cheese. Pour over salmon, and stir gently. Set aside to let flavors mingle.

Cook pasta in a large pot of boiling salted water with a little olive oil added, until tender. Drain pasta well, rinse with hot water, drain again, and toss with sauce in bowl. Serve at once with extra cheese — we use homemade cheddar.

Lavender

Lavender is a flowering plant of the mint family known for its beauty, fragrance, and multiple uses. It originated in the Mediterranean, the Middle East, and India, and its history goes back 2500 years. It is mentioned in the Bible in the Song of Solomon under the name of "spikenard." The Romans used lavender to scent their rooms, baths, beds, clothes, and hair. They also enjoyed its medicinal properties for healing wounds and promoting sleep. Today lavender is cultivated in its countries of origin, Europe, Australia, and in the Americas. Its widespread presence is due to the beauty of its flowers, scent, and multiple uses.

Lavender contains vitamin A, calcium, and iron. We grow lavender in our garden for its beautiful flowers and scent, and because it attracts pollinators; the bees practically line up for it.

Many claims are made for the beneficial effects of lavender oil, which is a commercial product we don't make at home, but is easily available at a natural foods store. Lavender oil is claimed to reduce anxiety, soothe headaches and migraines, aid in sleep, and to be beneficial to hair.

Tips for Lavender

~Some gardeners believe that planting lavender under rose bushes will prevent rust on the rose leaves.

~For drying, cut lavender before individual buds open.

~To hang in the house, bundle lavender by the stems and hang blossom-side down. Its scent is quiet and pleasant.

~Lavender can be placed into lingerie drawers for its subtle perfume, or used as a fragrance in soap.

~It is important to distinguish between edible lavender and lavender prepared for things like potpourri which can be treated with oils or chemicals.

~There are recipes for cooking with culinary lavender available online.

Marjoram

Marjoram is a sweet perennial herb of the mint family. Its fresh or dried leaves are used to season foods, imparting a warm, aromatic flavor.

Marjoram is indigenous to Cyprus and Turkey, and was known to the Greeks and Romans as a symbol of happiness; wreaths of marjoram were placed on the heads of bridal couples. The ancient Greeks used it as a treatment for poison, convulsions, and edema.

Marjoram made its way to England in the 10th or 11th century, where it was used in beer to add taste and as a preservative, and scattered on floors to sweeten the air as it was walked on. Dried leaves perfumed bed linens and were sewn into pillows.

Marjoram contains vitamins A, C, K, calcium, potassium, manganese, copper, zinc, and magnesium.

Tips for Marjoram

~Marjoram tastes similar to oregano and can be used interchangeably in many recipes; oregano has a stronger flavor.

~This herb is a common ingredient in German and Polish sausage recipes. In French cooking, it is frequently included in the *Herbes de Provence* blend.

~Dried marjoram is used in marinades, salad dressings, and soups, where it adds a nice mild flavor. It is also a key ingredient in stuffing for turkey. It enhances pork and tomato dishes, spaghetti sauces, and cheese and egg dishes.

~We cut fresh marjoram to put in green salads. It adds a warm, spicy flavor to the mild greens.

Basque Salad

For the Salad:
1 each green, red, and yellow bell pepper, thinly sliced
4 medium fresh tomatoes, thinly sliced
1 large cucumber, peeled, seeded and thinly sliced
1 red onion, peeled, halved, and thinly sliced
For the Dressing:
1/4 C red wine vinegar
1/2 C olive oil
1 t salt
1/2 t pepper
1 t sugar
1 T each minced fresh oregano, basil, and marjoram
Chopped fresh parsley

In a large bowl, toss together the green, red, and yellow peppers with the tomato, cucumbers, and onion.

In a medium bowl, whisk together the vinegar and olive oil. Season with salt, pepper, and sugar. Whisk in oregano, basil, and marjoram. Continue whisking until the oil and vinegar emulsify.

Pour enough dressing over vegetables to moisten but not swamp them, and toss gently with a wooden spoon. Cover and marinate at room temperature for 1-2 hours, stirring frequently.

Refrigerate until 1 hour before serving, then let sit at room temperature. Add more dressing at that point, if desired, or reserve it for future use.

Garnish salad with chopped parsley.

Marjoram Pasta Sauce with Tomatoes & Cheese

1/2 C chopped onions
2 carrots, scrubbed and diced
2 stalks celery, diced
4 T olive oil, divided
6 ripe tomatoes, chopped
2 T finely chopped fresh marjoram
1 lb cooked pasta
1/2 C grated Parmesan or other hard cheese

Sauté onions, carrots, and celery in 3 tablespoons olive oil in a large pot over medium heat for about 5 minutes. Reduce heat to low, add tomatoes and simmer for 30 minutes.

While the sauce simmers, cook pasta until tender. Put vegetable mixture in a food processor and puree. Return pureed mixture to pot and add marjoram. Serve over cooked pasta.

Sprinkle pasta with remaining 1 tablespoon olive oil and grated cheese, then cover with sauce. Toss together well, and serve immediately. At the table, sprinkle with extra grated cheese.

Runner Beans with Bacon and Marjoram

This recipe calls for fresh runner beans when the beans are small and tender in the pod and before they have matured to the drying stage. Treat them as you would green beans.

4 quarts water
1 T salt
1 lb fresh runner beans with flat pods and small seeds
2 slices bacon, finely diced
2 cloves garlic, finely chopped
2 T fresh marjoram, coarsely chopped
Pepper, to taste

Bring the water and salt to a boil in a large pot. Trim the stems from the beans and cut them diagonally into 2-inch lengths. Heat a large skillet over medium-low heat. Add the bacon and cook, stirring, until it renders its fat and is nearly crisp. Add the garlic to the skillet and sauté until it is softened but not browned. Remove skillet from heat.

Drop the beans into the rapidly boiling water and cook until they are tender but still have a snap to them, 2-4 minutes. Drain, rinse with cold water to stop the cooking process. Place the skillet with bacon and garlic back over medium high heat. Add the beans and marjoram and toss to heat and blend the flavors. Season with pepper and additional salt, if needed.

Mint

Mint originated in Asia and the Mediterranean region, and has been used throughout history. Greeks cleaned their banqueting tables with it, and added it in baths to stimulate their skin. Romans used it in sauces, as an aid to digestion and a mouth freshener. The name comes from the Greek name Minthe, a river nymph. Mint is found all over the world except in the coldest regions.

The plant grows extravagantly and must be cut back in most gardens to keep it under control. The most common types of mint grown for culinary purposes are spearmint, peppermint, apple mint, lemon mint, and chocolate mint.

A mint bush can act as a repellent to cabbage moths, aphids, flea beetles, and ants, and is especially effective to ward critters off tomatoes and cucumbers.

Mint has been used to treat indigestion, stomach cramps, and nausea. Some find that a postprandial cup of peppermint tea aids digestion. It is claimed that mint oil rubbed into the skin works as a pain reliever for joint pain and arthritis.

Mint is rich in carotenes and vitamin C, magnesium, calcium, phosphorus, iron, copper, and potassium.

Tips for Mint

~Add chopped mint to sauces for vegetables such as peas, green beans or new potatoes.

~Mint adds a zing to a raw, fresh vegetable salad, particularly with cucumber and tomato.

~Dried peppermint leaves make a pleasant tea that may aid digestion.

~Henning gathers fresh lemon mint to steep in boiling water and then strains it for a refreshing tea.

~Gather mint stalks early in the morning and place them in a glass of water in your kitchen for easy access.

~To dry, bundle stalks together, place them in a paper bag with holes in it, and tie from a rod to dry. When they are dry and crumbly, store in a jar and make tea from them all winter.

~Chopped mint and sliced cucumbers make a

quick, cool salad. Just add a simple vinaigrette dressing.

~Mint is wonderful in cooling summer drinks, from iced tea and water to gin and tonic.

~Berries and mint pair beautifully. Mix plain yogurt with any berries you like and sprinkle with chopped mint.

Chopped Vegetable, Bean, and Herb Salad

1 lb cooked garbanzo beans (see *Dried Beans* in *Vegetables* for cooking instructions)
1 medium zucchini, chopped into 1/4-inch cubes
1 medium cucumber, peeled and chopped into 1/4-inch cubes
1 yellow, orange, or red bell pepper, finely chopped
1/2 large red onion, finely chopped
4 large leaves kale, stemmed and chopped into 1/2-inch pieces, and then massaged with your fingers to soften
1 T each fresh dill and mint, finely chopped
1 1/2 T olive oil
1 T fresh lemon juice
1 1/2 T red wine vinegar
Salt and pepper, to taste

Rinse and combine beans, vegetables and herbs in a large salad bowl. Mix oil, lemon juice, vinegar, salt and pepper, and drizzle over the salad. Let sit for 15 minutes before serving, adjusting seasonings to taste. Will keep in the refrigerator in a glass container for days.

Mint Jelly

1 C fresh mint leaves, tightly packed
1 C water
1 C apple cider vinegar
3 1/2 C sugar
Sure Jell® pectin (dry)

Place mint leaves in a large pot. Add water, apple cider vinegar, and sugar. Stir constantly, dissolving sugar completely. Bring to a boil. Remove from heat. If desired, add a few drops of organic green food coloring, and stir in pectin until dissolved. Reheat to a boil, and boil for 30 seconds.

With a slotted spoon, remove mint leaves, and strain liquid through dampened cheesecloth and a strainer into a large measuring cup. Pour liquid into hot sterile jars, leaving 1-inch headroom. Wipe rims and seal with clean lids and rings.

Place jars in water-bath canner, cover with at least 2 inches of hot water, bring to a boil, cover the pot, and process for 10 minutes. Let cool in canner before removing.

Mint Sauce

1 C cider vinegar
1/4 C sugar
1/2 C finely chopped mint leaves

Put ingredients in a sauce pan and bring to a boil. Remove from heat and cool. Serve with lamb dishes.

Watermelon, Mint, & Cucumber Salad

8 C cubed seedless or seeded watermelon
2 cucumbers, peeled, halved lengthwise and sliced into half moons
6 scallions, chopped
1/4 C minced fresh mint
1/4 C white balsamic vinegar
1/4 C olive oil
1/2 t salt
1/2 t pepper

In a large bowl, combine watermelon, cucumbers, scallions and mint. In a small bowl, whisk remaining ingredients. Pour over salad and toss to coat. Serve immediately or refrigerate, covered, up to two hours before serving.

Oregano

Like marjoram, oregano is closely related to mint, thyme, basil, sage, and lavender. It is native to Southwestern Europe and the Mediterranean. Its name means "delight of the mountain" in Greek. It grows easily in any home garden, but its flavor and strength vary according to climate and regions. The hot and dry Mediterranean oregano yields a robust, full flavor with a peppery taste. The cooler regions of Europe and North America yield a more delicate aroma and sweeter taste.

Oregano contains vitamins A, C, E, K, dietary fiber, folic acid, beta carotene, iron, manganese, magnesium, potassium, riboflavin, thiamin, iron, and is high in antioxidants.

Tips for Oregano

~1 teaspoon dried oregano equals 2 teaspoons chopped fresh oregano.

~Sprinkle over pizza or add to spaghetti sauce.

~Sprinkle over fish, tomatoes, potatoes or rice.

~Add to dishes of zucchini, squash, or mushrooms, or to fresh salad.

~Add crushed oregano leaves at the end of the cooking process for vegetables such as zucchini, eggplant, and cauliflower.

~To dry, bundle fresh oregano sprigs, and hang upside down in a dry, sunny room until completely dry, 1-2 weeks. Strip the leaves, and crush until powdery. Store in an airtight container for 6-12 months.

Baked Cod with Feta Cheese & Oregano

2 lb cod filets
1/2 C diced onions
3 cloves garlic, minced
2 T olive oil
4 ripe tomatoes, chopped
2 T tomato paste
2 T drained capers
4 T finely chopped fresh oregano
1/3 C finely chopped parsley for cooked dish,
1/4 C finely chopped parsley for garnish
Pepper, to taste
1/4 lb feta cheese, crumbled

Butter a casserole dish and lay washed and dried cod fillets in dish. In a skillet, sauté onions and garlic in oil over medium heat for 2-3 minutes.

Reduce heat to low, add tomatoes, tomato paste, capers, oregano, parsley and pepper, and simmer until well cooked. Pour contents of skillet over cod in casserole dish, and bake casserole in oven at 425 for 15 minutes.

Remove from oven and sprinkle with feta cheese. Bake for an additional 5 minutes, and garnish with parsley. Serve with rice or boiled new potatoes.

Balsamic Potato Salad with Oregano

You can serve this salad at once, or let its flavors marry all afternoon, or refrigerate until the next day (warm to room temperature before serving).

1/2 medium onion, thinly sliced
1 red bell pepper, seeded and cut into matchsticks
1 clove garlic, minced
1/4 C white balsamic vinegar
2 1/2 t salt
2 lb small red potatoes

1/4 C olive oil
1/2 C coarsely chopped Kalamata olives
1/2 C coarsely chopped fresh mint
1/4 C coarsely chopped fresh flat-leaf parsley
2 T coarsely chopped fresh oregano
Pepper, to taste

Combine the onion, red pepper, garlic, vinegar, and 1/2 teaspoon salt in a large bowl and let sit uncovered at room temperature for one hour to soften and mellow the onion.

Quarter the red potatoes and put them in a 4-quart saucepan. Fill the pan with cold water, add the remaining 2 teaspoons salt and bring to a boil. Reduce heat and cook until potatoes are tender but still hold their shape. Drain.

Stir the olive oil, olives, and chopped herbs into the onion mixture. Add the warm potatoes and toss gently. Season with pepper, as needed. Serve warm or at room temperature.

Fresh Summer Pizza

1 pizza crust (See *Bread & Grains*)
5 T olive oil
5 ripe tomatoes, sliced
5 large mushrooms, cleaned and sliced
4 T finely chopped fresh oregano
1/2 C grated mozzarella cheese
1/2 C grated Parmesan or other hard cheese

Preheat oven to 500. Sprinkle cornmeal on lightly oiled pizza pan. Roll out pizza crust on a floured work surface. Put crust on pan, spread with fingertips, and brush with oil. Bake crust for 5 minutes, remove pan from oven and overlap tomato slices on top of crust. Put mushroom slices on top of tomato slices, sprinkle with oregano, and cover with cheeses. Return pan to oven and bake on lower shelf for 15 minutes until crust is browned and pizza is bubbly. Serve immediately, ideally with garden salad.

Oregano Avocado Salad

4 large leaves of Romaine or butterhead lettuce
2 ripe avocados, peeled and sliced lengthwise
Juice of 1/2 lemon
2 ripe tomatoes, sliced
6 oz mozzarella cheese, thinly sliced
6 T olive oil
2 T white wine vinegar
2 T finely chopped fresh oregano

Put a large lettuce leaf on each of four serving plates, and place one quarter of the avocado slices on top of each lettuce leaf. Sprinkle with lemon juice to prevent discoloration.

Surround avocado with alternating slices of tomato and mozzarella cheese. Mix oil, vinegar and oregano, and drizzle dressing over each salad. Serve at once.

Parsley

Parsley is much more than just garnish on a plate — it is serious food. Originally a native of Southern Europe, this herb has spread all over the world. Used by Greeks and Romans for flavoring, it moved out to the rest of Europe and to its colonies starting in the 15th century.

Parsley contains vitamins A, B, C, calcium, iron, potassium, copper, magnesium, manganese, and iron. There are many health claims about parsley.

Parsley is a perennial that can easily be grown in the home garden, and will last through the winter. We grow both flat-leafed and curled parsley, and keep both plants in a growing pit outside our kitchen, to harvest just before serving a dish.

Tips for Parsley
~There is no need to dry parsley from your garden, because it will grow year round.
~Cut a bunch of parsley and keep in the kitchen in a jar of water for use with any meal.
~Sprinkle chopped parsley over eggs, in broth or soups, on potatoes, in salad dressings, even over meat. Its mild taste enhances flavors without being overpowering.
~Parsley makes a quick vegetable dip when mixed with equal amounts of yogurt and mayonnaise, salt and pepper to taste.

Green Herb Frittata
1/2 C sliced potatoes
3 T olive oil, divided
1 clove garlic, minced
1 1/2 C packed fresh greens (spinach, chard, and/or beet greens), washed and chopped
1/4 t salt
1 t white balsamic vinegar
5 eggs
Pepper, to taste
1/2 C chopped parsley

1 1/2 T chopped mint
1/4 C grated Parmesan or other hard cheese

Cook potatoes and drain. Sauté garlic in 1 tablespoon oil in a large cast-iron frying pan. Add chopped greens and salt, and sauté. Add vinegar.

Beat eggs with a bit of salt and pepper, chopped parsley, mint, and cheese. Stir into sautéed greens and add cooked potatoes. Add the remaining olive oil. Cook, lifting so that eggs flow to the bottom of the pan, until top is slightly runny, then put under the broiler for 2-3 minutes to brown.

Parsley Green Sauce
This sauce is great on fish, or as a dip for vegetables or chips. It will keep in the refrigerator for several days.

1 large bunch parsley, rinsed, dried, stalks removed
2 T chopped chives or dill weed
1 medium avocado
Juice of one lemon
1/2 C cold water
Pepper, to taste

Puree all ingredients in a food processor or blender. Transfer to a bowl, cover, and refrigerate until ready to use.

Parsley Pesto
2 cloves garlic
2 C packed parsley, flat or curly leafed
1 t salt
1/4 C walnuts
1/2 C Parmesan or other hard cheese, grated
1/3 C olive oil
In a food processor, process garlic, parsley, salt, walnuts, and cheese until they form a paste. Scrape down the sides and, with the machine running, slowly pour in olive oil until blended. Use at once or freeze in small jars.

Parsley pesto is excellent on pasta (add a little white wine to thin it), on a piece of bread, tossed with spinach, added to salad dressings, or dolloped on roast chicken or grilled or baked fish.

Pasta with Parsley and Garlic
12 oz pasta
4 T olive oil
5 cloves garlic, minced
Red pepper flakes (use sparingly)

1 1/2 C minced fresh parsley
1 C grated Parmesan or other hard cheese
Salt and pepper, to taste

In a large skillet, warm the olive oil, garlic and red pepper flakes over low heat (garlic should not brown).

Cook the pasta, adding a little salt and olive oil to the water before boiling. When pasta is done, drain it and add to oil and garlic in skillet. Add 1 cup of the parsley and a handful of the grated cheese. Toss to combine. Season with salt and pepper and toss again. Transfer the pasta to warmed plates, garnish with remaining parsley and serve at once. Top with remaining cheese.

Rosemary

The first mention of rosemary is found on cuneiform stone tablets as early as 5000 B.C. Egyptians used it in their burial rituals, and the Greeks and Romans burned it as incense and scattered it over the floors of prisons and courtrooms as a prophylactic against disease. It made its way to Britain in the 8th century, and to the Americas with the first European settlers.

The flowers of the rosemary plant are blue, said to have taken their color from the robe of the Virgin Mary when, on the flight to Egypt, she flung it over a bush to dry.

Rosemary contains vitamins A, C, pyridoxine, niacin, pantothenic acid, riboflavin, thiamin, sodium, copper, folate, calcium, iron, magnesium, manganese, and potassium.

Tips for Rosemary
~We grow a bush of rosemary in our garden, where the flowers draw bees by the hundreds. The flowers are edible, but we prefer the non-flowering, low-growing shrub in our little greenhouse for cooking purposes. There are many kinds of rosemary: check catalogs or your garden store to determine which ones will best suit your needs and growing conditions.
~Cut rosemary sprigs from the bush. In some dishes, use the whole sprig during cooking, and remove it before serving. If you want to use the leaves, snip them from the sprig with scissors or strip them off by hand.
~Use rosemary leaves to flavor lamb or goat meat. With a small knife, prick the meat in several places and press a sliver of garlic and a rosemary leaf into each cut.
~Scatter rosemary leaves over potatoes and vegetables before roasting; toss with olive oil.
~Tuck into focaccia (See *Bread & Grains*).

Roasted Carrots with Herbs
5 carrots, scrubbed, sliced into quarters
Olive oil
1/4 C fresh parsley, chopped
1 T fresh rosemary leaves, chopped
1 T fresh thyme leaves
Salt and pepper

Toss all ingredients to coat with olive oil and herbs. Place in roasting pan and roast at 400 for 30 minutes, until carrots are tender. Stir once during roasting.

Rosemary Chicken
This recipe can be used for chicken or Cornish game hens.

1 4-lb chicken
4 whole cloves garlic, peeled — 2 cloves whole, 2 chopped
4 T rosemary leaves
1/4 C olive oil
1/4 C dry vermouth

Rinse chicken inside and out under cold running water, pat dry and put in a roasting pan. Put 2 whole cloves garlic, one half of the rosemary and some pepper in the cavity of the chicken.

Rub one half of the oil on skin of the chicken. Sprinkle chicken with chopped garlic, remaining half of rosemary and pepper. Pour remaining half of oil in the bottom of the roasting pan. Bake at 375 for one hour, basting every 15 minutes.

When chicken is done, remove roasting pan from oven, and place chicken on a serving platter. Keep warm. Add vermouth to pan and cook on a burner on low heat, scraping up solids and stirring constantly. Carve chicken into serving pieces, and pour pan juices over the top.

Rosemary Potato Casserole
4 lb potatoes, peeled and cut into bite-sized pieces
8 t chopped rosemary leaves
1/2 C butter

Pepper
2 C milk

Layer potatoes and rosemary in a casserole dish. Dot each layer with butter and season with pepper. Pour milk over the top. Cover and bake at 375 for one hour. Uncover and bake an additional 30 minutes until browned.

Sage

Sage has a long and interesting history. Cultivated by ancient Egyptians, Greeks and Romans, it has been used in cooking and in medicine in almost every culture of the world. It is a perennial shrub, easily grown in the home garden.

Sage is a beautiful bush, with long, gray-green leaves. Its name comes from the Latin "salvare," which means "to save" or "heal." It was believed to cure ailments ranging from eye diseases to broken bones and loss of memory. The word "sage" also means "wise one." It is said of this herb, "How can a person die with sage growing in the garden?" Folk wisdom has it that when things are going well, sage plants will flourish; when things are going badly, the plant will droop its leaves.

Sage contains vitamins A, C, E, K, folate, niacin, riboflavin, thiamin, calcium, copper, iron, magnesium, manganese, and zinc.

Tips for Sage
~Harvest before flowering stage. Wash and pat dry. Keep between paper towels in refrigerator.
~Fresh leaves can be used as part of stuffing in sausages, on poultry, and fish.
~Cook beans with sage, garlic, and black pepper to create a richly flavored stew.
~Use finely minced fresh leaves in salads and omelets.
~Dry sage by cutting whole stems, and hanging them upside down in a paper bag with holes punched in it. When dry, crumble with your fingers and place in a jar for later use.
~Like thyme and rosemary, sage is one of those hearty herbs of which a little can go a long way and is best when cooked. If you use it raw, use only small, tender leaves and chop them finely.

Fettuccini with Sage Butter & Peas
1 1/2 C fresh garden peas or 8 oz frozen peas

6 T unsalted butter
1/2 C chopped fresh sage leaves
3 oz prosciutto, cut into thin strips, or smoked bacon
1 lb fresh homemade fettuccini (see *Bread & Grains*) or 12 oz dried
1/2 C grated Parmesan or other hard cheese
Pepper

Cook the peas briefly if frozen; if fresh, cook just until they rise to the top of the pan. Drain and set aside.

Melt the butter in a large skillet over low heat. Add the sage leaves and cook until the butter begins to brown slightly and the sage gives off a nutty, toasty aroma. Add the prosciutto and cook for about 1 minute.

If using bacon, cut and fry until barely done, or blanch in boiling water for a few minutes until the meat becomes tender and translucent; rinse and drain before cutting and adding. Add the peas and cook briefly.

While you are preparing the sauce, cook the pasta in 4 quarts of salted boiling water until tender. Rinse, drain, and add to the skillet. Sprinkle with cheese and pepper and toss gently. Place pasta in warmed bowls.

Green Beans with Sage
1 lb green beans, trimmed
2 T butter
2 t diced sage
1/4 C grated Parmesan or other hard cheese
Pepper, to taste

Steam beans until just tender. Melt butter in saucepan, and mix in cheese and sage. Season with pepper. Toss beans in the sauce and serve at once.

Sage Sausage Patties
1 T ground sage
1 t salt
1 t brown sugar
1/2 t pepper
1/8 t red pepper flakes
1/4 t ground marjoram
1 pinch ground cloves
1 lb ground pork
1 egg
Put spices in a bowl and mix well. Break up pork

and mix with the spices and the egg. Place on baking sheet lined with parchment or waxed paper and flatten to desired height. Cut rounds with a cookie cutter or drinking glass.

Fry at once on stove top in a little olive oil or wrap and freeze to cook later. Serve with fried potatoes and eggs.

Sage Tea
This aromatic tea can settle stomachs and soothe sore throats.

10 fresh sage leaves
1 C boiling water
1 t lemon juice
1 t honey

Steep sage leaves in boiling water for 5 minutes. Remove leaves and stir in lemon juice and honey.

Savory

Savory was first cultivated by the Romans, who introduced it to England, where it quickly became popular both as a medicinal and a culinary herb. Savory is thought to be a natural antiseptic, used as a remedy for sore throats and bacterial infections, and to provide relief for bites and stings. Savory can also help with digestive problems, which is one reason it is incorporated into bean dishes.

Savory contains vitamins A, C, pyridoxine, niacin, iron, calcium, magnesium, thiamin, and manganese.

Tips for Savory
~There are two savory plants — summer and winter savory. Both are easy to grow in the home garden. Summer savory is an annual plant, winter savory a perennial. Summer savory is sweeter than the spicy winter savory. Both are good in vegetable dishes, particularly beans.
~When cooking beans, throw in a few sprigs of summer savory. Remove sprigs before serving.
~Add summer savory to cold bean salads. Snip a few leaves over chicken as it is barbecuing.
~Winter savory is an herb that does well with long cooking times, for instance as a rub for roasts.

Pork Chops with Apples & Winter Savory
2 medium onions, chopped
4 T olive oil
3 apples, sliced

4 pork chops
2 T flour
1 T finely chopped winter savory
1 1/2 C homemade chicken broth
Pepper, to taste

Sauté onions and apples in oil until soft. Remove from skillet and set aside. Add extra oil if needed. Brown pork chops briefly on each side. Sprinkle flour and savory on top of each pork chop, then cover with onion and apple slices.

Season with pepper. Add chicken broth to skillet and simmer over medium-low heat for 20-25 minutes. Sauce will thicken. Add water to skillet if liquid evaporates before chops are done. Serve with rice. Spoon sauce over chops and rice and serve.

Runner Beans with Summer Savory & Bacon
4 quarts water
1 T salt
1 lb fresh runner beans with flat pods and small seeds, trimmed and cut diagonally into 2-inch pieces.
2 slices bacon, diced
2 cloves garlic, chopped
2 T coarsely chopped summer savory
Pepper and salt to taste

Cook the bacon until crisp. Remove bacon and sauté the garlic in the bacon fat until it is tender but not browned.

Boil the water with added salt. Add the beans, and cook for 2-4 minutes, until they are tender but still crisp. Mix bacon, garlic, savory, and beans together in the skillet. Warm, and season with pepper and salt, to taste.

Tarragon

The Greeks knew tarragon as early as 500 B.C. The Arabs in the 13th century believed it fought pestilence. When it reached Europe in the 16th century, the French called it "estragon" (fr. Greek *drākon*, meaning dragon or serpent). The name possibly refers to the serpent-like roots, or because of its fierce flavor.

Tarragon contains vitamins A, C, calcium, magnesium, iron, manganese, copper, potassium, zinc, folate, niacin, riboflavin, thiamin.

Tips for Tarragon

~Unlike sage and rosemary, the tarragon in our garden does not produce leaves in winter, but we fall upon it in spring, when its tall, leafy branches appear, and before it sets seed. Our two favorite uses for it are to flavor chicken and fish, and to make the vinegar we use all year.

~Harvest tarragon in late spring and early summer.

~The leaves can be dried for storage in a perforated bag in a well-ventilated area.

~Tarragon can be used in salad dressings, eggs, cheese dishes, and chicken, and as a flavoring base for marinades for fish, lamb, and poultry.

Creamy Tarragon Dressing

This dressing can be used over sliced tomatoes, green salads, and cooked vegetables.

2 shallots, minced
2 T minced fresh tarragon
1 t Dijon mustard
3 T fresh lemon juice
1/2 C olive oil
Salt and pepper, to taste

Combine all ingredients in a food processor and process until smooth. Season to taste with salt and pepper.

Herbed Shrimp

1 lb raw large shrimp or prawns, peeled
3 T olive oil
2 cloves garlic, peeled and diced
4 T each finely chopped fresh tarragon and parsley
2 T freshly squeezed lemon juice

Sauté shrimp or prawns in a skillet in oil for 3-4 minutes, tossing constantly until done. Add tarragon, parsley, and lemon juice to skillet and simmer for 5 minutes. Serve on pasta or toasted French bread (see *Bread & Grains*) with a green salad.

Tarragon & Shallot Butter Sauce

This sauce can be served over fish, rice, potatoes, or meat, and as a dip for bread. Excess can be frozen for future use.
1/2 C unsalted butter, softened
1 1/2 t lemon juice
1 T dried tarragon

1 t pepper
2 T minced shallots
Salt to taste

In a food processor or blender, cream butter, lemon juice, tarragon, pepper, and shallots. Season with salt to taste. Chill before using.

Tarragon Vinegar

8 C white vinegar
1 t sugar
1 large bunch fresh tarragon
1 large piece of red pepper
1/2 t whole black peppercorns
1 t celery seed
2 cloves garlic, peeled

Warm vinegar and sugar. Place all other ingredients in a large glass jar with a tight-fitting lid. Pour warm vinegar into the jar and put the lid on tight. Store in a dark cool place for four weeks. Then strain vinegar into a bottle with a tight-fitting lid. Add a sprig of fresh tarragon, a fresh clove of garlic, and a new piece of red pepper. The vinegar will age and mellow on the shelf, and is best when a light golden color.

Thyme

Historians believe that the ancient Sumerians were the first to cultivate thyme, possibly as early as 5000 years ago. The ancient Greeks believed that thyme imparted courage and fortitude, a notion that was carried into medieval Europe, where women embroidered scarves showing bees hovering over branches of thyme, and gave them to knights as tokens of bravery. Thyme tea was believed to prevent nightmares, and people tucked sprigs of it under their pillows to induce sleep.

Thyme contains vitamins A, C, folate, niacin, riboflavin, thiamin, calcium, iron, magnesium, manganese, and zinc.

Tips for Thyme

~Thyme is a member of the mint family, and like its relatives, is rich in oils. The chief oil, thymol, is a powerful antiseptic and is used in salves.

~There are more than 400 types of thyme, some ornamental, some culinary. Ornamental thyme plants are beautiful in rock gardens, low growing and quick to spread. The flowers attract bees and other pollinators.

~We have bushes of culinary thyme in our garden, and use it in soups, stews, and salad dressings.

~Thyme pairs well with meat, tomatoes, and beans.

~Thyme enhances the flavors of vegetables, meats, and seafoods without overpowering the taste of the food.

~Add a sprig of fresh thyme right at the end of cooking dishes with lentils and split peas. Remove the dish from heat, cover, and remove sprig before serving.

~Add a couple of pinches of dried thyme to herbed bread before baking.

~Lemon thyme is a particular favorite for cooking.

Beef Stew with Beer & Thyme

2 lb stewing beef, cut into bite-sized pieces
1/4 C flour
4 T olive oil
2 medium onions, finely chopped
2 C dark beer or stout
2 T each finely chopped thyme and parsley
Pepper and salt, to taste
3 each medium potatoes and carrots, plus
1/2 lb mushrooms, to add during the last hour in the oven.

Dredge pieces of beef in flour, shaking off excess. Brown beef in oil in an ovenproof pot, such as a Dutch oven. Add onion and sauté. Add beer or stout, thyme and parsley and bring to a boil. Season with salt and pepper. Place pot in oven at 350 and bake for 2 hours or until beef is tender. Add potatoes, carrots, and mushrooms during the last hour of cooking.

French Onion Soup with Thyme

4-5 medium onions, thinly sliced
1 T butter
1 T olive oil
1 t sugar
3 C homemade beef stock
1/4 C dry white wine
3 T finely chopped lemon thyme
Pepper to taste
4 slices toasted French bread (see *Bread & Grains*)
2 C freshly grated Gruyere cheese

Cook onions in butter and oil in a large, heavy pan over medium heat until onions are soft, about 15 minutes. Stir occasionally. Remove one half of the onions and set aside. Add sugar to remaining onions and cook on low heat for an additional 15 minutes, stirring often. Onions should be a deep golden color.

Add beef broth and wine to pan and simmer for 40 minutes. Return first half of onions to pan, add thyme, and season with salt and pepper. Heat through. To serve, ladle into ovenproof bowls and put a slice of toasted bread on top of each bowl. Cover bread with cheese and broil briefly until cheese has browned. Serve immediately.

Roasted Carrots & Parsnips with Thyme

1 lb carrots
1 lb parsnips
3 T olive oil
2 T honey
6 sprigs fresh thyme
Salt and pepper

Peel carrots and parsnips and quarter them lengthwise. Place vegetables in a roasting pan, and drizzle with olive oil and honey. Season with salt and pepper and toss to coat. Scatter thyme sprigs on top. Roast at 400 for 10 minutes; toss vegetables and return to oven.

Continue roasting 15-20 minutes, until vegetables are tender and slightly caramelized. Serve warm.

Notes:

Wildcrafting

There are many useful and edible foods in fields and forests in the Pacific Northwest. On Lopez Island alone, there are blackberries, calendula (a garden escape), chamomile, comfrey, dandelions, elderberries, huckleberries, nettles, mint, mushrooms, Oregon grape, rose hips and salmonberries, to name a few. Most were part of the diet and medicinal practices of indigenous people here, and many folks gather and use them today.

In harvesting and processing any wild mushroom, plant, or berry, know how to identify and cook or process it properly. Wild plants, because they have not been bred for domestic use, are powerful, and should be treated with knowledge and respect.

Blackberries

Blackberries are among Nature's gifts: you don't have to water or weed them; they grow prolifically along roadsides and in meadows. However, in our part of the state, blackberries need rain at the right time to get plump and juicy, and you have to avoid wasps and thorns when you pick them. As with any crop, morning is the best time to harvest.

There are two kinds of wild blackberries in the Northwest. The Himalayan blackberry, which was introduced to the Northwest, is the one we know best — the berries are large and sweet. The native blackberry, called the Pacific blackberry, is smaller, more flavorful, and prized by chefs for pies and tarts because the seeds are smaller and the berries more firm. They ripen earlier than the Himalayan blackberry, so if both grow in your area, you can have two harvests.

Blackberries contain vitamins A, most B vitamins, C, E, potassium, magnesium, and calcium, and are a rich source of antioxidants.

We like both our garden-grown and wildcrafted berries frozen rather than processed, but blackberries can be made into excellent jam. Follow directions on the jar or package of pectin.

Calendula

Calendula is an ancient plant, a relative of the ornamental marigold (but the two should not be confused). The flowers of both were given as a birthday celebratory salute during the Roman Empire, made into wreaths and put around the necks of holy statues in India, and placed by early

Christians next to statues of the Virgin Mary ("Mary's Gold").

Claims for the healing properties of calendula for internal problems are legion, but little scientific documentation is available; there is historical and anecdotal evidence, but also strong cautions against ingesting raw or processed calendula without the advice of a health professional.

Calendula contains vitamins C and E, both healthful for skin. The topical use of calendula for skin care is well known: the flower is made into oils, ointments, creams, salves, and lotions. The calendula cream we use at home (produced by an island grower) contains olive oil, purified water, herbal extracts of calendula, Oregon grape, comfrey, aloe, vegetable glycerine, beeswax, vitamin E, lecithin, and lavender oil. We find it hydrating and soothing. Some folks find it beneficial for sunburn, dermatitis, or psoriasis. There are cautions about using it topically on small children, so applying it on diaper rash may not be wise.

As a garden plant, calendula has many uses: the flowers attract beneficial insects, and form active relationships with soil fungi. The flowers are easy to grow, and will last a long time providing beautiful colors! As a culinary plant, the flower petals are used in cooking, giving a bright color and taste to foods. The yellow flowers have been used to color butter and cheeses.

When used in stews, broths and salads, they add a spicy taste similar to saffron. Calendula should be used sparingly in cooking.

Calendula blossoms can be dried for tea, but should be mixed with other herbs. This tea can cause complications with pregnancy because it has a notable effect on hormone levels, and can induce menstruation. Some people ingest it without difficulty, others experience stomach upset. Wild plants and their domesticated cousins are powerful, for good or ill. Proceed with caution, enjoy when possible.

Chamomile

Most folks associate chamomile with commercial and homemade tea as a soothing, soporific beverage. There are many kinds of chamomile, a member of the daisy family; the two best known in the United States are Roman chamomile and

German chamomile. Roman chamomile is a perennial that grows close to the ground and is often used as a ground cover. German chamomile is an annual, with longer stems and smaller flowers. Both are used to make essential oils, teas, cosmetics and medicine, and both are renowned for health benefits, particularly for skin conditions.

Chamomile has small amounts of folates, iron, potassium, and calcium.

People taking extracts from chamomile should be aware of its potential interactions with prescribed medications, or its triggering of allergic reactions. Scientific research does not validate the use of chamomile tea to treat health conditions.

We harvest and dry German chamomile flowers from our garden for tea, and find it tasty and soothing.

Comfrey

Comfrey is a perennial shrub that, like nettles, grows prolifically in areas that have partial sun and shade. It has multiple uses for people, animals, soil, plants and compost piles. Comfrey regrows generously.

Comfrey contains vitamin A, nitrogen, potassium calcium, allantoin.

Tips for Comfrey
~For Human Use: because of the substance allantoin, which speeds cell and tissue growth, comfrey can be used as a poultice for burns, bruises, or skin inflammations, but should not be used on broken skin. Mince up a leaf, bind it to the affected area with another leaf, and be patient. Both leaves and stalk are prickly, and can be uncomfortable to apply for long periods. However, there are oils, ointments, tinctures and salves made from comfrey that can be applied topically with more comfort.

~Comfrey should not be taken internally (by people) because it contains alkaloids that can cause lung damage, liver damage, and cancer, according to some sources. The FDA has recommended that all oral comfrey products (tablets, liquid, tincture, teas) should be removed from the market.

~For Animal Feed: Comfrey is low in fiber and high in protein and minerals, and a good source of vitamin A. We feed small amounts (5-6 large leaves) of comfrey to our pigs, milk cow, sheep, turkeys and chickens on a daily basis. Some farmers use it for goats, ducks, rabbits, and other farm animals. Some folks dry it; we feed it fresh. It never comprises the whole of an animal's feed, nor are our animals allowed to free-range in a comfrey patch. We cut and give it to them, mixed with other feed.

~*In the Garden*: Comfrey can be put into a mixed compost pile; its high nitrogen and potassium content and quick decomposition add nutrients to the compost and aid in quicker breakdown of the mix.

~Some gardeners tear or macerate leaves to use as mulch around garden plants.

~Comfrey can be used for a biodynamic compost tea, combined with an equal part of nettles, soaked in a barrel or bucket of water. Let it sit for three to five weeks to ferment (it becomes quite smelly). When ready to apply, strain out the leaves and mix tea with soft water (from a pond). For soil, mix a ratio of one part tea to eight parts water; to apply around seedlings, mix one part tea to thirty-six parts water. Put the strained leaves in the compost pile.

~The flowers attract pollinators, particularly bumblebees.

Dandelions

Dandelions are considered a "weed" in most gardens and yards — that is, a plant growing where you don't want it. However, it is a useful and nutritious plant, containing vitamins A, C, E, K, thiamin, riboflavin, pyridoxine, folic acid, calcium, iron, magnesium, manganese, potassium, and zinc.

You can eat all parts of the plant, whose flowers, leaves, and roots have been used as diuretics, appetite stimulants, laxatives, and stabilizers for blood sugar.

Making these remedies at home requires expertise, and awareness of how parts of the plant made into medicaments might interact with conventional medicines or supplements.

The leaves are the most nutritious part of the dandelion, and should be harvested while young — as they mature, they become bitter. They can be eaten raw as a spicy addition to a green salad, or steamed, sautéed or boiled. You can sauté the greens with minced garlic and onions. Add broth to the pan and steam until they are tender and the liquid has decreased a little. Add salt, pepper, a

dash of white balsamic vinegar and serve as a side dish or over pasta.

Dandelion leaves, fresh or dried, can be made into tea, by themselves or mixed with other herbs. The flowers can also be made into tea. Some people make dandelion wine, and recipes and procedures can be found online.

For us, the most important use of dandelions is the Biodynamic Preparation 506 (see sshomestead.org/offerings/biodynamic-products/). The entire process can be accessed online, as can uses for yarrow, chamomile, nettle, oak bark, valerian and horsetail for other biodynamic preparations. Your soil, plants, and compost piles will benefit greatly in fertility and health from these inputs.

Growing and harvesting the plants is easy — most are wild anyway — and the processing not difficult. By following these procedures, you will not need fertility from a bag, and you will protect your plants from disease. The biodynamic preparations essentially function as homeopathy for the soil. The Biodynamic Association site is a good place to begin finding information.

Elderberries

Elderberry bushes are prolific on Lopez Island. They produce clusters of white flowers and blue-to-black berries. Native Americans used elderberry to treat infections. It was used in folk medicine in many parts of Europe for relief from pain, swelling, inflammation, and as a laxative and diuretic.

The flowers can be eaten raw or cooked, and make a delicious cordial; the berries must be cooked or dried before eating, and can be processed into syrup or wine.

Elderberry contains vitamins A, B, and C, and antioxidants. There is anecdotal evidence that commercially produced elderberry extracts reduce cold and flu symptoms.

There is strong caution against using elderberries as a home remedy; the only research regarding health benefits have been performed on commercial products, and there is little information about the safety or efficacy of homemade remedies. Consumption of uncooked berries, leaves and stems may result in cyanide toxicity, inducing vomiting and diarrhea. Commercial preparations generally do not cause adverse reactions if taken at the recommended dosage.

For us? We enjoy looking at the flowers and berries on our walks. We do not eat or process them; however, others do. Research advised.

Huckleberries

You do have to leave Lopez Island to gather huckleberries, which can be grown in our gardens, but in the wild prefer high elevations. We consider a hike on Mt. Baker to be an occasion to gather huckleberries. While related to blueberries, huckleberries are smaller, sweeter, and grow at the edges of coniferous forests in partial sun and shade. The bushes range from high to low-growing, most less than four feet tall, and the leaves are oval in shape, one to two inches long, and smooth. The berries range in color from red to blue-black. Be sure not to strip an entire plant when you gather them; the berries are also eaten by birds and animals, and the seeds they leave behind help the plant reproduce.

Do not eat any berry in the woods that you cannot identify.

Huckleberries can be grown in the home garden. Both wild and domesticated huckleberries are valued for their use in jams, compotes, muffins, cobblers and pies, over ice cream, or as part of a fruit salad.

Huckleberries contain vitamins A, C, K, thiamin, riboflavin, pyridoxine, niacin, iron, sodium, potassium, calcium, magnesium, and phosphorus.

Mint

Several kinds of mint grow wild in the Northwest, and can be easily grown in your garden, either by transplanting wild mint or purchasing a domesticated plant (which will soon proliferate in your yard or garden unless you plant it in a container or cut it back on a regular basis).

For general and culinary information and recipes for mint, see *Herbs*.

Mushrooms

Anyone who is serious about collecting mushrooms should consult David Arora's *All That the Rain Promises, and More…,* which is a wonderful field and cooking guide.

There are many kinds of mushrooms growing in our pastures and woods, some edible, some toxic. We gather button mushrooms, also known as meadow mushrooms or champignons. These usually appear in September after rain, ranging in size from a button to a hat. At their peak, the crown is white, with the gills scaling from pink to light brown. Among toxic mushrooms on our farm, the most dramatic is the bright red, white-dotted Fly Agaric (*amanita muscaria*), famous from fairytales, from traditions about Viking warriors who ate the mushroom to "go berserk" (put on the bear shirt), and from Native American shamanistic practices. As Madrona Murphy, a local botanist, told our farm class, the mushroom is dangerous because it makes people feel invincible.

Mushrooms contain vitamin D, thiamin, riboflavin, niacin, pantothenic acid, folate, biotin, sodium, potassium, calcium, iron, zinc, magnesium, and selenium.

Tips for Mushrooms
~The mild flavor of mushrooms makes them useful in many dishes, such as Beef Stroganoff, or they can be sautéed and added to a green salad or used in omelets, quiches or crepes.
~Remove the stalks from mushrooms before slicing or stuffing. They can be fibrous and tough.
~Drop fresh mushrooms into cold water and gently rub off dirt before slicing.
~You can store fresh mushrooms in the refrigerator, but only for a few days; they will become slimy.

Cream of Mushroom Soup
5 C sliced fresh mushrooms
1 1/2 C homemade chicken broth
1/2 C chopped onion
1/2 t dried thyme
3 T each butter and flour
1/4 t each salt and pepper
1 C half-and-half
2 T dry sherry

In a large pot, cook mushrooms with broth, onion

and thyme until tender. In a food processor or with an immersion blender, puree the mixture, leaving some chunks in it. Set aside.

In a saucepan, melt the butter, and gradually whisk in the flour until smooth. Add the salt, pepper, half-and-half, and combine with the pureed soup.

Stirring constantly, bring the soup to just below boiling, and cook until thickened. Adjust seasonings to taste, and add sherry.

Crepes with Mushrooms

This dish is easy to make and satisfying to eat.
For the Crepes: (Makes 4)
1 C flour
1 T sugar
3 eggs
1 C milk
2 T melted butter

Mix all ingredients with a whisk. Place a large ladle of the batter into a heated nonstick pan. Swirl the batter until it is thin and covers the lower part of the sides of the pan. Cook crepes on both sides until light brown; remove to a plate.

For the Filling:
1/2 medium onion, minced
1/2 C butter
16 oz mushrooms, cleaned, stemmed, and sliced
1/2 C sour cream
Salt and pepper, to taste

Sauté the onion in the butter, add the sliced mushrooms, and sauté until liquid has emerged and the mushrooms are tender. Add sour cream, salt and pepper, and stir until combined. Fill crepes. Serve with green salad or a vegetable of your choice.

Mushrooms and Baby Spinach

3 C sliced mushrooms
3 cloves garlic, minced
1 1/2 T butter
Salt and pepper, to taste
6 C small spinach leaves, stalks removed, torn into pieces.

Sauté sliced mushrooms in butter. Do not crowd; you want them to brown, not steam. Stir in the minced garlic and cook for about one minute.

Season with salt and pepper. Stir in the spinach and cook until it just starts to wilt.

Nettles

Nettles are an "opportunistic" plant, growing just about everywhere that is damp and has partial shade and sun.

Nettles contain vitamins A, C, K, riboflavin, niacin, calcium, magnesium, phosphorus, potassium, and sodium. Claimed health benefits from stinging nettles are legion. Nettles have long been used as a tonic, being loaded with minerals and beta-carotene, flavonoids, and are also an excellent detoxifier and diuretic. We know that it makes delicious tea and can be used in a number of ways. On a biodynamic farm, it is the most important wild plant. Made into Biodynamic Preparation 504, it is used to enliven the soil.

Tips for Nettles

~For culinary use, nettles must be harvested while young: choose only the tops and tender leaves. The season for gathering nettles is spring, and fairly short.

~Use heavy gloves; the nettle releases formic acid, which causes blistering and pain. (It should be noted that the formic acid and histamine in the stinging hairs of the fresh nettle have a long history of therapeutic use.)

~The acid dissipates with cooking and drying. To dry, spread on a screen in the sun or hang in a paper bag with holes until the nettles are dry. Use for tea.

~Nettles used for biodynamic compost tea (see *Comfrey* above) can be harvested at any stage of growth. Again, beware of the sting.

Nettle Pesto

3 garlic cloves, chopped
2 T pine nuts or chopped walnuts
2 T grated hard cheese
2/3 C blanched, chopped nettles
Salt
4 T olive oil
Blanch for one minute, drain and chop the nettles. Put them with all other ingredients into a food processor. Warm and serve over fresh pasta or spread on bread or use as a garnish for soups.

Like other pestos, this can be frozen for future use.

Nettle Soup

1/2 large shopping bag of fresh nettle tops and leaves
Salt
1 T olive oil
1 t butter
1/2 C each chopped shallots and celery
1 lb Yukon Gold or russet potatoes, peeled and chopped
4 C homemade chicken stock
1-2 C water
1 bay leaf
1 t dried thyme or 2 sprigs fresh thyme
Pepper
1 1/2 T lemon juice
2-3 T
Cream

Blanch the Nettles:
Bring a pot of lightly salted water to a boil. Wearing protective gloves, transfer nettle tops and leaves into the water. Blanch for two minutes.

Drain nettles and place in cold water to stop the cooking process. Drain in colander. Cut away and discard stems from the nettles. (They will have lost their sting.)You should have three to four cups of blanched nettles for the soup. Extra nettles can be frozen for future use.

Make the Soup:
Sauté the shallots and celery in the olive oil and butter in a large soup pot for about five minutes. Add the chopped potatoes, chicken broth, bay leaf, and thyme. Simmer five minutes. Roughly chop the blanched nettles, and add three to four cups of them to the pot. Add just enough water to cover the potatoes and nettles, 1-2 cups. Simmer for fifteen minutes, until potatoes are soft and nettles are tender.

To Finish:
Remove the bay leaf and sprigs of thyme (if using instead of dried thyme), and puree the soup. Return to the pot. Add salt, pepper and lemon juice to taste. Swirl in cream. Reheat, do not boil. You can add a sprig of mint to each bowl for garnish.

Nettle Tea

Immerse dried nettle leaves or seed in boiling water, and steep. The tea has health benefits and a bright taste.

Oregon Grape

Oregon grape, the state flower of Oregon, is a broadleaf evergreen shrub that grows well in shady spots in the woods and can be cultivated in the home garden. It has prickly, holly-like leaves, yellow flowers that attract pollinators, and blue berries.

The berries of the Oregon grape are rich in vitamin C, and the roots and stems of the plant have been used for their anti-inflammatory, anti-bacterial, and anti-fungal properties to treat a variety of skin conditions, such as psoriasis, eczema, and athlete's foot, for example. Claims are made for the efficacy of berberine, an active compound in Oregon grape.

When a girl, Elizabeth used to harvest the berries from Oregon grape, a time-consuming but rewarding endeavor. The berries are deeply flavored but very tart, so should be harvested when they are fully ripe and dark blue. To make jelly, you need:

6 C cleaned berries
2 C water
1 oz liquid pectin
1 T lemon juice
3 C sugar

Put cleaned berries in a pot and add water; bring to a boil and simmer for 15 minutes. Mash the berries to extract the juice; put berries and juice through a food mill or squeeze through a jelly bag to remove the skin and seeds. Measure the juice you have left — should be around three cups. An alternative is to put berries in a juicer to extract the juice through steam (see *Keeping the Harvest*). Using this process, you do not have to clean the berries or pull off stems.

Put the juice (adding water if necessary to make 3 cups) into a pot on the stove. Add the lemon juice and pectin and bring to a boil. Stir in the sugar and boil for one minute, then remove from heat. Pour jelly into sterilized canning jars, clean rims, seal, and process in a water-bath canner for ten minutes.

Rose Hips

Rose hips are the seed pods of roses — the fruit that remains after the blooms fade. They are bright red, and are best harvested after the first frost, when they will have developed the most flavor. Rugosa roses, a native shrub rose species, are said to have the best tasting hips, which are also the largest and the most abundant.

Rose hips are extremely high in vitamin C and also contain vitamins A, D (made by sunshine and often missing in the winter months) and E, as well as antioxidants and pantothenic acid. The syrup makes a great winter medicine to help ward off coughs, colds and flu. In Scandinavia, rose hips have been the most important source of vitamins during the long winters.

Tips for Rose Hips

~To harvest, pluck or cut them off the rose canes, remove the seeds (a digestive irritant), and wash the fruit before processing. They should not be eaten raw.

~Rose hips can be cooked or steamed to extract the juice for jams, jellies, and syrup, with only a slight loss of vitamin C. The juice can be used immediately or frozen for up to a year. It can be mixed with other fruits, such as apples or cranberries, for a more complex flavor. Avoid using aluminum pans, which will discolor the rose hips and give them a metallic taste.

~To make syrup, add sugar or honey to the juice and cook down until it reaches the desired consistency. Use fresh or freeze.

~Rose hips can also be dried in an oven or dehydrator until they are brittle; when they are completely dry, store them in jars. They can be used in stir fries or mixed with other fruit for smoothies or sauces, jams or compotes. Note: drying rose hips causes them to lose most of their vitamin C.

~Tea is one of the most popular ways to use rose hips. For fresh rose hip tea, simmer four to eight rose hips in water for ten to fifteen minutes. This tea has been used to soothe upset stomachs. You can add honey for sweetness or a slice of lime for extra vitamin C.

Salmonberries

Salmonberries, like blackberries, are common in our part of the Northwest, growing in damp woodland places. Although they have prickly stems, they do not have thorns. When ripe, their color ranges from yellow to red. They can be eaten raw or made into jellies, jams, and wine. Native Americans often ate them with salmon (hence the name). We like to eat them from the bush on our hikes. They can be made into preserves, used for pies and tarts, or rendered into syrup. Their flavor is mild, so you might want to mix them with other fruits, such as gooseberries or currants, when you bake or sauce them.

Salmonberries contain vitamins A, C, E, K, calcium, iron, magnesium, phosphorus, potassium, zinc, copper, and manganese.

Notes:

Tree Fruits and Berries

Apples

Domestic apples originated in Central Asia, where trees threw off fruit in all colors and sizes from marbles to softballs. Forests of wild apple trees (*Malus sieversii*) sixty feet high can still be found in Kazakhstan today. Cultivation of the species progressed over thousands of years, with significant genetic exchanges with the crabapple (*Malus sylvestrys*). Travelers on the Silk Road probably gathered the most attractive of these fruits and deposited seeds along the way home. The crabapple native to Britain crossed with descendants of the Asian ancestor and in turn became the progenitor of most cultivated apple varieties known today (*Malus domestica*). Apple trees brought by early settlers to America crossed with native crabapples, producing a small, sour apple used in low-alcohol, fermented cider that could be stored all year.

The apple trees seeded by Johnny Appleseed (John Chapman) throughout the West were planted for cider, not fresh eating. He collected seeds from cider mills, covering baskets with mud and moss to protect the seeds as he moved from western Pennsylvania through central Ohio and into Indiana. Appleseed left a chain of tree nurseries behind him, waiting for coming settlers.

The modern apple, prized for its wholesome sweetness, was an invention of the 1900s. When alcohol was demonized and Prohibition was close at hand, apples were raised as edible fruit as well as for fermented juice, and both have been enjoyed in America ever since.

Due to their genetic variability, apples thrive in almost any climate and are grown in every state of the U.S. But, due to their heterozygosity, meaning that their genetic makeup includes ancestral variations that combine randomly, cultivated apples must be propagated by grafting.

Today apples are second only to bananas in popularity in America, and the maxim "An apple a day keeps the doctor away" is sound. Apples are low in calories and free of fat, sodium and cholesterol. They are rich in fiber, and contain vitamins A, C, E, K, potassium, folate, calcium, phosphorus, iron, and niacin.

However, health benefits are reduced if you purchase non-organic apples, which rank as one of the most contaminated foods in the market. Apples are the fruit most consumed by children, and a two-year-old eating half a non-organic apple ingests more than the government's daily allowance of "safe" pesticide exposure. The USDA lists 46 different pesticide residues found on non-organic apples: these include carcinogens, hormone disruptors, neurotoxins, reproductive toxins, and honeybee toxins.

Over the last 50 years, we have grown a number of apple varieties, including Oriole, Melrose, Mutsu, Liberty, Anna, Akani, Black Cider, and local heirlooms Gravenstein and Olympia. We chose varieties to provide us with fresh apples from early summer to early winter. The earlier apples are for juice, cider, drying and fresh eating, the later ones are "keepers." We keep them in cool storage, separated with layers of newspaper, and eat them until spring. By early summer they get a bit wrinkled, at which time we turn them into pies, cakes, applesauce, and dressings. Pigs, sheep, cows and chickens appreciate any we can't use.

Tips for Apples
~Eat apples with the skin on. Almost half of the vitamin C in apples is just beneath the skin, and the skin contains fiber.

~If you dry apples, slice them thin and immerse them in lemon juice before putting them on the dryer racks. This will keep them from oxidizing (turning brown) and add a wonderful tartness to the dried apple. We like them dried, not desiccated, so we store them in the freezer. Henning carries a bag of these in his pocket when he is out working on the farm.

~Add chopped apple to sauerkraut, cooked cabbage, and liver dishes to make their flavor milder.

~When cooking fresh apples for pies or sauces, the yield is about 50%. 1 cup sliced or chopped apples equals 1 medium apple. 1 pound raw equals 1/2 pound cooked.

~Choose the right apple for your purpose: firm apples for pies and cakes, softer ones for sauces and dressings and cooking with other foods. Apples are a good addition to green, vegetable, or fruit salads.

Apple & Blackberry Pie
Dough for a 10-inch, two-crust pie:
2 1/3 C flour, plus some for rolling out the dough
1 t salt
1 C butter or
1/2 C each homemade pork lard and butter
Enough cold water to make the dough cohere — be sparing; too much water will make the pie dough tough.
For the Filling:
6 C sliced apples
2 C fresh or frozen blackberries

1/2 C sugar
1/3 C flour
1 t each salt, cinnamon, and nutmeg
1/4 C butter
2 t granulated sugar, for sprinkling on finished pie
For the Dough:
Mix flour with salt. Slice lard or butter into small pieces with a knife, and use a pastry cutter to mix the dough and shortening until the dough resembles fine meal.

Stir in water, a little at a time, until dough can be formed into two balls. Flatten one ball on a floured counter, and roll out with a rolling pin (put flour on dough to keep rolling pin from sticking). If the dough will not cohere, press it with your fingers into the bottom of the pie dish.

Mix apples with berries. Mix sugar, flour, salt, cinnamon and nutmeg; stir into apples and blackberries. Spoon filling into pie shell. Dot the top with butter; roll out top crust and place on top of filling. Tuck the top crust into the bottom crust, and slash in four places. Cover the crust with aluminum foil. Place on the middle rack of the oven, preheated to 425 degrees, and put a cookie sheet on the rack below it to catch juice spills. Bake for 30 minutes, remove foil, and bake for another 20 minutes or so, until the crust is brown and juices have begun to bubble through. Remove pie from oven and sprinkle lightly with granulated sugar. Cool before serving.

Apple Sauce
See *Keeping the Harvest* for making and canning applesauce.

Applesauce Oatmeal Muffins
For the Muffins:
1 1/2 C regular oats
1 1/4 C flour
3/4 t cinnamon
1 t baking powder
3/4 t baking soda
1 C applesauce
1/2 C milk
1/2 C brown sugar, packed
3 T grapeseed oil, or other unflavored vegetable oil
1 egg
For the Topping:
1/2 C regular oats
2 T packed brown sugar
1/8 t cinnamon

2 T melted butter

Mix all ingredients for the muffins, and place the mix into twelve greased muffin cups. Mix ingredients for topping, and spoon a little topping over each muffin. Bake at 400 for 20 minutes.

Baked Apples

1/3 C finely chopped pecans or walnuts
1/3 C brown sugar
1/2 t each cinnamon and nutmeg
4 firm ripe apples, tart or sweet
Vanilla
Butter
1 1/2 C water

Scoop seeds and core from apples, using a knife or a melon baller. Keep bottom intact. Fill apples with nuts, sugar and spices. Top with a bit of vanilla, and a small pat of butter. Place in baking dish; add water. Bake at 350 for 50 minutes or until apples are soft. Remove from oven, baste with juices. Serve with cream or ice cream.

Hood River Fresh Apple Cake

Elizabeth grew up in Hood River, Oregon, a valley between the Columbia River and Mount Hood. She remembers its four distinct seasons, and the wonderful fruit her family grew on their farm. It was a pleasure to discover *A Taste of Oregon,* a book of recipes from Oregon chefs, and to adapt the following recipe, which we make every year when apples are in season.

1 C wheat bran flakes
1 C sugar
1 C melted butter
2 eggs
2 C flour
1 t cinnamon
1/2 t salt
4 C chopped apples
1 C chopped walnuts
Powdered sugar for topping

Cream together bran, sugar, butter, and eggs. Sift the dry ingredients and add to mixture. Add chopped apples and nuts. Bake in a buttered 9x13-inch pan at 350 for 45 minutes. Remove from oven and sift powdered sugar over the top while the cake is still warm.

Cherries

Cherries originated in the region of Greece and Turkey; since ancient times, their indigenous range has extended through most of Europe, western Asia, and northern Africa. In fact, it has been suggested that the forbidden fruit in the Garden of Eden was not an apple, but cherries.

Cherries arrived in North America with Dutch settlers and spread across the U.S. Cherries can be difficult to cultivate because of their need for a chilling period before blossoming and their susceptibility to frost and rain damage. But they are in high demand because of their taste and nutritional benefits.

Cherries contain vitamins A, C, K, thiamin, riboflavin, niacin, pantothenic acid, pyridoxine, calcium, iron, magnesium, manganese, phosphorus, potassium, sodium, and zinc.

Tips for Cherries

~We grow both pie and sweet cherries. Cherries are Henning's favorite fruit, so we have little occasion to preserve them. However, if you have an abundance, see *Keeping the Harvest* for tips about canning and freezing.

~You can bake with whole cherries, but you will have to contend with the pits. Use a cherry pitter, a chopstick or paper clip to push the pit through the stem end. (Wear an old shirt — cherry juice stains.)

~You can use sweet or pie cherries interchangeably in recipes; adjust the amount of sugar.

~Cherries should be stored in a cool place; unlike strawberries and tomatoes, they won't lose flavor or texture in the refrigerator.

~Non-organically raised cherries are high in pesticide residue. While some surface pesticides and herbicides can be removed by a thorough washing or soaking in a little cold water and baking soda, "systemic" pesticides are absorbed by plants and fruit. Pesticides kill pollinating insects, particularly honeybees. Buying organic fruits and vegetables is a good practice.

Cherry Cobbler

For the Filling:
2 1/2 C pitted fresh cherries
1 T fresh lemon juice

1 t vanilla extract
1/2 C sugar
1/4 C flour
For the Dough:
1 1/2 C flour
1/2 C sugar
1 1/2 t baking powder
1/4 t salt
1/2 C melted butter
1/3 C cream
For the Topping:
1/2 C sliced almonds
2 T sugar
1 T butter, melted

In a large bowl, toss pitted cherries with lemon juice and vanilla. Add sugar and flour and stir to combine. Pour into a greased 9x13-inch baking dish.

In a medium bowl, combine flour, sugar, baking powder and salt. Add melted butter and cream, and stir to form a soft dough. Scatter pieces of the dough over the top of the cherries.

In a small bowl, combine the almonds, sugar, and melted butter. Scatter the mixture over the top of the cobbler dough.

Bake at 375 for 30-35 minutes until the cherry filling is bubbly and the topping is golden brown. If the top seems to be getting too dark, cover with foil to finish baking.

Allow cobbler to cool. The juices will thicken and set up, and it will still be warm for serving.

Cherry Crisp
3 C cherries, pitted
3 T sugar
1 T cornstarch
1/2 T fresh lemon juice
1/8 t almond extract
1/2 C brown sugar, packed
1/2 C flour
1 C oatmeal
1/3 C butter, cold
1/2 t cinnamon
1/4 t nutmeg

In a large bowl, gently toss first five ingredients together. Place in a greased 8-inch casserole. In another bowl, mix the rest of the ingredients, using

a pastry cutter or fork. Spread over the filling. Bake at 375 for 30 minutes or until brown.

Cherry Pie
Dough for 10-inch two-crust pie (see *Apple & Blackberry Pie,* above)
6 C washed and pitted cherries
1 C sugar
1/2 C flour
1 t almond extract (optional)
3 T butter
Granulated sugar

Stir together sugar and flour; mix with cherries and proceed as with *Apple & Blackberry Pie* (above).

Fruit Soup
This soup is a good summer dish, eaten cold.

1 lb fruit (berries, apples, plums, rhubarb, cherries, apricots, melons, peaches)
1 piece of lemon peel
3 pints water
1/4-1 C sugar as needed, depending on sweetness of fruit
3 T cornstarch
Lemon juice or white wine, to taste

Wash fruit and chop (leave berries whole). Add water and lemon peel, simmer until soft. Pass through a sieve, as desired for clear or chunky soup. Add sugar to taste; bring to a boil. Add cornstarch, dissolved in a bit of water; bring to boil again. Flavor with lemon juice and/or wine. Let cool. Serve with French bread (see *Bread & Grains*) and butter for a main meal, or by itself as a dessert.

Grapes

Grapes, while technically not a tree fruit, are included here because they grow on tree-like vines. The cultivation of grapes began 6000-8000 years ago in the Near East. The natural yeast in grape skins led to grapes' being used for wine-making as well as fresh eating. In America, native grapes grew wild across the continent, and were an important part of the Native American diet. In the 19th century, a citizen of Concord, Massachusetts, cultivated the Concord grape from native grapes (*Vitis labrusca*), which became an important agricultural crop in the United States. The colors of grapes include black, dark blue, crimson, blue, yellow, orange, green, and pink.

Grapes contain vitamins C, E, K, thiamin, riboflavin, niacin, pantothenic acid, pyridoxine, folate, choline, calcium, iron, magnesium, manganese, phosphorus, potassium, sodium, and zinc.

Tips for Grapes

~According to the Food and Agriculture Organization, some 75,000 square kilometers of land in the world are dedicated to grapes. About half of production goes to making wine, one third to fresh fruit, and the rest to raisins and juice.

~Table grapes, unless organically grown, may contain pesticides, herbicides and fungicides. Wine may contain the same: chemicals permitted by law for use in wine-making include pesticides, herbicides, equipment cleaning chemicals, and sulphate preservatives.

~That said, wine, especially red wine, is considered good for your health, if taken in moderation. And it does add pleasure to a meal or a social gathering.

~We grow Interlaken grapes, both purple and green. We eat as many fresh as we can — competing with the birds — and make the rest into juice, using the steamer method described in *Keeping the Harvest*. One year we had so many grapes we ran out of canning jars for juice, and so we made wine, with the guidance of local vintner Brent Charnley (Lopez Island Vineyards). The white wine we produced by very simple methods turned out to be delicious, a little dry, and high in alcohol content. We saved it for special occasions, and served it in small glasses.

~Grapes do not continue to ripen after they have been picked.

~Store grapes in the refrigerator. Wash before serving, but not before refrigerating.

~Grapes can be frozen and eaten straight from the freezer.

~Grapes paired with cheese and pears make a wonderful dessert.

~Overripe grapes can be used in smoothies, spooned into melon halves and topped with yogurt for a light breakfast.

~Do not let your dog eat grapes or raisins; the exact toxin is unknown, but the results — often fatal —are well documented.

Peaches

Peaches originated in China as early as 2000 BC. The clingstone and freestone types identified in archaeological excavations there are the same that are cultivated today. Persians introduced them to the Romans, who took them to southern Europe. Spanish explorers took them to Latin America, from there they made their way to England. In the 17th Century, they were brought to Virginia by an English horticulturist and were carried by Native Americans across the country. In the 19th century, commercial production began.

Today there are many variations in peaches: flesh that may be white, yellow, or shading to red. Textures range from "melting" — very soft and juicy — to nearly as firm as an apple. There is also a range of flavors, from very sweet to slightly tart. All peaches are fuzzy (nectarines are a mutation). Peaches you buy in the store have had most of their fuzz mechanically removed.

Peaches contain vitamins A, C, E, riboflavin, thiamin, pyridoxine, and niacin.

Tips for Peaches

~Peaches picked from your orchard or found in a farmers market will be ripe and succulent; peaches found in stores were picked before ripening so they could be transported without bruising.

~Peaches will ripen off the tree. When you take home firm peaches from the store, or pick your own before they are ripe, put them on a linen or other porous cloth (not a paper bag), separated from each other and out of the sun. Place another cloth over the peaches to protect them from fruit flies. Check them every day by smell, color at the stem (a nice yellow stripe for yellow peaches, white stripe for white peaches). Ripen, then refrigerate. If you refrigerate them before they are ripe, they will turn mealy.

~Redness does not signal ripeness; the red on a peach is blush from the sun. Green peaches will not ripen. If peaches are fully ripe, they will peel easily; just start with a knife at the base and peel toward the stem end.

~If you want to peel peaches (as for canning) that are not fully ripe, ease them into boiling water for about 30 seconds. Remove with a slotted spoon, and immediately place into cold water. The peels will slip off easily.

~To remove the pit from a peach (best done with the peel still on) cut the peach all the way around (North to South Pole) and give a little twist. This method does not work well with clingstone peaches. For canning tips, see *Keeping the Harvest*.

Peach Cobbler

For the Filling:
1/2 C sugar
1 T cornstarch
4 C sliced peaches, peeled
1 t lemon juice
For the Topping:
1 C flour
1 T sugar
1 1/2 t baking powder
1/2 t salt
3 T butter, sliced
1/2 C milk

Blend sugar and cornstarch in a medium saucepan. Stir in peaches and lemon juice. Cook, stirring constantly, until mixture boils. Remove from heat and stir until ingredients are well combined. Pour into an ungreased 2-quart casserole. Measure flour, sugar, baking powder and salt into a bowl. Add butter slices and milk. Cut butter into the mix until dough forms a ball. Drop dough in spoonfuls on hot fruit.

Bake at 400 for 25-30 minutes or until biscuit topping is golden brown. Serve warm, with cream.

Peach Melba

For the Peaches:
3 C water
3 C sugar
1 vanilla pod, split lengthwise
2 T lemon juice
8 peaches
For the Raspberry Sauce:
3 C raspberries
1/4 C powdered sugar
1 T lemon juice

Put the water, sugar, lemon juice, and vanilla pod into a wide saucepan and heat gently to dissolve the sugar. Bring the pan to a boil and let it bubble for about 5 minutes, then turn the heat down to simmer.

Cut the peaches in half; if the stones come out easily, remove them. If not, get them out later.

Poach the peach halves in the sugar syrup for 2-3 minutes on each side, depending on the ripeness of the fruit. When the peaches are soft, remove them to a plate with a slotted spoon.

When all the peaches are poached, peel off their skins and remove stones. You can freeze excess syrup for the next time.

To make the raspberry sauce, blend the raspberries, powdered sugar and lemon juice in a food processor. You can put the sauce through a strainer to remove raspberry seeds, or leave them in.

Allow 2 peach halves per person and serve them on a plate alongside a scoop or two of ice cream or frozen yogurt. Spoon raspberry sauce over each.

Peach Shortcake

This dish makes a wonderful breakfast.

For the Biscuits:
2 C flour
2 t baking powder
1 t salt
1/4 C butter
1 C milk
For the Topping:
Several fresh peaches, peeled and sliced
Butter
Warm milk or cream

Measure flour, powder, and salt into a bowl. Cut in butter thoroughly. Stir in the milk. Drop dough by spoonfuls onto a greased cookie sheet, lightly flattening each round so the biscuits cook through completely. Bake at 450 for 10-12 minutes or until golden brown.

Cut the hot biscuits in half and spread with butter. Top with fresh peaches and milk or cream.

Pears

Pears are one of the world's oldest cultivated and beloved fruits, originating in the Mediterranean region and spreading from there to Europe and America. In the paintings of Renaissance masters, pears are often featured in still-life paintings. "A Partridge in a Pear Tree" is part of an 18th-century Christmas carol, still sung today.

Early colonists brought pear trees to America, from

where they migrated to the Northwest. Pears are presently one of the most important crops produced in Washington and Oregon.

Pears contain vitamins A, C, K, potassium, calcium, iron, magnesium, riboflavin, pyridoxine, and folate.

Tips for Pears

~As healthy as they are in their natural state, conventionally raised pears are covered with pesticides. The amount of pesticides on pears is greater than on most other tree fruit crops, including peaches, nectarines, apples and cherries. The amount of pesticides has more than doubled since 2010. 49 pesticides and fungicides were found on pear samples in the most recent study. Some chemicals are applied after harvest to keep pears from spoiling in storage. Purchase local, organically-grown pears; or, better, plant your own trees.

~Pears ripen from the inside out. If you pick and store pears (separated by layers of newspaper), be vigilant. The pear can look and feel firm on the outside but be browning and softening on the inside.

~It is best to pick pears before they are fully ripe. If you need to hasten ripening, place them in a paper bag for a day.

~The most common pears in the Northwest are Anjou and Bartlett; both are good for eating, cooking, and canning

~See *Keeping the Harvest* for tips on canning pears.

~Asian pears differ from European pears: they are round, turning from green to golden as they ripen. They are a firm fruit rather like an apple in texture, and keep for a long time after picking.

~Asian pears do not ripen off the tree. We had to rescue the pears (and the branches of the tree) from raccoon predation this year, while the pears were still green. We put them in paper bags with apples, so that the ethylene gas would help the pears ripen. They did so, and were edible, but they lacked the sweetness that tree ripening gives them. They are good for baking, especially with apple dishes.

Baked Pears

4 pears, halved and cored
1/2 t cinnamon
1/2 C walnuts, chopped
1/4 C raisins
Honey

Cut pears in half; scoop out center. Sprinkle prepared pear halves with cinnamon, and fill with walnuts and raisins. Drizzle with honey. Pierce pear halves with a knife along the sides. Place on a baking sheet covered with parchment paper. Bake at 350 for 30 minutes.

Curried Butternut Squash & Pear Soup

2 lb butternut squash
3 T butter
1 onion, diced
2 cloves garlic, minced
2 t minced fresh ginger root
1 T curry powder (we use a sweet curry powder)
1 t salt
4 C homemade chicken broth
2 firm pears, peeled, cored, and diced
1/2 C half-and-half

Cut squash in half lengthwise; put seeds and membrane into compost. Place squash halves, cut sides down, on a baking sheet covered with parchment paper or aluminum foil, coated with water to steam the squash. Roast at 375 about 45 minutes, until very soft. Scoop the pulp from the peel, and reserve.

Melt butter in a large soup pot over medium heat. Stir in the onion, garlic, ginger, curry powder, and salt. Cook until onion is soft. Pour chicken broth into the pot and bring to a boil. Stir in the pears and the reserved squash, and simmer until the pears are very soft.

Puree the soup in a food processor or with an immersion blender in batches until smooth, return to pot, stir in the half-and-half, and reheat.

Fresh Apple & Pear Salad

4 medium apples, thinly sliced
2 medium pears, thinly sliced
1 medium cucumber, peeled, seeded and chopped
1 medium red onion, thinly sliced
1/4 C apple cider or juice
1 T snipped fresh dill or minced fresh tarragon
1 T olive oil
1 T spicy brown mustard
2 t brown sugar
1/4 t pepper

In a large bowl, combine apples, pears, cucumber and onion. In a small bowl, whisk remaining ingredients until blended. Pour over fruit mixture and toss to coat. Refrigerate until serving.

Pears & Cottage Cheese

When Elizabeth was a girl, fresh or canned pears over cottage cheese was a regular treat in her home. Canned pears (see *Keeping the Harvest*) are better for this combination, because the juices soak into the cottage cheese. Wonderful for lunch or dessert.

Roquefort Pear Salad

1 head leaf lettuce, torn into bite-size pieces
3 pears, cored and chopped
5 oz Roquefort cheese, crumbled
1 avocado, diced
1/2 C thinly sliced green onions
1/4 C sugar
1/2 C pecans
1/3 C olive oil
3 T red wine vinegar
1 1/2 t each sugar and prepared mustard
1 clove garlic, chopped
1/2 t salt
Pepper to taste

In a skillet over medium heat, stir 1/4 cup sugar together with the pecans. Continue stirring gently until sugar has melted and caramelized the pecans. Transfer to waxed paper, allow to cool, and break into pieces.

For the dressing, blend oil, vinegar, sugar, mustard, chopped garlic, salt, and pepper.

In a large serving bowl, layer lettuce, pears, cheese, avocado, and green onions. Pour dressing over salad, sprinkle with pecans, and serve.

Melons

Melons are an ancient fruit, that, like grapes, grow on vines. They were developed in the Middle East, and widely grown throughout Europe by the third century A.D. They came to America on Columbus' second voyage, were well known on the east coast of the U.S. by the 17th century, and widely grown by the 19th. The category of melons includes watermelons, cantaloupe, and honeydew, which contain varying amounts of vitamins and minerals: A, C, K, thiamin, niacin, folate, pyridoxine, iron, magnesium, potassium, copper, calcium, and manganese.

Tips for Melons

~Conventionally grown melons contain up to 23 pesticides (some carcinogenic), hormone disruptors, and honeybee toxins. Photographs on the internet show people in hazmat suits spraying poisons on the industrially grown melons you might find in the market. Buy local, organic melons, or, better, grow your own.

~Melons are ripe when the stem side is closed and they come easily off the vine. Commercial melons are often harvested unripe, which means that the stem side is open and can absorb bacteria, such as E-coli. In 2019, pre-cut melons and pre-cut medley fruit products supplied by Caito Foods caused an outbreak of salmonella. Buy from a local farmer, or, best, grow your own.

~Melons don't store well. Don't keep them for more than two days in the refrigerator.

~Melon halves filled with ice cream, yogurt, or cottage cheese make a wonderful breakfast, lunch, or snack.

~Slices of melon with other fresh fruit in a salad are great for any meal. We salt melon lightly; others like ginger, or pepper.

~We grow cantaloupe and honeydew melons, and eat them fresh. The results of freezing and juicing have been disappointing, so we eat them as they ripen.

Cucumber Melon Salsa

This refreshing salsa can be served over fish, pork or chicken, or used as a dip for tortilla chips.

2 cucumbers, peeled and diced
3 C diced fresh cantaloupe
1 T olive oil
1/2 jalapeño pepper, seeded and minced
Juice of one large or two small limes
1 small red onion, minced
1 plum tomato, *or* 1/2 red pepper, chopped
1/2 C cilantro *or* 1/2 C parsley, chopped
A pinch of salt, a pinch of pepper

In a large serving bowl, mix all prepared ingredients. Cover the bowl and chill in the refrigerator for 2 hours to let the flavors blend.

Melon Salad

Mix pieces of cantaloupe, honeydew, and watermelon — using a melon baller produces uniform pieces — and toss with a little honey, lime juice and fresh mint leaves.

Rhubarb

Although technically a vegetable, rhubarb is prepared as a fruit. The exact origin of culinary rhubarb is unknown, although by the 18th century, it was grown in Europe and used for medicinal purposes.

Rhubarb contains vitamins A, C, E, K, folate, pantothenic acid, pyridoxine, riboflavin, thiamin, sodium, potassium, calcium, copper, iron, magnesium, manganese, phosphorus, selenium, and zinc.

Tips for Rhubarb

~Rhubarb leaves contain oxalic acid, and should not be consumed by people or animals. We put them in the compost pile, where the acid breaks down and becomes harmless.

~There are recipes online for homemade pesticide sprays made from rhubarb leaves.

~Rhubarb can be frozen; unlike other vegetables, it does not need to be parboiled first. Just cut the stalks into half-inch pieces and put into a freezer bag. Defrosted, it is good for any of the following recipes.

~Steaming or cooking rhubarb briefly before using it in a dish is a matter of personal taste. We prefer steaming rhubarb to cooking it in water — there is no liquid to pour off, and the pieces retain more texture.

~Rhubarb breaks down quickly when cooked or steamed.

Rhubarb Coffee Cake

1/2 C butter, softened
1 C sugar
1 egg, beaten
2 C flour
1/2 t salt
1 t baking soda
1 C buttermilk
2 C rhubarb, chopped
1 t vanilla
Extra sugar and some cinnamon for topping

Cream butter and sugar, add egg and beat together. Sift dry ingredients and add to the mix alternately with buttermilk. Gently blend in rhubarb and vanilla. Pour into a greased 9x13-inch baking pan. Sprinkle top with a bit of sugar and cinnamon.

Bake at 350 for 45 minutes, or until a knife inserted in the cake comes out clean.

Rhubarb Crisp

1/2 C sugar
2 T cornstarch
3 C rhubarb, cut into 1-inch slices, briefly steamed
2 C sliced apples (or strawberries, or a mix of the two)
1 C oats
1/2 C packed brown sugar
1/2 C butter, melted
1/3 C flour
1/2 C minced walnuts

In a large bowl, combine sugar and cornstarch. Add rhubarb and apples and/or strawberries, toss to coat. Spoon the mix into an 8 or 9-inch oven-proof baking dish.

In a small bowl, combine oats, brown sugar, butter, flour and cinnamon. Sprinkle over fruit. Bake at 350 for 45 minutes, until bubbly.

Rhubarb Fool

There are two versions of the origin of this name: one is that the second word comes from *fouler* — French for "to mash" or "to press." The other is "any fool can make it." Both are apt.

There are many elaborate recipes for Rhubarb Fool. The simplest — and one of the best — is just to fold stewed rhubarb into stiffly whipped cream, and top with minced candied ginger. The contrasting textures and flavors make this a toothsome, light dessert, best served in parfait glasses.

Rhubarb Pie

A tart, delicious pie. You can balance the tartness of the rhubarb by using half strawberries, fresh or defrosted, for the filling.

Pastry for a two-crust, 10-inch pie. (See *Apple & Blackberry Pie*, above).
For the Filling:
1 C sugar
1/2 C flour
5 C stewed rhubarb, *or*
3 C stewed rhubarb and 2 C strawberries
3 T butter

Prepare pastry, and stir the sugar and flour into the fruit. Spoon the fruit into the bottom pie crust, dot with the butter, and cover with the top crust. Tuck the top crust into the bottom crust, and cut slits in it to release juices.

Cover the top of the pie crust with aluminum foil to prevent excess browning; remove the foil 20 minutes before the pie comes out of the oven. Place a cookie sheet on the lower oven rack to catch the juicy spills. Bake at 425 for 40-50 minutes.

Stewed Rhubarb

This is the simplest way to prepare rhubarb. Cut the stalk into 1-inch pieces and steam or cook gently in just enough water to cover. Add sugar, honey, cinnamon, ginger, or orange juice, as desired. Serve on pancakes or waffles, over ice cream, or mixed with strawberries and topped with cream.

Berries

Berries have been a valuable food source for humans since before the start of agriculture, when they were a seasonal staple for early hunter-gatherers. Many can still be found wild (see *Wildcrafting*) and many can be cultivated in your garden. All are sources of good health and delightful eating. Berries are high in nutrients, varying with different kinds of berries.

Black Currants

Black currants are native to northern Europe and Asia. They were developed in Russia by the 11th century when they were cultivated in monastery gardens and grown in towns and settlements. Popular in Europe since the 17th century, the black currant was used for food, and decoctions of leaves, bark, and roots were used for medicinal purposes. Early in the 20th century, black currants were popular in the U.S. But in 1911, the commercial cultivation of currants was outlawed by an act of Congress for the bushes' alleged part in spreading white pine blister dust, which threatened the timber industry.

Because of its high vitamin C content, the black currant was cultivated in England during WWII, when other sources of the vitamin were hard to come by. New types of the bush, which do not threaten trees, have been developed in the U.S., so the berry is enjoying a comeback. Black currant

seed oil is used in cosmetic preparations and the leaves and fruit are sources for dyes.

Black currants contain vitamins C, E, pyridoxine, thiamine, riboflavin, niacin, pantothenic acid, calcium, iron, magnesium, manganese, phosphorus, potassium, sodium, and zinc.

Tips for Black Currants
~We grow black currants, and try to get them picked before the birds do. We process them into a potent juice (using a juicer, described in *Keeping the Harvest*). The juice can be mixed with water when serving.
~Black currants are acidic, so we mix the juice with milder juices, such as grape, pear, or apple juice.
~Fully ripe black currants are delicious to eat by themselves; less ripe currants can taste sour, and may best be used in compotes or juices.
~You can make black currants into jam, teaming them with raspberries, red currants or strawberries.
~Compote made with black currants, blueberries, red currants, and/or strawberries is easy to make and freeze. Briefly cook the berries of your choice with enough sugar to sweeten, then cool and freeze for winter. Spoon over yogurt or ice cream, or use as a topping for shortcake.

Blueberries

Blueberries originated in North America. They were used as a dye as well as a food staple by Native Americans, who taught European settlers how to harvest and dry the berry. The wild berries were domesticated in 1911, and cultivation was so successful that the U.S. now grows over 90% of the world's blueberries.

Blueberries are packed with antioxidants and there are many claims for their ability to boost the immune system, fight cancer, and promote heart health. They contain vitamins C, E, K1, pyridoxine, manganese, and copper.

Tips for Blueberries
~We grow several types of blueberries, both to eat fresh, and freeze. Unlike strawberries and raspberries, which when defrosted tend to collapse and produce a lot of juice, blueberries stand up to the freezing process. They remain firm, ready for

pies or muffins or to serve with yogurt or sweetened quark.

~To freeze blueberries, simply pluck any stems and put the berries (unwashed) in a freezer bag. They will keep in the freezer for up to two years.

~Fresh blueberries keep in the refrigerator, unwashed, for one to two weeks. Wash just before using.

~Blueberry jam can be made with or without pectin, since the blueberries will thicken on their own. Find recipes and methods online, or on containers of pectin.

~If you bake with frozen blueberries, fold them into the batter before they thaw.

~Blueberries are a wonderful addition to a summer fruit salad and fruit-based smoothies.

Blueberry Cobbler

For the Fruit:
1 1/2 C fresh or frozen blueberries
1 t vanilla
Juice of 1/2 lemon
1 C sugar, or to taste
1/2 t flour
1 T butter, melted
For the Topping:
1 1/3 C flour
4 t baking powder
6 T sugar
5 T butter
1 C milk
2 t sugar
1 pinch cinnamon

Lightly grease a 9-inch baking dish. Place the blueberries into the baking dish, and mix with vanilla and lemon juice. Sprinkle with 1 cup sugar and 1/2 teaspoon flour, then stir in the tablespoon of melted butter. Set aside.

In a medium bowl, stir together flour, baking powder and sugar. Rub in the butter using your fingers, or cut in with a pastry cutter until dough is crumbly. Make a well in the center, and quickly stir in the milk. Mix just until moistened. You should have a very thick batter. Let it rest for 10 minutes.

Spoon the batter over the blueberries, leaving only a few small holes for the berries to peek through. Mix together the cinnamon and the remaining sugar; sprinkle over the top.

Bake at 375 for 20-25 minutes, or until the top is golden brown. Insert a knife in the topping to ensure doneness. Let cool until just warm before serving. Cobbler can store in the refrigerator for 2 days.

Blueberry Muffins

There are simpler recipes for blueberry muffins available, but none we have tried result in the deep flavor, crunchy top and tender texture of this one.

1 C sugar
1/2 C butter, softened
2 large eggs
2 T grapeseed oil (or other flavorless vegetable oil)
3/4 C sour cream
1/2 C milk
2 T grated lemon peel
3 C flour
1 T baking powder
1/2 t baking soda
3/4 t salt
2 C fresh or frozen blueberries

Grease 16 muffin cups. Beat butter and sugar in a large bowl until light and fluffy. Stir in one egg at a time until well mixed. Add oil, and stir to combine — an electric mixer works well. Whisk sour cream, milk, and lemon zest into butter mixture until smooth. In a separate bowl, sift together flour, baking powder, baking soda, and salt.

Stir half the flour mixture into the butter mixture until combined. Add remaining half of flour mixture and blueberries into the batter, folding together until just combined. (If you over stir, the batter will toughen.)

Spoon batter into prepared muffin cups. Place muffin tins on the center rack of the oven and bake at 375 until tops are golden, and a knife inserted in the center of a muffin comes out clean, 20-30 minutes. You can sprinkle muffins with sugar before baking.

Blueberry Nut Bread

2 C sifted flour
1 C sugar
1/2 t each baking powder and baking soda
1 t salt
Juice and grated rind of one lemon
2 T melted butter
1 egg, well beaten

1/2 C chopped walnuts
2 C fresh or frozen blueberries

Sift together flour, sugar, baking powder, soda, and salt. Combine lemon juice, rind, melted butter and enough water to make 3/4 cup juice. Stir in beaten egg. Pour mixture into dry ingredients, mixing just enough to dampen. Fold in blueberries and nuts. Spoon into greased loaf pan, making sides higher than center. Bake at 350 for 50-60 minutes.

Blueberry Parfait
You can make this end-of-the-meal delight with almost any fruit, but blueberries, fresh or defrosted, add color and texture.

1 qt quark, sweetened with sugar or honey, and softened with yogurt or cream
2 C blueberries

Place prepared quark and blueberries alternately in parfait glasses. Add a sprig of mint for a bit of color.

Gooseberries

Gooseberries grew wild in Europe, Africa, and Asia. The berries were first cultivated in the 16th century in English and Dutch gardens before they were brought to America.

Gooseberries contain vitamins A, C, thiamin, riboflavin, niacin, pantothenic acid, pyridoxine, folate, calcium, iron, potassium, manganese, copper, phosphorus, magnesium, and zinc.

Tips for Gooseberries
~Gooseberries appear in June when they are small and green, but they are sour and should be cooked or processed, and need some sugar. Wait until July, when the berries are softer and golden in color, and they are sweet enough to eat right off the bush.
~If you are going to serve them uncooked, in a parfait or over ice cream or with yogurt, let them lie in the sun for a while to bring out the sweetness and flavors.
~Gooseberries have a stem and a flower end; you can pinch off both with small scissors or your fingernails before serving. If you are going to freeze the berries for desserts, you can leave flower and stem ends on; they will soften in freezing.

~Gooseberries can be made into excellent wine, compote, or jam.
~Use gooseberries in cobblers, crisps and pies (see recipes for *Rhubarb Crisp*, *Blueberry Cobbler* and *Apple-Blackberry Pie*).

Raspberries

Raspberries originated in eastern Asia. The red raspberry may have been brought to North America by prehistoric people who crossed the Bering Strait, but the wild black raspberry is believed to be native to the West.

There are over fifty kinds of cultivated raspberries, ranging in color from gold to black. Red raspberries are the most common, and are selected for their fruiting times, from early summer to fall.

Raspberries contain vitamins C, E, K, thiamin, riboflavin, niacin, pantothenic acid, pyridoxine, folate, choline, calcium, iron, magnesium, manganese, phosphorus, potassium, and zinc.

Tips for Raspberries
~Although raspberries are cultivated primarily for their fruit, their leaves are also used in medicinal teas.
~Raspberries should be picked every day as they ripen. They can be eaten fresh, made into jam, or popped into freezer bags to save for winter. When berries are ready, they pull easily off the hull. Pick only ripe berries, as they will not ripen off the vine.
~Avoid washing raspberries, if possible. If it is necessary, use little water, because the berries are delicate. Dry, spread on paper towels. They will keep in the refrigerator for 1-2 days.
~One pint of fresh raspberries equals 1 3/4 cups.
~Raspberries can be sweetened with a little sugar and served with ice cream, yogurt, sweetened quark, over pancakes, cereal, or waffles.
~Raspberries can be substituted for strawberries in many recipes.

Fresh Raspberry Vinaigrette
6 oz fresh raspberries
4 T olive oil
1 T red wine vinegar
Salt and pepper to taste
Honey to taste (optional)

Push berries through a fine mesh strainer into a small bowl, first with a fork (to mash) and then with the back of a spoon to push all the berries through. If a few seeds squeeze through, that's fine. This should yield about 1/2 cups raspberry puree.

Whisk in red wine vinegar, olive oil, salt, pepper, and honey (if used). The vinaigrette can be stored in the refrigerator for up to a week. The oil will solidify, so warm it to room temperature before serving over green salad, vegetables or fruit.

Raspberry Crumble
For Topping:
6 T melted butter, plus more for baking dish
1 1/2 C rolled oats, divided
1/2 C sliced almonds
1/4 C brown sugar
1/2 t salt
For Filling:
6 C fresh raspberries
1 t vanilla
1/3 C brown sugar
2 T cornstarch
A pinch of salt
For Serving:
Plain yogurt

Brush an 9-inch baking pan with melted butter. Pulse 1/2 cup rolled oats in a food processor until finely ground. Transfer to a bowl; stir in 1 cup oats, the almonds, brown sugar, salt, and melted butter.

In another bowl, gently combine all filling ingredients.

Transfer filling to baking pan. Sprinkle top with oat mixture; bake at 350 for 45-50 minutes, until top is golden brown and filling is bubbling. Let cool; serve with plain yogurt or ice cream.

Raspberry Muffins
2 C flour
1/2 C sugar
2 t baking powder
1 t salt
6 T butter
1 egg, beaten
1 C buttermilk
1 C fresh raspberries

Combine flour, sugar, baking powder and salt. Cut in butter until mixture resembles coarse meal. Add egg and buttermilk; mix just until dry ingredients are moistened. Fold in berries. Fill 12 greased muffin cups two-thirds full. Bake at 400 for 20 minutes or until browned.

Red Currants

Red currants, related to black currants and gooseberries, are native to Europe, Asia, and North America. Wild varieties have been cultivated for larger berries and fewer thorns, and can be easily grown in the home garden.

Red currants contain vitamins C, E, K, thiamin, riboflavin, niacin, pantothenic acid, pyridoxine, folate, choline, calcium, iron, magnesium, manganese, phosphorus, potassium, sodium, and zinc.

Tips for Red Currants
~Pick red currants from the bush by the cluster, then remove stems by pulling a fork through the berries. Use fresh, or freeze for later.
~If you want to keep them in the refrigerator for a few days, wrap them loosely in paper towels; do not wash them until just before use.
~Red currants can be made into jelly or jam; see instructions in the packet of pectin.

Henning's Red Currant Sauce
1 pint red currants, fresh or thawed
3 T sugar
1 t cornstarch whisked with a little water

Mash the currants with a potato masher and then strain through a sieve to separate seeds from juice. Add the sugar, and cook gently for about 2 minutes. Add the cornstarch that has been mixed with water, and cook until the sauce is thickened. Spoon over ice cream or yogurt or sweetened quark, or over a plain cake, such as sponge cake. This thickened juice keeps well in the refrigerator.

Strawberries

Strawberries are native to North America, and were used by Native Americans in many dishes. Wild strawberries were so plentiful that colonists did not start to cultivate domesticated varieties until the 19th century.

Strawberries contain vitamins A, C, E, K, thiamin, riboflavin, niacin, folate, pantothenic acid, pyridoxine, potassium, magnesium, calcium, sodium, iron, selenium, manganese, copper, and zinc.

Tips for Strawberries

~Wild strawberries are smaller and more flavorful than those that are cultivated, and local custom is that folks do not tell where their favorite patches are, anymore than they tell where they find mushrooms. Cultivated strawberries are larger and less intense in flavor. They are easily grown in the home garden, and will reproduce through runners, so original plants will replace themselves.

~Commercially grown strawberries can contain 20 different types of pesticide residues, and lead the list of most-pesticide-laden foods. Buy organic, or better, grow your own.

~Fresh local strawberries, like fresh local tomatoes, are worth waiting for. The commercially grown strawberries available in stores in the winter are large, and have the consistency and flavor of styrofoam. Freeze your own strawberries and eat them in December, rather than the "fresh" ones in the market.

~Don't wash strawberries unless there is a real need, because their flesh is porous and will absorb water.

~Stem strawberries with a sharp knife or your fingernails. You can serve them with stems on for a fruit and cheese plate.

~Strawberries are fragile, and mold on a few berries will contaminate the rest. If you are not going to eat them within a few days, freeze or process them.

~Putting sugar on fresh or frozen strawberries will draw the juice.

~One pint of fresh strawberries is equal to 2 1/2 cups whole, 1 3/4 cups sliced, 1 1/4 cups puréed.

~Strawberry jam is a favorite. Find recipes and instructions on containers of pectin.

Strawberry & Avocado Salad

1 T sugar
2 T olive oil
4 t honey
1 T cider vinegar
1 t lemon juice
2 C torn salad greens
1 avocado, peeled, pitted, and sliced
10 strawberries, sliced
1/2 C chopped pecans

In a small bowl, whisk together the sugar, olive oil, honey, vinegar, and lemon juice. Set aside.

Place salad greens in a serving bowl, and top with sliced avocado and strawberries. Drizzle dressing over salad, then sprinkle with pecans. Serve immediately.

Strawberry Crepes

For the Crepes:
1 C flour
1 T sugar
3 eggs
1 C milk
2 T melted butter

Whisk together all ingredients. One ladle at a time, spoon into a nonstick pan that has been preheated over medium heat. Swirl until batter is spread thinly and evenly over the bottom and sides of pan. Cook until lightly browned on both sides.

For the Filling: Sliced fresh or defrosted strawberries. If using fresh strawberries, mix with a little sugar ahead of time to draw the juice. You can add other fruit, such as fresh or defrosted blueberries, blackberries, streamed rhubarb, or raspberries.

Cook crepes, place on a plate, and fill each with the fruit. Fold or roll, and top with whipped cream.

Notes:

Dairy

Our decision to purchase a dairy cow and produce our own milk products was a natural step toward self-sufficiency. We already produced beef, lamb, pork, chickens, eggs, vegetables, fruit, and herbs. We were still dependent on outside sources for organic grain and dairy products. So Henning planted a two-acre field to barley, and we went in search of the perfect cow. We found Loveday, a beautiful Jersey, at Our Lady of the Rock, the farming monastery on Shaw Island.

Jerseys are an heirloom strain, bred for their high butterfat milk, their hardiness, and their gentle nature. A DNA test of a hair sample from Loveday assured us that she would only produce milk that contains A2 protein, unlike the milk from cows (Holsteins, for instance) that produce A1 protein associated with symptoms of lactose intolerance. Jerseys are also beautiful: brown, with distinctive black and white markings on face and legs.

Loveday and her offspring have supplied us for 30 years with the best milk, butter, buttermilk, cream, sour cream, ice cream, yogurt, whey, and cheeses that can be had. Owning a cow also kept us from participating in a particularly abusive aspect of agribusiness — commercial dairy farming.

The contrast between a family cow and cows exploited by commercial dairies was beautifully expressed by Tanya Barnett, who wrote an article for *Earth Ministry*. After she spent a weekend on our farm, she wrote:
"(Given what) I know about the dairy industry in this country, I realized how unique it is for a cow to be treated as a co-worker rather than a machine — or, more accurately, a dispensable cog in a larger industrial machine. This industrial dairy machine works to produce the greatest quantities of milk with the smallest input costs (e.g. feed, acreage, buildings, etc.) For decades, farm policies in our country have supported and subsidized this mechanistic model, which requires placing large numbers of cows on as little land as possible. Most cows in our country (over 85 per cent) now live in Concentrated Animal Feeding Operations, or 'CAFOS.' But such a mechanistic system is actually 'too' productive: milk quantities far exceed consumer need. Our current oversupply of milk floods the national economy and threatens to supplant remaining small-scale, sustainable milk production here and around the world. The problem of over-production is so great that, for example, in 1985 our government paid over fourteen thousand dairy farmers to kill their cows and get out of the dairy business. These cows were 'dispensable cogs' and their milk a waste product.

CAFO cows don't live like Loveday. Loveday produces a quantity of milk that's natural to her body (about 20 pounds a day). After receiving stress/disease producing (e.g. mastitis, uterine disorders, enlarged internal organs) injections of recombinant Bovine Growth Hormone (rBGH), her commercial cow sisters can produce a painful 49 pounds of milk. Loveday grazes freely and eats food that her body was created to consume; CAFO cows typically never taste fresh grass — they're confined to small areas and fed a highly concentrated diet that is foreign and stressful to their bodies. Loveday's manure is a blessing to the land; the enormous quantity of CAFO manure is almost always an air/water pollutant, an environmental curse. Loveday is treated as a co-worker and source of God's grace; CAFO cows are treated like expendable chattel, and their abundant milk like a problem to be solved. Loveday can expect to produce a calf every year for at least 12 years; her CAFO counterparts usually "wear out," cease milk production, and are slaughtered within two years."

The sad news about dairy cows merges right into sad facts about the fast food industry. Consumers not only ingest hormones and antibiotics with the non-organic milk, but also with the hamburger they eat — much of the hamburger served in fast food restaurants comes from slaughtered dairy cows. The U.S. Department of Agriculture's Economic Research Service reports that in 2019, over three million dairy cows were slaughtered under federal inspection for sales to restaurants, 77% of the total beef production. "Cheap" hamburgers come with a substantial health cost — meat laced with hormones and antibiotics.

The good news — although we don't hear much about them —is that family cows are not uncommon. In *The Family Cow*, Dirk van Loon notes that when he set out to find a dairy cow for his family, the county extension agent told him that there were none. That is, none had made it into the records. But van Loon knew of many such cows, and secured one without trouble. So did we.

Loveday, who gave us milk for fifteen years, was the first of many of our dairy cows: we are now milking Persephone, daughter of Ceres (granddaughter of Loveday), whose calf, Penelope, will soon become another milk cow when she freshens next spring.

Milking sets the morning schedule: cutting up "treats" for the cow — typically potatoes, sugar beets, apples, greens, pumpkins, cabbage, or whatever else is in the garden — getting her in from the pasture, cleaning, grooming and milking her,

returning her to pasture, decanting the milk, and cleaning the milking stall. Two months before parturition we dry the cow off so that all of her energy can go into growing the calf, but we continue grooming, petting, and giving her treats. We make butter, cheese, yogurt and quark from her milk for ten months of the year, so that we have stored dairy products to see us through the time of her late pregnancy.

The cow's milk changes with her natural cycles and the seasons. When the calf is born, the colostrum in the first milk provides natural antibodies to build the calf's immune system. After about three weeks, the antibodies dissipate enough for the milk to ferment into quark, yogurt, or cheese. In the meantime, the colostrum provides us with delicious pancakes. In winter, when the cow is fed on hay, the butterfat content is relatively low; but with the flush of spring grass, you can stand a spoon in the cream, and make plenty of butter. Milk from a family cow keeps us in touch with seasonality as milk from the store never could.

Raw milk from grass-fed cows is one of the best foods we ingest. High in omega 3s (from grass), it also provides vitamins A, D, E, K, cobalamin, calcium, thiamin, riboflavin, phosphorus, and protein. Raw milk has been credited with reducing allergies, psoriasis, eczema, and acne, and boosting the immune system.

However, it is important to note that while the natural bacteria in raw milk strengthen an adult's immune system, it should not be fed to a child under two years of age, whose immune system still needs to develop, and whose digestive system cannot process the enzymes and proteins in raw milk. Other natural products, such as egg whites, unpasteurized fruit juice or honey, pose the same risks for a baby.

If you have a cow (or other milk-producing animal), a strict milking and processing protocol is essential. The milking parlor, milk pails, wash buckets, and other equipment must be scrupulously clean, and the procedure for cleaning the animal and the milker's hands rigorously observed. If you get milk from a local farmer, observe the process or participate yourself so that you will know that the milk is safe. Our dairy is inspected and licensed by the Washington State Department of Health — the first such licensed facility in San Juan County since WWII.

Pasteurization

For us, "food security" means that we grow and process our own food, and know what it contains. In the commercial dairy industry, "food security" means that milk products other than some long-fermented cheeses have been pasteurized; in other words, they are enzymatically dead. Pasteurization requires heating the milk so that bacteria, pathogens, and all the enzymes are destroyed. Without enzymes, however, no metabolic life process can take place (see Edward Howell, 1946. *Food Enzymes: Health and Longevity*). Pasteurization halts that process so that milk can be shipped over long distances and refrigerated for extended periods.

Enzymes are the complex proteins that act as catalysts in every biochemical process in our bodies. If not present in foods like dairy products, the pancreas must supply them. Not surprisingly, many Americans suffer from pancreatic disorders — including cancer — at much higher rates than in cultures whose food traditions emphasize non-pasteurized and fermented foods.

Furthermore, in pasteurized dairy products, vitamin C has been reduced by 50%, other water-soluble vitamins by up to 80%, and the availability of minerals such as calcium, magnesium, chloride, and potassium is compromised. Calcium, the mineral people are most concerned about because of its bone-building function, cannot be absorbed in the body without vitamin D, which is destroyed in the pasteurization process. So two different forms of synthetic vitamin D are added to commercial, pasteurized milk. However, one form of the synthetic vitamin (D2) is a toxin linked to heart disease; the other (D3) is difficult for the body to absorb (see Sally Fallon, 2001. *Nourishing Traditions*).

Proponents of pasteurization are as fierce about the dangers of raw milk as are proponents of raw milk about the dangers of pasteurization. But note that pasteurization did not become necessary until the 19th century when dairy cows were moved into confinement in burgeoning cities, fed brewery wastes, and milking practices became careless in the extreme. Raw milk carries pathogens that can produce listeria, tuberculosis, and other illnesses, and can be dangerous, depending on how it is produced. Pasteurization kills bacteria; however, it also gets careless dairy producers off the hook while compromising the quality of the milk.

When building our processing kitchen, we worked closely with the Washington State Department of Health to set up protocols to keep the cow, the milk parlor, and milk and cheese rooms scrupulously clean, thereby eliminating the need to pasteurize our milk. Furthermore, pasteurizing milk does not guarantee its safety: the only known cases of milk-borne salmonella have occurred in commercial dairies practicing pasteurization. Johne's disease, a wasting disease affecting the intestinal system of cows, and para-tuberculosis, also survive pasteurization.

Homogenization

Commercial milk is usually homogenized, a process in which the fat particles are forced through tiny pores at great pressure to keep them in suspension rather than rising to the top as in natural milk. This process changes the cell structure of the fat particles, potentially interfering with the capacity of the fat globules to bind with essential nutrients like vitamins A and D. The appeal of homogenized milk to the consumer is purely cosmetic and is desired by the dairy industry because homogenized milk can be shipped without incurring separation of fat and liquid.

Raw, responsibly produced milk from sheep, cows, or goats is a living food, and it is an indispensable part of our diet.

Milk Recipes

Colostrum Pancakes

This recipe replaces the butter and eggs in a conventional recipe with the rich colostrum from the first milk of a lactating cow.

2 C colostrum
1 C flour
1 T sugar
1 t baking powder
1/2 t each soda and salt

Sift together dry ingredients and beat in colostrum until batter is smooth; add more flour or colostrum as needed for desired thickness. Spoon into hot buttered frying pan to fry. Serve with yogurt, berries, or syrup. The pancakes will not need butter because of the richness of the colostrum.

Custard

This is a good dish for desserts, lunches, or a quick breakfast. Top the custard with raspberries.

2 C milk
2 eggs
1/4 C honey
1/8 t salt
1/2 t vanilla
Nutmeg

Beat together the milk, eggs, honey and salt, then add the vanilla and beat again. Pour the custard into six custard cups, and sprinkle nutmeg over the top. Place the cups on a rack over a baking dish filled with an inch of water. Bake at 300 for 40 minutes or until custard is firm. It will finish cooking out of the oven.

Rice Pudding

Rice pudding is a comfort food. Elizabeth's mother made it when her children were in need of something wholesome and easy to digest. In Henning's childhood, it was served once a week as a main dish.

1/2 C uncooked regular white rice
1/2 C sugar
1/2 t each cinnamon and nutmeg
1 generous T butter
4 C milk
1 C raisins

Mix ingredients, except raisins, in two casserole dishes. Bake at 350 for 2 hours, stirring every half hour. Add raisins the last half hour. Place the casseroles on a cookie sheet to prevent spills.

Butter

Next to long-fermented sourdough rye bread, butter is the most important food in our household. The first move we made was from margarine to commercial butter. The second was from conventional to homemade butter. The difference in flavor was tremendous, as was knowing that in our own butter, we were not ingesting trans fats, synthetic hormones, or antibiotics. Butter made from our Jersey cow's milk is as superior in taste as fresh milk is to commercial milk. Fermented butter does not need to be refrigerated; it stays wholesome because of the enzymatic balance in the raw product.

People make butter by using hand churns, or just shaking cream in a jar. We use a food processor. The procedure is easy. Skim cream from the milk, add a teaspoon of whey from the last cheese making to ferment the cream, and let it sit on the counter for a couple of days, until slightly soured.

Pour a quart of that cream into a 14-cup food processor, and let the machine run until the cream has separated into buttermilk and butter. The speed by which cream turns into butter is determined by room temperature. Around 70 degrees is ideal; any higher or lower will slow the churning process.

Henning recalls the Norwegian tradition of butter theft by witchcraft. If the cream would not turn to butter after long churning, witchcraft by an envious neighbor was suspected, and the remedy was to drive the witch from the cream by thrusting a heated scythe into the churn. This would raise the temperature of the cream, of course — and the next day the suspected neighbor would complain about a cut wound having appeared on her thigh.

With churning complete, drain off the buttermilk, reserving it for various baked goods (see below). Then "wash" the butter by pouring a pint of cold water into the bowl and push the "pulsing" button on the food processor for a few seconds. Repeat three to five times until the water runs clear.

Put the butter in a bowl and press out the water with a spatula, being careful not to spread the butter up the sides of the bowl (so it does not become oily).

Divide the butter into chunks, and knead out any remaining water with cold hands (moisture will make the butter hard). Freeze whatever you don't use right away.

The deep yellow color, full, rich taste, and vitamin content of homemade Jersey butter are gratifying. It contains vitamins A, D, E, K2, and cobalamin. It has only trace amounts of lactose, so people who are lactose intolerant can digest it.

The wash water can be given to pigs or chickens, or poured on the compost pile. Drink the buttermilk fresh, or use it as in the following recipes. Commercial buttermilk, so-called, is made from cultured pasteurized milk and therefore an entirely different product.

Buttermilk Biscuits

2 C white flour
2 t each sugar and baking powder
1 t salt
1/2 t baking soda
1/3 C butter
2/3 C homemade buttermilk

Measure dry ingredients into a bowl. Cut in butter, and stir in buttermilk. Round up the dough on a lightly floured board, and knead gently for a minute, then roll out the dough to 1/2-inch thickness. Cut with a biscuit cutter or the top of a quart jar. Place biscuits on an ungreased baking sheet. Bake at 450 for 10-12 minutes, until golden brown.

An alternative is to make drop biscuits. After mixing ingredients, drop large spoonfuls of dough onto a lightly greased baking sheet. Bake as above. These are superb for shortcake.

Buttermilk Pancakes

1 C white flour
1 t sugar
1/2 t salt
3/4 t baking powder
1/2 t baking soda
1 egg
1 C homemade buttermilk
1 t melted butter

Combine dry ingredients in a bowl. In a second bowl, beat egg, and mix with buttermilk and melted butter. Combine dry and wet ingredients with a few swift strokes. Cook in a little butter on medium heat, or in a non-stick pan. We like to serve these with butter, applesauce, yogurt, and a little maple syrup.

Buttermilk Spice Cake

This cake is very easy to make, and feeds a crowd.

2 1/2 C white flour
1 C white sugar
3/4 C brown sugar (packed)
1 t each baking powder and soda
1 t salt
3/4 t each cinnamon and allspice
1 1/3 C homemade buttermilk
1/2 C butter, melted
3 eggs

Grease and flour a 9x13-inch baking dish. Measure all ingredients into a large electric mixing bowl. Blend 1 minute on low speed, scraping bowl constantly. Beat 3 minutes on high speed, scraping bowl occasionally. Pour into prepared baking dish, and bake at 350 for 45 minutes, or until a knife inserted into the center of the cake comes out clean. Cool before serving.

Cheese

Cheese, fundamentally, is the fermented, compressed, and ripened curd of milk separated from the whey. The fermentation process is initiated by mixing fresh milk with rennet, which traditionally was derived from the lining of the calf's stomach. Until the calf is weaned, it lives mostly on its mother's milk which coagulates into a cheese in the calf's fourth stomach (abomasum) and is then gradually digested.

Early on, pastoralists learned that the stomach lining could be used for making cheese for human consumption. Today, rennets are often derived from plants. People the world over have been making cheese for thousands of years and the basic process is simple, but over time many refined variations have evolved, depending on bacterial cultures native to particular regions. Examples are the famous Camembert of France, Emmental of Switzerland, Mozzarella of Sicily, and Geitost, the canonical whey cheese of Norway. Not all cheeses, however, require rennets or starter cultures — for example, cottage cheese.

Cottage Cheese

Like homemade sour cream (below), homemade cottage cheese is better than the commercial product. It is something to make while you do other things in the kitchen, so that you monitor the curds warming on the stove.

You will need a glass or ceramic bowl that will fit on top of a stove-ready pan. We use a crock pot that balances nicely by its handles on top of a water bath canner.

1/2 gallon raw milk
2 t sea salt
Fresh cream (optional)
1 C cold water

Heat the milk on the stove in a pan to 80 degrees. Transfer the milk to the ceramic pot and place it in a warming cupboard or any other warm place for 1-3 days, until the milk is clabbered: that is, forms a solid cake floating in whey, from the action of the bacteria naturally occurring in the milk.

Cut the curd into 1/2-inch strips in a crisscross pattern and on the diagonal. Fill the water bath canner with hot water and balance the ceramic pot on top by its handles. The hot water in the canner should go up the sides of the ceramic pot containing the curds. Slowly raise the temperature to 110, stirring occasionally. Hold the temperature of the curd at 110 for five hours by placing a heavy towel over the top.

Drain the curds into a colander lined with cheesecloth set over a bowl until most of the liquid is gone. Reserve the whey for smoothies, bread starter, or soup base. Pour cold water over the curds and drain, gently moving the cheesecloth to get the liquid out, breaking up the curds with your fingers.

Place the curds in a bowl. Sprinkle salt over the curds a bit at a time, stirring to combine. Transfer the cottage cheese to a glass jar, cover, and refrigerate. Mix with a little fresh cream to sweeten and soften the cheese, if you like.

Quick Cottage Cheese

This method is faster than the cottage cheese recipe above, but results in less cheese, and acidified whey that is not usable for cooking or animal feed.

8 C milk
1/2 C white vinegar
1/2 C whole milk or cream
1/8 t salt

Heat milk to 120 degrees, stirring constantly. Pour in vinegar, stirring to separate curds and whey. Let sit, covered, for 1/2 hour. Drain in a cheesecloth-lined colander over a large bowl and discard the whey. Leaving the curds in the cheesecloth, rinse in cool water, then massage the bag with your fingers to break up the curds and remove any remaining whey. When the curds are rinsed and dry, place in a bowl, and stir in whole milk or cream, and salt. Cover and refrigerate.

Quark

Quark is a German-style light cheese, also made by fermenting raw milk without adding a starter culture or rennet. It has great food value — four times the protein of whole milk or yogurt, four times the folic acid, and twice the riboflavin and cobalamin, but one-tenth or the fat and cholesterol. Because of its digestibility, quark is especially good for children, the old, and for convalescents. It also contains a number of trace minerals required for healthy bone development, particularly calcium and phosphorus. Next to sauerkraut, quark is the most important probiotic food in German food culture.

Some uses of quark:
~Mix with honey or fruit to make a delicious breakfast or dessert.
~Mix with herbs and minced garlic and serve over baked or boiled potatoes.
~Spread on bread (and butter) and cover with jam.
~Combine with other soft cheeses for a sandwich spread.
~Use in place of ricotta — quark is especially good in lasagna.
~Mix with minced onion and a bit of salt, and stuff celery with it. Sprinkle with paprika.

To make quark, skim the cream from raw milk (1 half to a full gallon of milk is the best quantity) and heat the milk slowly to 85 degrees. Pour it into an enamel or ceramic pot, cover and let it sit in a warm place until clabbered, usually 2-3 days. We use a warming cupboard with a 70-watt lightbulb, but the top of a water heater, a gas stove with a pilot light, or a heated floor may work. If the heat is not constant, the milk will sour without solidifying. When the quark is ready, it forms a solid cake floating in whey, with a bit of fermented butter on top. Skim off the butter and use it as sour cream.

Drain the curd in a cheesecloth or a linen bag, tied closely and suspended on a string, and put a bowl underneath to catch the whey for other uses. Refrigerated, the quark will keep for weeks.

Henning's Cheese Cake

For the Crust:
6 T butter
1 egg
1 1/2 C flour
1 T baking powder
4 T sugar

A dash of salt
(All ingredients should be at room temperature.)

Sift flour, salt, and baking powder onto a counter-top and make a shallow well. Put in the egg and sugar, then cut the butter into flakes around the rim of the flour. With a fork, mix eggs and sugar, distributing small amounts of flour into the mix until it is like fine meal.

With your hands, rapidly incorporate the remaining flour and butter into the egg and sugar mixture. Knead briefly until the dough is smooth but remains cool. Use a little of the flour to dust hands and board to keep dough from sticking.

Form dough into a ball and place on a foot-long sheet of waxed paper dusted with a little flour. With a floured rolling pin, roll dough into a round shape about 2 inches larger than a 9 or 10-inch springform pan.

Grease the pan and place it upside down on the dough and, placing one hand gently under the waxed paper, turn the dough upside down so that it settles evenly on the bottom of the pan. With your fingers, press a 2-inch high edge in place. With a fork prick the dough on bottom and sides, and bake at 350 for 15 minutes. Remove from oven.

For the Filling:
3 C quark
3 T vegetable oil (we use grapeseed oil)
1 1/2 C sugar
3 egg yolks
1/4 C cornstarch
1/2 t vanilla extract
3 egg whites
Grated peel of one small lemon

Place the quark in a mixer. Add oil, sugar, egg yolks, cornstarch and vanilla. Mix until airy, but do not over mix. Beat the egg whites separately and fold, with the lemon peel, into the filling. Using a spatula, spread filling into crust, mounding it slightly to the middle. Bake at 350 for about 45 minutes on the middle rack. Do not open oven door until the last 10 minutes of baking. Test for doneness with a knife. Let the finished cake cool in the turned-off oven with the door open. The filling is a custard, and will collapse if the cake is removed too early.

The cake can be served immediately, but is best after it has rested in a cool place at normal room temperature for at least 12 hours.

Mozzarella

This recipe is the creation of Nathan Rausch, father of our apprentice, Joel. Nathan based the recipes for mozzarella and ricotta on David Asher's book *The Art of Natural Cheesemaking*. Asher's discussion on acidity in mozzarella and ricotta is key to success with these recipes. We find this mozzarella to be the most flavorful and tender we've tasted. Inexperienced cheesemakers are advised to read the book before trying the recipes.

1 packet thermophilic culture or 1 T plain yogurt
2 gallons of raw milk
1/2 t animal rennet, diluted

Heat 1/2 gallon of milk to 105 degrees, and inoculate it with culture or yogurt. After 2 minutes, stir thoroughly. Keep the milk at 105 degrees for 60 to 90 minutes. (If you forget about it, it will turn to yogurt).

When the inoculated milk is ready, heat the remaining milk to 105 degrees, and combine the cultured milk with the sweet milk. There needs to be a high enough population of thermophilic bacteria in the milk to sour the curd so that it will stretch.

To set the curd, add diluted rennet. After 10 or 15 minutes, when it "breaks clean," cut the curd with a bread knife into 1/2-inch cubes in a criss-cross pattern and on the diagonal. Stir every few minutes for about 30 minutes. Then stop stirring and let the curd knit together in the bottom of the pot for about 10 minutes. Pour off the whey, and save it for ricotta.

Drain the curd in a colander lined with cheesecloth and save the whey. Keep the curd in a warm place (105 degrees) overnight or even a whole day, so the heat-loving culture will continue to sour the curd — the curd must be acidic when stretching it into cheese. Once soured, the curd can be stored in the refrigerator up to a week or even frozen, but it is best to stretch it when it is still warm.
The next day, cut the curd into 1/2 inch slices and heat consecutive 1-pound portions in 150 degree whey.

Once the slices stick together when hot, roll them into a ball and stretch at once. Brine the mozzarella in a saturated salt brine. Sticks of string cheese brine for about 20 minutes.

Raw Milk Cheddar

This is the cheese we eat almost daily and sell to two stores on the island as state-certified cheese. You can use this cheese in any recipe that calls for hard cheese, such as Parmesan. The texture varies from creamy to crumbly, and the flavor is superb.

For this cheese, you will need a press. These are available for purchase online, but homemade presses work admirably. There are many online demonstrations and instructions about how to make your own press. Ours consists of a wooden base, a perforated 4-inch piece of PVC pipe, a frame with arms to hold the pipe that has a top to hold weights. The weights consist of 10- and 25-pound weights our son once used for weightlifting. (You can use appropriately-sized rocks, but the weights are flat and easier to position.)

Before making this or other hard cheeses, we strongly recommend that you read about cheesemaking — for example, Ricki Carroll's *Home Cheese Making*. There are clear explanations and diagrams of every procedure that take the mystery out of the process.

2 gallons whole cow's or goat's milk
1 packet direct-set mesophilic starter or 1 C whey
1/2 t liquid rennet, diluted in 1/4 C cool, unchlorinated water
1 T sea salt

Heat the cow's milk to 90 degrees (for goat's milk, heat to 85 degrees.) If you have just milked, there is no need to heat the milk. When milk reaches 90 degrees, add the starter and stir thoroughly. Cover and allow the milk to ripen for 45 minutes. Check temperature periodically and gently warm, if necessary.

Add the diluted rennet and stir gently with an up and down motion for 1 minute. If you are using farm-fresh whole milk where the cream rises to the top, top-stir for 1 minute with the flat side of a perforated spoon to blend in the butterfat. Cover and let set at 90 degrees (or 85 degrees for goats' milk) for 45 minutes, or until the curd gives a clean

break. During this process, we cover the pot with a heavy towel.

Using a bread knife, cut the curd into 1/2-inch cubes, side to side and on the diagonal. Slowly raise the temperature of the curds to 100 degrees. You can do this on a gas or electric stove, or in a sink full of hot water. Increase the temperature no more than 2 degrees every 5 minutes. This should take about 30 minutes. Gently stir to keep the curds from matting. The curds will shrink and the yellow whey will grow in volume as you stir.

Cover the pot and let the curds set for 5-10 minutes. Scoop the curds into a cheesecloth-lined colander set in a large bowl. Tie the corners of the cheesecloth with string to hold the bag together firmly, and hang the bag to drain overnight. Do not hang in a drafty spot — the curds need to stay relatively warm.

The next day, place the drained curds in a bowl and break them up gently with your fingers into walnut-sized pieces. Mix in the salt.

Firmly pack the curds into a 2-pound mold lined with cheesecloth, then neatly fold the cheesecloth over the top. Place a flat pan under the mold to receive the whey that will be expressed from the cheese. Apply 10 pounds pressure for 10 minutes.

Remove the cheese from the mold and gently peel away the cheesecloth. With your hand, turn the cheese, re-dress it with the cheesecloth, place it back in the mold, and press it at 20 pounds pressure for 10 minutes. (If the cheese falls apart when you turn and re-dress it, just repack it and keep going.)

Repeat the process, pressing the cheese at 50 pounds pressure for 12 hours.

Remove the cheese from the mold and carefully peel away the cheesecloth. Air dry the cheese at room temperature on a bamboo mat (you can purchase these as sushi mats). Morning and evening, turn the cheese and replace the moist mat with a dry one. Repeat for 2-4 days, until a nice rind has formed.

To store the cheese, you can wax it, or shrink-wrap it. If any mold has developed (as it can in warm months) be sure to cut it off or pick it out of the rind. If you have a persistent mold spot, put raw butter into it — butter resists mold and bacterial growth. Store in a cool place (not a refrigerator, which is too cold for the maturation of the cheddar). We use a wine "cave" that keeps the cheese at 50-52 degrees.

Turn the cheese daily, and age it for at least a month before eating. We age cheese for 6 weeks before selling it, by which time the bacteria are balanced. Once mature, cheddar will keep in your refrigerator indefinitely.

Ricotta

This recipe is also from Nathan. It produces an excellent ricotta.

Heat the whey left over from the mozzarella recipe above to the verge of a boil. As it begins foaming, reduce the heat, and quickly remove from the burner once it reaches 200 degrees, because the residual heat of the burner makes the whey "churn" more and disrupts the delicate curd. Let it set for 20 minutes for the curd to knit together. Drain in a cloth-lined colander for a day at room temperature. Mix in 2% salt by weight: 3 teaspoons per pint.

Sour Cream

Sour cream is very easy to make, and tastier than what you can buy.

1 C minus 2 T cream
1 C whole milk, preferably raw milk
1 T plus 2 t commercial buttermilk (unlike homemade buttermilk, commercial buttermilk is cultured)

Sterilize three half-pint jars and lids. Heat the cream and milk to 72 degrees, and add the cultured buttermilk. Fill the jars and place at 72 degrees for 16-18 hours. Stir the cream and place the jars in the refrigerator to set for 48 hours.

An alternative is to combine 2 cups heavy cream with 4 teaspoons of lemon juice in a jar. Screw on the lid and shake lightly until combined. Remove lid and use a rubber band to secure a thin piece of cloth over the jar to allow the mixture to breathe, and to keep out bugs. Set jar at room temperature for several hours or overnight until thickened.

As one of our interns discovered, a third alternative is just to leave a quart of cream on the counter in warm weather to sour beautifully — no need for additions. This is the same method Henning's mother used when he was a child.

Whey and Fruit Smoothy (with egg)

All cheesemaking produces whey. Whey can be used as high protein feed for pigs and chickens, in breads, in soups, or in other cheeses, as in the ricotta above, or for delicious, high protein drinks.

Place a cup of fresh or frozen berries — we like raspberries best — in a food processor, and add 1/3 C honey. With the machine running, pour 1 or more cups of whey through the feeding tube. The mixture will foam up immediately. For a real power drink, add a raw egg to the berries and honey before mixing with the whey.

Yogurt

People who are lactose intolerant and cannot digest fresh milk can usually digest fermented milk products, yogurt especially.

1 gallon raw milk (you can use pasteurized milk, as long as it is not ultra-pasteurized)
1/2 C yogurt saved from an earlier batch (or purchased).

Heat milk to 180 degrees over medium heat, monitoring the temperature with a dairy thermometer, and hold at that temperature for 30 minutes by covering the pot with a large heavy towel. Heating the milk pasteurizes it to eliminate natural bacteria that might fight off the probiotic bacteria in the added culture. After 30 minutes, cool the milk to 115 degrees by immersing an ice-filled plastic jug into the milk. Use any food-grade jug; we use empty vinegar bottles. Do not use glass containers — they will break in the freezer or in the hot milk.

Whisk in the culture and put the cultured milk in a warming cupboard or other warm place for 2-3 days. It will be done when it is thick. The amount of time will be determined by the ambient temperature; a cooler place will take longer to get a firm set. We use a 70-watt light bulb in a closed kitchen cupboard and 2 days is usually sufficient. Drain the yogurt in cheesecloth or linen bag, tied to hold the yogurt and suspended by a string over a bowl until the yogurt nearly stops dripping, which provides a creamy yogurt. Draining for a longer time produces a dry, crumbly yogurt. Reserve the whey for other uses.

Other Cheeses

If you are interested in making other homemade cheeses, such as panir, queso blanco, cream cheese, Parmesan, manchego, cheeses from goats' milk — the list is endless — there are two books we recommend: Ricki Carrol's *Home Cheese Making*, and David Asher's *The Art of Natural Cheese Making*. If you feel daunted by the idea of making cheese at home, remember that people have been doing it for thousands of years without elaborate equipment, and nearly every cheese has variations.

Cheesemaking begins with separating curds from whey, and goes on from there. Cultures and rennet are available online. On Lopez Island, folks make cheese from goat, cow, and sheep milk, have fun doing it, and would be happy to share their expertise. Experiment, and enjoy!

Eggs

We raise chickens mostly for egg production, although we enjoy the occasional Coq au Vin or Roasted Chicken (see *Poultry*). We know that both chickens and their eggs are healthy, because the chickens are glossy of coat, contented, and eat the same things we do: grain, vegetables, potatoes, fruits, and milk products. Their eggs have high orange yolks and firm whites.

Eggs contain vitamins A, D, cobalamin, pyridoxine, riboflavin, folate, thiamin, pantothenic acid, selenium, and iron. Eggs are among the most important and useful foods the farm provides, each containing 7 grams of high-quality protein (but only 75 calories). They are flavorful and versatile.

Tips for Eggs

~Brown eggs are no healthier than white ones; the color reflects the color of the chicken, not the nutritional value of the egg.

~If you get eggs from your own chickens or from a neighbor, do not wash them until just before using. They have an outer protective membrane that prevents bacteria from entering the egg. Commercial eggs need to be refrigerated because that protective layer has been removed.

~For perfect boiled eggs, steam them. Put the eggs into a basket steamer or pot, turn water on high, wait until it boils, then turn it to medium, and steam eggs for 20 minutes. Plunge into cold water.

When eggs are cold, the peel will slip off easily.

Bauernfrühstück (Farmer's Breakfast)

This is a hearty, simple dish that can be served for breakfast, lunch, or dinner — one of Henning's favorite meals.

Olive oil or bacon drippings
1 onion, sliced
2 large potatoes, peeled and cut into long pieces, as for French fries
5-6 eggs, beaten
Salt, pepper, garlic granules, paprika
Bundle of chives, chopped

You can add cooked bacon or ham, or leftover vegetables, if you like. Sauté the onion in oil or drippings. Add sliced potatoes, sprinkle with salt, garlic and paprika, and cook gently, lifting and turning until they are fork tender. Add cooked meat or vegetables, if used. Add beaten eggs seasoned with salt and pepper. Gently lift mixture so that eggs run to the bottom of the pan. Cook until eggs are set but still moist. Sprinkle with chives.

Deviled Eggs

12 eggs
1/2 medium onion, minced
Mayonnaise (preferably homemade, see *Vegetables*)
Honey mustard
Pinch of salt, pepper, and paprika

Steam a dozen eggs, peel, halve lengthwise, and slip out the yolks. Place whites on a platter, yolks in a bowl. To the yolks, add minced onions, mayonnaise, mustard, salt, and pepper. Mash until you have a creamy filling. Place the filling into the egg whites, heaping it high. Sprinkle with paprika.

Egg Salad

12 eggs
1 C diced celery
1/2 C diced pickles
1/2 C diced onion
1/4 C prepared mustard, salt, pepper, garlic granules
1/2 C mayonnaise (preferably home made, see *Vegetables*)

Steam eggs, cool, and peel. Dice and place in a bowl. Add celery, pickles, and onion. In a separate bowl, mix mayonnaise, mustard, salt, pepper, and garlic. to taste. Blend with diced eggs. Serve by itself or on sandwiches.

Fried Eggs

We find that adding fried eggs to another dish (such as crepes with mushrooms) gives us the protein we need without eating meat. We fry eggs gently and slowly in a non-stick pan, using butter and olive oil.

4 fresh eggs (ideally from your own chickens)
1 T butter
1 T olive oil
Salt and pepper on the table

Crack the eggs into the heated butter and oil. Gently use a spatula or wooden spoon to move them as needed. When the whites are set, the yellows still soft, scoop them onto a plate with whatever else you are serving, or leftover mashed potatoes, or vegetables of your choice.

Poached Eggs on Toast

We use an egg poacher for this breakfast dish.
4 fresh eggs
Butter
Salt and pepper
4 slices of toast

Put water into the bottom part of an egg poacher, butter into each cup. Melt the butter over low heat, and crack an egg into each cup. Cover pan, and cook eggs until whites are set, but yolks are still

soft. Place eggs onto toast — we prefer homemade sourdough rye bread (see *Bread & Grains*).

Polenta and Eggs

Polenta (also known as corn grits) is made of stone-ground dried flint corn. While instant, quick-cooking, or tubed polentas are available in stores, they tend to be bland and mushy, and it is easy to make your own. We grow the flint corn, dry it, and and grind it fresh for each polenta meal, using a countertop German mill with a stone burr which keeps the grain cool (see *Corn* in *Vegetables*).

Just like rice, potatoes or noodles, polenta can serve as a base for many sauces and meat. It will support either rich or mild foods. The following dish is simple to make, and good for lunch or dinner.

For Polenta:
6 C water
1 t salt
2 C polenta
3 T butter
A few shakes of red pepper flakes
For Main Dish:
6 eggs (2 or 3 per person)
Butter
Grated cheese

In a large, deep pan, bring water and salt to a boil. Gradually stir in dry polenta, using a long spoon, because mixture will pop and bubble during cooking. Reduce heat and simmer gently, stirring frequently to prevent sticking. As the polenta begins to firm up, stir in the butter and pepper flakes.

When the polenta is really firm, in about 30 minutes, you can either place it in a linen towel or in a bread pan. Henning likes to use the towel because it shapes the polenta into an appealing traditional loaf; Elizabeth likes to use the bread pan because the polenta can be kept warm in the oven, and you don't wind up with a messy towel. (You won't if the polenta is sufficiently firm.)

Fry the eggs in butter in a non-stick pan, sunny-side up. Just before they are done, cut the polenta into thick slices, put on plates and top with butter and grated cheese. Place the eggs on top of the cheese. Serve with a green salad.

(Leftover) Potatoes and Eggs

Occasionally, we have cooked potatoes left over from the previous day; here's how we turn them into a meal:

Leftover potatoes, any amount
Cooking fat (butter, olive oil, or bacon grease)
3 eggs per person, beaten
Salt, pepper, red pepper flakes
Salsa (preferably homemade. See *Keeping the Harvest*).

Slice potatoes, and fry them in preferred fat. Add eggs, seasoned with salt, pepper, and red pepper flakes. Pour the eggs over the potatoes and lift gently, letting the eggs run under the potatoes until a little browned, and the dish forms a soft cake. Top with salsa.

Quiche

Quiche can have ingredients as minimal as onion, cheese, and the egg and milk mixture. We prefer a heartier quiche, adding grated cheese, cooked bacon, sautéed mushrooms and onions, marinated artichokes, dried tomatoes and defrosted spinach or broccoli. We make two 10-inch pies at a time, because this dish is good for leftovers.

Prepared pie crust (see *Apple&Blackberry Pie* in *Tree Fruits & Berries*)
1 egg, divided into yolk and white
3 pints defrosted vegetables, such as spinach or broccoli
6 slices thick-cut bacon
1 medium onion, diced
1 C mushrooms, sliced
1 C hard cheese, grated
1 C dried tomatoes, diced
1/2 C marinated artichokes, chopped
4 C milk or cream
6 eggs
1 t each of salt, pepper, and nutmeg

Brush pie crust with egg white and prick with fork. Dice vegetables, squeeze out moisture and dry between paper towels. Dice bacon, cook until done, and place on a paper towel. Sauté onion in bacon fat. Remove with slotted spoon, place on paper towel. Sauté mushrooms in remaining fat, remove to paper towel.

Place the cheese — we use our own cheddar, but any firm cheese will do— on the bottom of the crust, followed by bacon, onion, tomatoes, artichokes, mushrooms, and vegetables.

In a saucepan, scald milk or cream. Cool, then beat together with the eggs, salt, pepper, and nutmeg. Using a ladle, cover the filling with egg and milk mixture. Sprinkle paprika over the top, and bake at 375 for 40 minutes or so, until the top puffs and is firm. Cool before serving. Quiche can be served warm from the oven or at room temperature.

Russian Eggs

8 fresh eggs
Herbed mayonnaise (preferably homemade. (See *Vegetables*).
Strips of smoked salmon

Steam and peel the eggs, and cut them in half. Layer with strips of smoked salmon and cover with herbed mayonnaise. Serve as an hors d'oeuvres.

Spanish Tortilla

A Spanish tortilla has nothing to do with Mexican tortillas. It is a special kind of omelet.

2 T olive oil
1 large onion, peeled, halved, and thinly sliced crosswise
1 1/2 lb potatoes, peeled and thinly sliced
1 t salt
1/2 t pepper
5 large eggs

Pour olive oil into a 10 or 12-inch ovenproof frying pan over medium heat. Sauté onion until translucent. Add potatoes, half the salt and pepper, and stir to coat. Add 1/3 cup water, bring to a boil; reduce heat to medium, cover, and cook until potatoes are fork tender, about 10 minutes. If any liquid remains in pan, cook uncovered until evaporated.

In a large bowl, beat eggs with remaining salt and pepper. Add potato mixture to the eggs and mix gently. Set unwashed frying pan over medium heat; when hot, pour in egg and potato mixture. Reduce heat to low, lifting mixture to let liquid eggs flow to the bottom. Cook until eggs begin to set and bottom is lightly browned. Transfer pan to oven and broil about six inches from the heat until top is set. Remove from oven and run a spatula around the side to loosen. Cut into wedges and serve.

This makes a full meal if served with a salad or peas. We put chili sauce on the table to spice up the mild eggs and potatoes.

Spinach Omelet

2 eggs
Handful of raw or frozen spinach, sliced
2 T milk or more, as needed
Pinch of salt
Butter
Chives or other herbs
Sour cream

Beat the eggs with milk and chives and cook in a frying pan in butter until nearly firm. Place the uncooked spinach on half of the omelet and fold the other half over the top. Brown briefly, turning once. Top with sour cream.

Alternative: fill the omelet with leftover ham, other vegetables, or mushrooms.

Tomatoes and Scrambled Eggs

5 eggs
4 tomatoes
Butter
3 T milk
4 strips of bacon or slices of cooked ham
1 medium onion, diced
Pinch each of salt and paprika
Minced chives

Pour boiling water over tomatoes, plunge into cold water, skin and slice. Fry bacon, or sauté ham with onion and chives. Add tomato slices, salt and paprika. Beat eggs together with milk, and pour over top of bacon or ham, onions and tomatoes. Cook gently until eggs are set. Top with a pinch of salt and paprika and sprinkle with the remaining chives.

Yorkshire Pudding

6 eggs
6 T flour
Pinch of salt
Bacon fat for the pan

Yorkshire pudding is actually a casserole baked in a pan. Gradually mix the flour and eggs into a thin dough. Grease a cast-iron pan with a generous amount of bacon fat. Pour the dough into the pan

and bake in the oven at 350 until golden brown. Serve immediately to keep pudding from collapsing. Best served with beef roast and flavored with the drippings from the roast.

An alternative recipe for Yorkshire pudding uses fewer eggs but adds milk and water, and makes individual servings, baked in a muffin tin.

1 C flour
2/3 C milk
1/3 C cold water
2 eggs
Leaves from 1 sprig of thyme
2 t salt
2 T reserved drippings from roast

While the beef is roasting, make Yorkshire pudding batter. Whisk flour, milk, water, eggs, thyme, and salt in a bowl until smooth; let rest for 30 minutes.

While beef is resting, increase oven temperature to 425. Divide 2 tablespoons of fat from the roasting pan among 8 muffin-tin wells. Place muffin tin in the oven to heat until fat is hot, 5-10 minutes.

Carefully remove tin from oven and quickly divide batter among prepared wells, filling half full. Bake puddings until puffed and golden brown, 20-25 minutes. Serve with drippings from the roast spooned into each pudding.

For *Pickled Eggs*, see *Keeping the Harvest*.
For *Whey and Fruit Smoothy with Egg*, see *Dairy*.
For *Cheesecake with Eggs*, see *Dairy*.

Notes:

Poultry

Chicken

We raise chickens for egg production, turkeys for meat. The layers are replaced every three years, and we process the old hens and roosters for broth (see *Keeping the Harvest*). Since most layer breeds no longer have a strong brooding instinct, we usually buy our replacement chicks from a commercial breeder; however, we encourage any hen showing signs of wanting to brood by placing her and a clutch of eggs in a separate broody box. Naturally brooded chicks are healthier and they benefit from protection by the hen. If we get roosters in a naturally brooded run, we raise them for roasting or frying.

Poultry contains vitamins A, C, D, E, and K, niacin, pantothenic acid, folic acid, biotin, and zinc. Chicken soup is a time-honored remedy for relieving the symptoms of colds and flu because it is hydrating, and clears nasal congestion. No one claims that chicken soup will actually cure the illness, but it does make people feel better. Homemade soup, with vegetables and a carbohydrate such as noodles or rice, is preferable to soup from a can.

Chicken Soup
Bones and leftovers from a roasted or fried chicken

2 medium carrots, sliced into 1/2-inch rounds
2 celery stalks, sliced into 1/2-inch slices
1 medium onion, chopped
1 bay leaf
5 peppercorns
1/2 C rice or 2 C egg noodles, uncooked
2 T chopped parsley
Salt, to taste

Cover the bones with water, salt, and peppercorns. Cook for several hours, until you have a flavorful broth. Strain, removing meat from the bones and setting it aside. Add carrots, celery, onion, bay leaf, rice or noodles to the broth, and simmer until vegetables are tender and the rice or noodles are cooked. Add the meat, and season to taste. Top with parsley and serve.

Chicken Stew

In order to make this dish come together quickly, cook the kidney beans the day ahead, or use home-canned kidney beans from your shelf (see *Keeping the Harvest* for pressure-canning dried beans.) Rather than cooking a whole chicken for this dish, you can use leftover chicken or turkey.

2 T olive oil
2 stalks celery, cut into bite-size pieces
1 carrot, scrubbed, cut into bite-size pieces

1 small onion, chopped
Salt and pepper
1 quart chopped tomatoes, fresh or canned
1 quart homemade chicken broth
1/2 C fresh basil leaves, torn into pieces
1 T tomato paste
1 bay leaf
1/2 t dried thyme
1 small chicken (about 1 1/2 lb), separating thighs, breast, legs, neck and back
1 1/2 C cooked kidney beans (see *Vegetables*)
A dollop of sour cream for each serving

Heat the oil in a large heavy saucepan or Dutch oven. Add the celery, carrot, and onion. Sauté the vegetables about 5 minutes, until onion is tender. Season with salt and pepper to taste.

Stir in tomatoes with their juice, chicken broth, basil, tomato paste, bay leaf, and thyme. Add the pieces of chicken, covering them with the liquid.

Simmer gently, uncovered, until the chicken is cooked through, turning the pieces over from time to time and stirring the mixture occasionally, about 30 minutes. Transfer the chicken to a bowl, and allow to cool.

Discard the bay leaf. Add the prepared kidney beans to the pot and simmer until liquid attains a stew consistency, about 10 minutes. Do not overcook the beans — you want them to remain firm.

Pull or cut the chicken off the bones, removing or retaining skin as you like. Cut or tear the meat into bite-size pieces, and return to the stew. Bring the stew just to a simmer. Adjust seasonings. Ladle into serving bowls, and serve with a crusty bread (see *Bread & Grains)* and a dollop of sour cream.

Coq au Vin

1 chicken, cut into pieces (use back and neck for broth. See *Keeping the Harvest*).
2 T olive oil
1/4 lb chopped bacon
Salt and pepper
1 onion, sliced
1/2 lb carrots, cut diagonally into 1-inch pieces
2 garlic cloves, minced
1/4 C cognac or good brandy (optional)
2 C dry red wine
1 C homemade chicken broth

3 sprigs of fresh thyme (or 1 t dried)
2 T butter, softened
1 1/2 T flour
1/2 lb mushrooms, sliced

In a Dutch oven, brown bacon in the oil. Remove with slotted spoon and set aside. Sprinkle salt and pepper over the chicken parts and brown them in the fat in batches (do not crowd). Remove and set aside.

Add the carrots, onion, 2 teaspoons salt, and 1 teaspoon pepper to the pan and cook over medium heat for 10 minutes, stirring occasionally, until the onions are lightly browned. Add the garlic and cook for 1 more minute. Add the cognac or brandy (if used) and put the bacon, chicken, and any juices from the plate into the pot.

Add the wine, chicken broth, and thyme, and bring to a simmer. Cover the pot and place in the oven to bake at 350 for about 45 minutes until chicken is done. (Or simmer on stove). Remove sprigs of thyme, if used instead of dried thyme.

Mash 1 tablespoon butter into the flour and stir into the stew. In a separate pan, sauté sliced mushrooms in the remaining butter, and add to the stew. Simmer for another 10 minutes. Serve hot.

Roasted Chicken

Preheat oven to 450. Put the bird on a rack in a small roasting pan, rub it with butter, salt, and powdered sage. Reduce the heat to 350, and roast until the internal temperature reaches 180-185.

An alternative is to use a *Römertopf* (Roman pot best known by its German designation), an unglazed clay pot with a domed lid. Romans cooked with clay pots for centuries, and they are used today all over the world. The top and bottom parts of the pot must be soaked in cold water for at least 20 minutes; the clay soaks up the water, and slowly releases it during roasting, so the food will not burn, and will come out moist and tender.

The pot, with its food, must be put into a cold oven before raising the temperature. The same cooking method works well for fish and red meats, and for sweet as well as for savory dishes. The pots are readily available online or in stores specializing in cooking wares. There are many recipes for poultry: we give just one here.

Chicken in Burgundy in a Römertopf

2 small roasting chickens
4 T butter
1 onion, sliced
1 C sour cream
1 C Burgundy wine
1 shot glass of brandy
1 bay leaf
1 bunch parsley
Thyme, tarragon and nutmeg, to taste
1 C sautéed mushrooms
4 slices raw bacon
Juice of one lemon

Wash chicken, cover with lemon juice, place in soaked *Römertopf*, cover with bacon. Mix the sour cream with the Burgundy, add herbs and spices, pour into *Römertopf,* and bake at 450 for 1 hour. Open lid and test for doneness. Remove chicken and pour out sauce. Return chicken to pot and, without the lid, brown at 350 for 10 minutes.

In the mean time, put sauce through a sieve and refine with mushrooms and butter. Thicken with a little flour, if needed. Flavor with brandy and serve with crisp French bread (see *Bread & Grains*).

Turkey

Turkeys were first domesticated in ancient Mexico, taken back to Europe by the Spanish and returned to the New World with the first settlers, where they mated with wild turkeys. Their offspring are known as Heritage Turkeys, different from the white Butterball turkeys, which are bred for a lot of breast meat, but whose bodies get so bulky they are often unable to walk, and cannot breed naturally; the hens must be artificially inseminated. Our turkeys are the Bronze Heritage, whose meat is succulent and tender. They are beautiful and gentle, a pleasure to care for.

Roasted Turkey

It is better to use a fresh rather than a frozen turkey. In either case, carefully remove the giblets and neck from the cavities and wash the turkey, inside and out. Pat dry. Put the neck and giblets in a small saucepan, cover with water, and cook for gravy.

For the Turkey:
Cover the whole turkey with melted butter. Place uncovered on a rack in a greased roasting pan, and place in an oven at 450. Reduce the heat to 350.

Allow 20-25 minutes per pound, or until a meat thermometer inserted in the thigh registers 185. At that point, if you wiggle a leg, the flesh should part easily. Add 5 minutes to cooking time if the bird is stuffed. Stuffing should reach 165.

For the Stuffing:
There are many stuffings or dressings for turkey. Our favorite is *Apple and Onion Dressing.*

1/2 C raisins, briefly boiled, and drained
3 C soft bread crumbs
1/2 C minced onion
1 clove garlic, minced
1/2 C chopped celery
1 C diced apple
1/4 C chopped parsley
1/2 t salt
1/4 t paprika

Sauté the onion, garlic, and celery in melted butter, and add to the bread crumbs. Add apple and parsley. Spoon the dressing into the large cavity of the turkey; do not pack. Wrap the remaining dressing in foil and place on roasting rack with turkey.

For the Gravy:
Strain the cooking liquid from the giblets and neck; if you like, shred the meat to add to the gravy. After removing the turkey from the oven (it should rest before carving), drain the juices from the pan, cover the turkey with a roasting lid, and make the gravy.

To 1/4 cup of the pan drippings, add and stir 1/4 cup flour, until blended. Slowly stir in the broth from the giblets. Add a bit of sour cream if you like. Add minced meat from neck and giblets. Season to taste.

Leftover Turkey Corn Chowder

2 C shredded leftover cooked turkey
3 C frozen corn, thawed
1 qt homemade chicken or vegetable broth
1 celery stalk, chopped
1 red bell pepper, diced
2 C cubed Yukon or red potatoes
1 t dried basil
1/2 t dried sage
1 t garlic granules
Salt and pepper to taste
1 T flour
1/2 C milk

In a large stock pot, combine broth, vegetables, herbs, and garlic granules. Cover and simmer over medium heat until tender, 20-25 minutes.

In a separate small pan, whisk flour together with milk and heat until thick and smooth. Gently stir into chowder. Add turkey and season with salt and pepper. Heat through; do not boil.

Turkey Soup

Meat from leftover cooked turkey (from a small bird)
Enough homemade chicken broth to cover the meat, rice and vegetables (1 or more quarts)
1/2 C uncooked white rice
1 medium onion, finely chopped
2 medium carrots, chopped into 1/4-inch pieces
4 celery ribs, finely chopped
1 bay leaf
A dash of powdered sage, or 1 fresh sage leaf
1/2 t garlic granules
1/4 t pepper
Salt to taste

In a pot, place broth, vegetables, rice, and herbs and spices. Cover and simmer over medium low until rice is cooked. Discard bay and sage leaves. Add diced meat. Season to taste.

Seafood

In the interest of rounding out our sources of food on the farm, we once stocked the pond with brown trout. Unfortunately, the eagles and otters went fishing before we could. So we content ourselves with getting halibut and fresh and smoked salmon from local fishermen. Friends supply us with the occasional trout, and crab from the pots they set out during the season. We purchase Alaskan wild-caught rockfish, cod, and sole from local stores. We dig for clams on Lopez beaches and buy oysters, mussels, prawns and scallops from island purveyors. We never buy farmed fish, such as Atlantic salmon. We avoid tuna, or any other fish that is endangered.

We eat fish at least once a week, in part because fish contains vitamins A, D, K, thiamin, riboflavin, pantothenic acid, biotin, pyridoxine, cobalamin, folate, calcium, magnesium, potassium, iodine, selenium, zinc and iron, and is a good source of omega 3 fatty acids. Fish with high levels of mercury are not on our list, nor readily available on the island.

Fish

Baked Fish with Lemon, Garlic, and Chives
We like cod for this dish because of its firm texture, but you can use any white fish, such as Dover sole, rockfish, or halibut.

4 6-oz fish filets
4 t olive oil
Salt and pepper, to taste
1 bunch fresh chives, coarsely chopped
Slices of fresh lemon, enough to cover the fish
3 cloves garlic, sliced

Wash fish and pat dry. Brush filets with olive oil and sprinkle with salt and pepper. Place each filet in the center of an aluminum foil square.
Sprinkle garlic slices and chives over the fish. Squeeze lemon slices lightly and lay them on the fillets. Fold foil over the fish and turn the edges over 2-3 times. Flatten to seal the packets, and place them in a baking pan. Bake at 400 until fish is opaque and flakes easily with a fork, 15-20 minutes, depending on thickness of the fish. Serve with potatoes or rice and salad.

Fish Casserole
2 lb filets from rockfish, cod, halibut, or any firm white fish
5 T olive oil, divided
1 t oregano
3 C thinly sliced onion
3 cloves garlic, diced
1/2 C finely chopped parsley
3 C thinly sliced potatoes, parboiled
1 medium green pepper, seeds and membrane removed, sliced
1 quart home-canned tomatoes
Salt and pepper

Cut fish into large chunks, coat with olive oil and oregano; set aside. Sauté onion and garlic in olive oil until transparent; add parsley and sauté briefly. In a shallow 2-quart baking dish, spread onion mixture followed by potatoes sprinkled with salt and pepper, green pepper, fish and tomatoes. Cover and bake at 350 for an hour.

Ceviche
Ceviche is a dish in which raw fish is autolyzed with lime and lemon juice — it is cooked by the

acid in the juice. You can use any firm fish or shell fish: shrimp, salmon, rockfish, halibut, or scallops, for example.

2 lb fresh fish
1/2 C each fresh lime and lemon juice
1 medium red onion, chopped and divided
2 medium tomatoes, cut into 1-inch pieces
2-3 green chili peppers, seeded, membrane removed, diced
1 small cucumber, peeled, seeded, and cubed
1/3 C chopped cilantro
1 large or 2 small avocados, peeled and chopped

Wash, dry and cut fish into 2-inch pieces. In a 2-quart glass casserole, place the pieces of fish, lime and lemon juice, and half the chopped onion. Be sure the juices coat the fish. Cover and refrigerate 4 hours, gently stirring each hour. Drain.

In a large bowl, mix together tomatoes, cucumber, chiles, cilantro, and the remaining onion. Gently stir in avocado. Add to fish.

This dish can be served as an hors d'oeuvre or as a main dish, if accompanied by a warm, crusty bread (see *Bread & Grains*), and green salad.

Fish in Tomato Sauce

2 lb filets of rockfish, cod, halibut, or any firm white fish
Flour, seasoned with salt, pepper, garlic granules and paprika
3/4 C olive oil
1/4 C flour (for sauce)
2 T red wine vinegar
2 t tomato paste
1 1/2 C water
1/2 t sugar
2 cloves garlic, sliced
2-3 bay leaves
1/4 t each dried basil, tarragon and rosemary
Salt and pepper

Wash fish and pat dry, dredge in seasoned flour. Heat oil in skillet, fry fish until golden, remove. In the same skillet, blend the flour into the oil, then slowly add vinegar, tomato paste, water, sugar, garlic, bay leaves, basil, tarragon, rosemary, salt and pepper. Simmer 5-10 minutes. Add fish and heat through. Serve over potatoes or rice.

Barbecued Salmon

When we purchase salmon from a local fisherman, we like to barbecue the whole fish or fry the steaks.

1 5-lb whole salmon
1 bundle each fresh dill, rosemary, sage and thyme
Olive oil
Salt and pepper to taste
1 lemon, sliced

Wash and clean the salmon, setting aside head and tail for broth. Rub inside and out with salt and pepper, put lemon slices inside the fish, and cover the outside with bundles of herbs. Sprinkle with oil. Wrap the prepared salmon in chicken wire and cook on the grill over fire that has burned down to coals (fire will briefly flare up and sear the fish when the oil drops into the coals). Cook over reduced heat under cover. Turn once during cooking. Serve with potatoes and green salad.

We combine the bones, head and tail with herbs, vegetables and seasonings to make broth. Use for soups or stews. Freezes well.

Broiled Salmon Steaks with Beurre Blanc

We cut larger salmon into chunks that we freeze and later divide into steaks for broiling.

For the Salmon:
4 1-inch salmon steaks
2 T butter, melted
Salt and pepper to taste
For the Sauce:
3 cups Sauvignon Blanc or similar white wine
2 sticks of butter, sliced
1 shallot, minced
2 cloves of garlic, minced
4 red bell peppers roasted until blackened, peeled, seeds removed, and diced (see *Vegetables*)
1 bunch of chives, chopped
2 T olive oil
Salt and pepper, to taste

To Make the Sauce:
This recipe makes 32 servings. We use two for the meal and freeze the rest in small jars for later use. Heat the olive oil in a pan, sauté shallots and garlic until opaque. Deglaze with wine, reduce by two-thirds and puree with the bell peppers. With the food processor running, add the butter through the feeding tube. Season with salt and pepper. Serve over fish. Use sauce for pasta or chicken as well.

To Broil the Salmon:
Brush each steak with melted butter and place on a cookie sheet. Broil on the middle rack, turn once to brown on both sides. Salmon should flake when pierced with a fork. Serve with potato pancakes (see *Potatoes* in *Vegetables*), green salad, or other fresh vegetables.

Fried Trout

We fish for local trout in Hummel Lake, or receive it as a gift from a friend. That failing, we occasionally buy the trout at the grocery store, if caught wild.

2 trout
Butter and olive oil
Salt and pepper to taste
Lemon wedges

Clean the fish and fry in olive oil and butter, season and serve with French fries (see *Potatoes* in *Vegetables*), and salad.

Fish Stew

We like to make our own fish broth for this dish — we cook heads, tails, and bones from salmon or trout with herbs and vegetables until we have a savory broth.

6 T olive oil
1 1/2 C chopped onion
3 large garlic cloves, minced
2/3 C chopped fresh parsley
1/2 C fresh chopped tomato or 1 pint home-canned tomatoes
2 t tomato paste
1 C fish broth (see above)
1/2 C dry white wine
1 1/2 lb firm white fish filets, such as cod, halibut, or rockfish, cut into 2-inch pieces
1 t each dried oregano and thyme
1/4 t pepper
1 t salt

Heat olive oil in a large, heavy pot. Sauté onion and garlic. Add parsley and stir. Add tomatoes and tomato paste, and simmer for 10 minutes. Add fish broth, wine, and fish. Simmer until fish breaks apart.
Add oregano, thyme, pepper, salt, and any other seasonings you like for a savory stew.
Serve with French bread (see *Bread & Grains*).

Poached Salmon, Halibut or Cod

Poaching is a great way to prepare fish. It is fast, simple, and keeps the fish moist. You can poach any firm fish, such as salmon, halibut, or cod.

2 lb fish filets
5 black peppercorns
1 t salt
1 bay leaf
1/2 onion, sliced
2 cloves garlic, sliced
Fresh lemon juice from a whole lemon
1/2 C dry white wine
Fresh chives, parsley, and basil, minced

Fill a deep frying pan half full of water. Add all ingredients except the fish and the minced herbs. Bring liquid to a boil, lower heat, and simmer 1 minute. Turn off the heat. Add the fish, skin-side down, and let it poach until it begins to separate. Remove from cooking liquid, top with minced herbs, and serve with new potatoes or rice and your vegetable of choice.

As an alternative to the minced herbs, serve the fish with Beurre Blanc (recipe above).

Dover Sole Roulade Baked in the Römertopf

Baking fish in a roll without immersing it in water keeps it moist while preserving all the flavors of a delicate fish like Dover sole. Online you can find recipes for cooking marinated, plastic-wrapped fish roulade sous vide. We prefer using the *Römertopf* (see p.130) because it is simpler and avoids using plastic. Instead of marinating the fish, the roulade is baked in wine.

4-6 Dover sole filets
2 T lemon juice
1/4 t each salt, pepper and paprika
1 thick slice of homemade French Bread (see *Bread & Grains*)
1/4 C minced parsley
2 T minced onion
3 anchovy filets, minced
1 T capers, minced
1-2 apples, cored and cut into 8 pieces
1/4 C sour cream
3/4 C dry white wine

Soak the *Römertopf* in cold water for 20 minutes. Sprinkle the filets with lemon juice and season with salt, pepper, and paprika. Let rest for a few minutes.

In the mean time, soak the bread in warm water and squeeze dry. Mix with parsley, onion, anchovies, and capers.

Spread the filling on the filets, roll them into rounds and pin them together with thin toothpicks.

Place the roulades open-side down in the *Römertopf* and surround the fish with the apples. Whisk the sour cream and the wine, and add. Put the pot in a cold oven, set the temperature at 350 and bake for 30 minutes. Check for doneness and serve.

Rockfish with Vegetables and Rice
You can also use sole or cod for this flavorful meal.

2 T each butter and olive oil
2 lb rockfish filets
Flour seasoned with salt, pepper, garlic granules, dill weed, and paprika
1 large red pepper, seeds and membrane removed, sliced
1/2 medium onion, diced
3 cloves garlic, minced
8 oz mushrooms, sliced
3 stalks celery, diced
1 1/2 C cooked white rice
1/2 lemon
Salt, pepper, garlic granules, dried basil, thyme, and oregano, to taste

Prepare vegetables and sauté in butter and olive oil until tender and mushrooms have released their juices, adding salt, pepper and herbs as needed. Place in a casserole and keep warm in the oven. Prepare rice.

Wash filets, dry on paper towels. Dredge in seasoned flour, and fry in butter and olive oil. On plates, place a mound of rice, cover with sautéed vegetables, and put fish over the top. Serve with slices of lemon.

Halibut Fried in a Jacket
Frying fish steaks or thick filets dredged in flour, beaten eggs and bread crumbs locks the flavors in a tasty crust. Halibut is our favorite fish to cook with this method, but you can also use cod or rockfish, for example.
2 halibut steaks or thick filets
1/4 t each salt, pepper, and garlic granules
1/2 C white or whole-wheat organic flour

1 egg, well beaten and thinned with a bit of milk or cream
1/2 C dried, fine bread crumbs from homemade French bread (see *Bread & Grains*)
Olive oil and butter for frying

Season the fish with the spices and dredge in the flour, egg and bread crumbs. Fry in olive oil and butter for a few minutes until golden and crusty.

Shellfish
Shellfish contains protein, B vitamins, copper, zinc, phosphate, sodium, potassium, selenium, iodine, and is rich in Omega-3 fatty acids.

Horse Clam Chowder
From June through December horse clams are plentiful on the sandy beaches of Mud Bay and Spencer Spit.

1 dozen horse clams
4 slices bacon, chopped
1 large onion, diced
Salt and pepper to taste
3-4 organic potatoes, diced
3 T organic flour
1 1/2 C each cream and milk
3 sprigs of thyme
2 bay leaves
Olive oil

Soak the clams in water until the shells open and release the sand. Remove the neck and mantle from the shell, peel the tough skin and chop the flesh coarsely. Place clams in a large pot and barely cover with water. Cover and cook over medium heat until tender, about 10 minutes. Strain liquid from the pot and reserve. Set clams aside.

Over medium heat, crisp the bacon in a little olive oil, sauté the onion until fragrant. Add the potatoes and cook for 5 minutes. Stir the flour into onions and potatoes and gradually stir in reserved clam juice. Whisk in the milk and cream, add bay leaves and thyme. Season as needed. Simmer until the potatoes are cooked, 10-15 minutes. Add the clams.

Cooked Crab
We learned from our neighbors, Joe and Oakley

Goodner, how to enjoy crab right out of the water off the beach in front of their house. They would kill the crab by piercing the ganglia from the underside of the crab with a sharp knife before dropping the crab into boiling water.

2-4 medium-sized local crabs
Garlic butter

Kill crabs and cook in boiling sea water, 15-20 minutes. Crack the shells, remove meat and dip into garlic butter or herbed mayonnaise (preferably home made — see *Vegetables*).

Sautéed Scallops

A scallop is the tender muscle holding the two halves of the mollusk together. Scallops are very rich and easy to prepare.

1/2 lb scallops per person
2 T butter
1 clove garlic, minced
1 T chopped green onion
1/8 t tarragon
2 T dry white wine
1 t fresh lemon juice
2 t chopped parsley
Salt and pepper, to taste
Lemon wedges

Wash and dry scallops. Sauté garlic, onions and tarragon in butter. Add scallops and sauté until transparent, about 5 minutes. Pour in wine and lemon juice, stir in parsley, simmer about 3 minutes. Serve with lemon wedges, French fries, and green salad.

Steamed Mussels

Mussels are mollusks abundant in our marine waters, particularly on rocks and pilings.

1 lb unshelled mussels per person
1/2 C water, or more
1/2 C dry white wine
1 t each thyme, tarragon, and basil
1 stalk celery, minced
1 small onion, diced
Salt and pepper, to taste
Lemon wedges
Sprigs of parsley
Beurre Blanc Sauce (see above)

Clean the shells of the mussels thoroughly. Heat water and wine to boiling. Add remaining ingredients and steam until mussels open, 5-7 minutes. Place cooked mussels in serving bowls, top with cooking water and wine. Serve Beurre Blanc on the side for dipping. Serve with crusty bread (see *Bread & Grains*) and green salad.

Prawns or Shrimp

This is our favorite midsummer food, using a recipe we brought from Norway and pairing it with the German tradition of *Erdbeerbowle* (Strawberry and Wine Punch). We serve it between May 1st and Summer Solstice to celebrate the beginning of the summer season. This moveable feast engages the farm family and neighbors, especially the children, in providing fiddle music and making a wreath and streamers for the Maypole.

1/2 lb uncooked whole prawns or shrimp per person
Salt and pepper, to taste
1 T butter
2 cloves garlic, minced
Juice of 1 lemon
2 t chopped parsley
1/4 C frozen or fresh strawberries per person
2 C dry white wine per person
1/2 shot of vodka per person
1 t sugar per person

To Prepare the Shrimp or Prawns:
Parboil shrimp or prawns and leave it to the guests to peel them.
To Make the Sauce:
Melt the butter, add garlic and parsley. Stir in lemon juice and season with salt and pepper. Serve with French bread (see *Bread & Grains*) and green salad.
To Prepare Strawberry and Wine Punch:
Put strawberries in a suitable glass bowl, sprinkle with sugar and add vodka. Steep in refrigerator for several hours, then add the wine. Serve in punch cups.

See *Herbs* for recipe for *Herbed Shrimp*.

Notes:

Meat

These days, eating meat — or not— is under serious discussion in light of climate change, nutritional health, animal rights, the need to feed a growing world population, and the use of limited natural resources. Different analysts come to different conclusions regarding the impact of eating meat on natural and human ecologies. Based on their assumptions, some advocate a non-meat diet, others for putting ever more burgers on the grill, and others for eating less but better quality meat raised in sustainable and humane ways.

Consumer decisions have serious environmental and economic consequences: producers will market what people buy. Personal choice is powerful. If consumers avoid certain products, those will disappear from the market. By contrast, the supply-side industry uses advertising to maximize consumption irrespective of impacts on animals, consumers, and the environment.

When it comes to beef, lamb, and pork, there is a fundamental difference between factory-produced animals and those raised on small sustainable farms. Factory-produced animals are confined in feedlots and are given antibiotics and feed that is not natural to their digestive systems. Their wastes despoil soil, air, and water. By contrast, animals raised on appropriately-scaled farms feed on what nature intended them to. Their manures enrich soils and composts, fertilize hayfields and pastures, and sequester carbon in the soil.

We raise our own animals from birth to slaughter, feed them with what the farm produces, and allow them to live as naturally as possible for domesticated animals. We have a symbiotic relationship with our animals: we provide them with feed, shelter, and protection from predators; they give us the food we need, and we know that their meat is healthy and clean. If you purchase meat that is locally raised, and you trust the farmer, you know that the meat you put on your plate is nutritionally whole, and that the way the animal was raised is humane and ecologically sustainable.

Beef & Veal

Unlike feedlot beef produced on concentrates, grass-fed beef provides the healthy balance of omega-3 and omega-6 fatty acids required for human health. Beef contains cobalamin, pyridoxine, zinc, selenium, iron, niacin, phosphorus, and is a great source of protein. Veal is the meat from a calf or young beef animal. Strictly speaking, a veal calf is raised until about 16 to 18 weeks of age on its mother's milk, which renders the flesh tender and pale in comparison to beef. Industrially raised veal comes from male calves separated from their mothers at birth. These calves are confined and fed on artificial milk substitutes, and are typically anemic. Our calves are raised naturally on their mother's milk and fresh grass.

Tips for Beef

~Be sure that the beef you buy comes from grass-fed animals.

~If you purchase your beef from a neighboring farmer, use the cut list provided by the butcher to determine your choice of roasts, steaks, hamburger, stew meat, and so on, over the course of the seasons. Think ahead to weekly family needs and holidays to decide on cuts and weights.

~Familiarize yourself with the cooking requirements of different cuts: steaks and ground meats can be barbecued or fried; chuck roasts need a long, slow cook with liquid, and so on.

~For meat broths, see the *Winter* section of *Seasonal Calendar*.

Beef (or Pork) Steak

1 large or 2 small tenderloin, New York, T-bone, ribeye, flank steaks, or similar pork cuts
2 T olive oil
Salt, pepper and garlic granules

To cook the steak, rub it on both sides with salt, pepper, and garlic, then brown it in hot oil in an ovenproof frying pan. Cover, and cook in the oven at 350 until the steak is finished to your liking — rare to well done. Pour the drippings over potatoes or the steak.

Beef and Beer Carbonnade

This dish is a wonderful variant of beef stew. The Flemish use beer as a cooking liquid the way Germans use broth, or the Italians wine. The results are delicious.

2 lb stewing beef, cut into bite-sized cubes and seasoned with salt and pepper
1 lb onions, sliced
2 T lard or olive oil
1 slice lean bacon, diced
1 sprig fresh thyme (or 1 t dried)
1 bay leaf
1 pint dark beer
1 t sugar
Salt, to taste
1 T malt or dark balsamic vinegar

Melt the lard or heat the olive oil in a heavy frying pan or Dutch oven. Sauté the onions until soft and golden. Remove from the pan and brown the seasoned meat in the oil. Add bacon and herbs, pour the beer over, and add vinegar. Sprinkle with sugar and a little salt. Return onions to pan and

cover. Cook on low heat on top of the stove, or in the oven at 325 for 2 hours. Serve with potatoes and sauerkraut, or some other vegetable that can stand up to a hearty meat dish.

Beef Brisket

Brisket is a cut of meat from the breast of the animal. The chest muscles help support the weight of the body, and so contain a lot of connective tissue. The meat is very flavorful, but tough, and requires a long, slow cook in liquid.

3 lb brisket
3 T bacon fat or olive oil
1/2 C chopped onions
2 C beef or other homemade broth

In a Dutch oven or other heavy pot, sauté the onions in the fat or oil. Add the broth, and bring to a boil. Add the brisket, cover, reduce heat and simmer for 2 hours or until the meat is tender. Serve with sauerkraut or other vegetables that go well with well-flavored meat.

Beef Pot Roast

Cuts of beef that come from the upper part of the animal are tender; those that come from the lower part, because they are used for movement, are more flavorful but less tender, and require a long, slow braising or roasting in liquid. Pot roasts can be made from chuck, shoulder, top or bottom roasts.

3-4 lb roast
Flour for dredging
Olive oil for browning
1 carrot, chopped
1 rib celery, diced
1 onion, chopped
2 cloves garlic, chopped
2 C homemade beef broth
1 bay leaf
3 peeled potatoes, cut into 3-inch pieces
3 carrots, cut into 3-inch pieces
2 turnips, 2 parsnips or other root crops, cut into 3-inch pieces
Sour cream, to taste
Salt and pepper, to taste

Dredge roast in flour. Heat olive oil in a Dutch oven and brown roast on all sides. Add carrot, celery, onion, garlic, beef broth and bay leaf.

Bake at 325 for 3-4 hours or simmer on top of the stove until meat is tender, turning it once or twice. When meat is fork-tender, remove from pot and cut into serving pieces. Add potatoes, carrots and other root crops to the broth, bring to a gentle boil, and cook until tender. Add meat to the pot and heat through. Remove meat and vegetables and place in a serving dish. Whisk sour cream into remaining broth, season with salt and pepper, and pour the sauce over meat and vegetables..

Beef Roast

For a dry roast, use cuts that come from the upper part of the animal, such as standing rib roast, sirloin tip roast, or rolled roast.

Place roast fat-side up on a rack in a shallow greased roasting pan. Place uncovered in a 550 oven and reduce heat immediately to 350. Roast for 20 minutes per pound or until a meat thermometer registers 140 for rare and 180 for well done. Remove from oven, cover, and let rest before slicing.

Serve with vegetables and potatoes of choice. We find that peas, corn, and mashed potatoes go particularly well with this roast. The juices from the meat can be dripped over the slices, or as an alternative, try a favorite recipe from Henning's family, a Madeira sauce:

Madeira Sauce

2 T butter
4 T flour
1 pint or more meat broth, as needed
Soup greens
6 peppercorns
6 whole allspice
1 bay leaf
Salt, as needed
A few grains of cayenne pepper
1 C Madeira or red port wine

Brown flour in butter and stir into simmering meat broth. Add soup greens, peppercorns, allspice berries and salt, and simmer for one half hour. Strain through a sieve, and return sauce to pan. Return to a simmer, finish with Madeira, salt, and cayenne.

Beef Stroganoff

1 1/2 lb filet of beef (top or bottom round)

3 T butter, divided
1/2 C minced onion
3/4 lb mushrooms, sliced
Salt, pepper, nutmeg, to taste
1/4 C dry white wine
1 C sour cream
Egg noodles (see *Bread & Grains* for making your own egg noodles or spätzle)

Cut the meat into 1/2 inch slices across the grain, and pound thin. Sauté onion in 1 tablespoon butter. Add beef strips, and sauté quickly until evenly browned, remove. Sauté mushrooms in 2 tablespoons butter, and add the beef and onion. Season with salt, pepper, and nutmeg. Add wine and stir. Cook until meat is tender. Add sour cream and heat through. Serve over noodles.

Braised Veal Shanks

2 veal shanks
Flour for dredging
Butter and olive oil, for browning
1 C chopped onion
2 garlic cloves, chopped
1 C red wine
1/2 t each salt, pepper, and dried thyme
1 sprig rosemary
2 potatoes, peeled and cut into chunks
2 carrots, scrubbed and cut into large pieces
2 turnips, peeled and cut into chunks

Dredge shanks in flour, shake off excess. In a Dutch oven, brown shanks thoroughly on all sides in butter and olive oil, then remove. Add onion and garlic to pot, cook until softened. Add wine, herbs, and spices. Bring to a gentle boil, remove from heat.

Add meat to pot, spoon liquid over. Cover and bake at 325 for an hour or until meat is fork tender. Remove from pot. Add carrots, turnips and potatoes, bake until tender. Replace meat in pot to warm. Remove rosemary and serve.

Chili con Carne. See *Dried Beans* in *Vegetables* for recipe.

German Meatballs (Königsberger Klopse)

This recipe has been derived from a variety of sources: a time-honored recipe in Henning's family, *Lüchow's German Cookbook*, and *The Joy of Cooking*, which claims that this recipe for meatballs is superior to all others. Unlike the Swedish recipe, it calls for cooking the meatballs in a vegetable broth instead of frying them. It recommends grinding the meats from scratch instead of mixing pre-packaged ground meat, and using sardines for flavoring the sauce. We serve this dish for holidays and special occasions over spätzle (see *Bread & Grains*).

For the Meat: (to make 12 2-inch balls)
1 thick slice of homemade French bread (see *Bread & Grains*), soaked in broth
1 1/2 lb veal (any cut suitable for grinding)
1/4 lb fatty pork
3 eggs, beaten
3 T butter
2 T minced onion
2 T chopped parsley
1/2 t pepper
1 t salt
1/2 t grated lemon rind
1 T lemon juice
1 t Worcestershire sauce

For the Broth: Use 1 1/2 quarts homemade vegetable broth (see *Vegetables* for recipe). If you grind the meat from cuts that are boned and trimmed for this purpose, add the trimmings to the stock as you prepare it.

For the Sauce:
5 C boiling homemade vegetable broth
1-2 small boneless sardines
4-5 T butter
4-5 T flour
Salt and pepper, to taste
2 t capers or chopped pickles
Sour cream, to taste
2 T chopped parsley
1/2 C buttered bread crumbs (see *Bread & Grains*)

To Prepare the Meat and the Sauce:
Grind meat twice using the finest plate on the meat grinder, and mix with 2 tablespoons melted butter. Squeeze excess liquid from the slice of bread, and mix bread with meat. Sauté onion in 1 tablespoon butter; add to meat with lemon peel, eggs, salt, pepper, lemon juice, Worcestershire sauce, and parsley. Mix with your hands and shape into twelve 2-inch balls. Simmer in broth for 15 minutes; remove with a slotted spoon.

For every 2 cups of broth, mix 2 tablespoons butter with 2 tablespoons flour. Stir into hot broth; cook and stir until smooth. Mash sardines with 1 tablespoon butter. Stir into sauce with capers and

parsley, and reheat meatballs in sauce. Cover top of the sauce with buttered crumbs.

Serve with noodles or spätzle.(See *Bread & Grains*)

Beef (or Lamb) Lasagna
Olive oil, for sautéing and browning
8 wide lasagna noodles (see *Bread & Grains*)
1 lb ground beef (or lamb)
1 quart basil and tomato sauce (preferably home made)
1 large onion, diced
4 cloves garlic, diced
1 t dried oregano
1 bay leaf
Salt and pepper, to taste
2 C ricotta or quark (see *Dairy*)
1 C shredded mozzarella (see *Dairy*)

In a Dutch oven or other heavy pot, sauté onion and garlic until soft; add ground meat and cook thoroughly, breaking up into a small mince. Add basil and tomato sauce, oregano, bay leaf, salt and pepper, and simmer until flavors mix, adjusting seasonings to taste.

Cook lasagne noodles until tender; drain, rinse under hot water, drain again thoroughly. Place 4 noodles in the bottom of a 9x13-inch baking dish; top with half of the meat sauce and spread 1 cup of the ricotta or quark over the top. Repeat with a second layer of noodles, meat sauce, ricotta or quark. Top with shredded mozzarella. Bake, uncovered, at 350 for 30 minutes. Let rest for a few minutes before cutting into squares and serving.

Meat Loaf
A homey dish prepared by Elizabeth's mother on Sunday afternoons.

1 lb ground beef (or lamb)
1 egg
3/4 C homemade chili sauce or ketchup (see *Keeping the Harvest*)
1/4 C milk
1/2 medium onion, minced
2 cloves garlic, minced
1/2 t each salt, pepper, garlic granules, dried basil, thyme and oregano.
Mix all ingredients together and bake in a covered casserole for an hour. Serve with baked potatoes and vegetable of choice.

Sauerbraten

A quintessential German dish, made known in America by Irma Rombauer's *The Joy of Cooking*. One of its virtues is that it can use a variety of cuts, from shoulder, chuck, and rump to round steak tenderized by marinating in wine or vinegar over several days. The recipe featured here comes from the kitchen of famous Lüchow's, a New York restaurant established by an immigrant in 1897 that survived two world wars and Prohibition, until it succumbed to urban blight in the 1980s. It was said that "Through the doors of Lüchow's pass all the famous people of the world," including, for example: Teddy Roosevelt, Mencken, Paderewski, Dvorak, Victor Herbert, Rogers & Hammerstein, Fritz Kreisler, Theodore Dreiser, John P. Marquand, and a host of others.

Lüchow's Sauerbraten

3 lb round steak, shoulder, rump, or chuck
1 T salt
1/2 t pepper
2 onions, sliced
1 carrot, sliced
1 stalk celery, chopped
4 each spice cloves and peppercorns
1 C red wine vinegar
2 bay leaves
2 T kidney fat (or butter)
6 T butter
3 T flour
1 T sugar
5 gingersnaps, crushed

To Marinate: wipe the meat with a damp cloth, season with salt and pepper. Place in a glass or enamel bowl. Combine onions, carrot, celery, cloves, peppercorns, bay leaves, vinegar and 2 1/2 pints of water, enough to cover the meat. Cover and refrigerate for two to four days.

To Prepare: After the final day drain and set aside the marinade, brown the meat in kidney fat (or butter), then add the marinade and simmer for three hours. In a small pan, melt the remaining butter and stir the flour into it, add sugar and brown, then add the mixture to the simmering meat. Cover and cook another hour until tender. Remove meat to a serving platter, add crushed gingersnaps to pot juices and cook until thickened. Pour the gravy over the meat.

Serve with boiled potatoes or potato dumplings, and with sweet-sour red cabbage (for both, see *Vegetables*).

Steak Tartare

This raw meat delicacy requires clean, high quality beef and fresh eggs.

1/3 lb beef top sirloin
1 egg
1/4 t whole capers
1 small yellow onion, minced
Salt, pepper and garlic granules, to taste
Thick slice of dense bread (see *Bread and Grains*)
Butter for the bread

Grind the sirloin twice using the finest blade on a meat grinder. Spread the bread generously with butter, followed by the ground meat. Top with onion, raw egg, capers, salt, pepper. Sprinkle with garlic granules. Serve with a good beer.

Swedish Meatballs

A great company meal. Uncooked ingredients can be frozen.

1 slice bread (preferably homemade sourdough (see *Bread & Grains*).
1/2 lb each ground pork, lamb, and beef, mixed
2 eggs, well beaten
1 T butter
1/2 C minced onion
3 T chopped parsley
1 1/4 t salt
1/4 t paprika
Rind from 1/2 lemon, finely grated
1 t lemon juice
1/4 t each nutmeg and allspice
2 T butter
2 C homemade pork, lamb, or beef broth
2 T sour cream

Soak bread in water, wring out and crumble. Mix eggs and bread with meat. Sauté onion in butter, and mix with meat. Add parsley, salt, paprika, lemon rind and juice, nutmeg, and allspice; mix well. Shape meat into one and a half inch balls, brown thoroughly on all sides in melted butter. Cover and simmer in broth, about fifteen minutes, and finish with sour cream. Serve over boiled or mashed potatoes.

Texas Hash

This is our go-to recipe for hamburger. It is a great comfort food, cold as well as hot.

1 lb ground beef (or lamb)
3 onions, sliced
1 large green pepper, seeds and membrane removed, chopped
1 quart home-canned tomatoes
1/2 C uncooked regular white rice
1 1/2 t chili powder
1 t salt
1/2 t pepper

In a large skillet, cook the ground beef until light brown. Add onions and green pepper. Cook and stir until onion is tender. Stir in tomatoes, rice, chili powder, salt and pepper, and heat through. Divide between two one-quart casserole dishes, cover, and bake at 350 for one hour, stirring once at the half-hour mark to be sure the rice cooks.

Wiener Schnitzel

Henning thinks of the Schnitzel as the crown of Austrian and German cooking — tender and delicately flavored, made from veal or pork.

2 veal or pork loin chops
Flour
Salt, garlic granules, freshly ground pepper, to taste
1 beaten egg, thinned with a little milk
Bread crumbs (preferably from homemade French bread (see *Bread & Grains*)
Butter for frying
2 wedges of a lemon

Debone chops and make a broth from the bones. Pound the meat to a thickness of 1/4 inch. Sprinkle with salt, pepper and garlic. Dredge in flour. Dip in egg and milk, and dredge in bread crumbs. Let sit for a quarter of an hour, then fry in butter, 2-3 minutes per side. Serve with wedges of lemon, green salad, peas, and mashed or new potatoes garnished with butter and parsley.

While the meat is resting, season the broth with salt, pepper, and garlic granules. Sprinkle with chopped parsley. Serve before the main meal.

For corned beef, and pickled beef tongue, see *Keeping the Harvest*.

Lamb

Up to about a year old, a sheep is called "lamb." Older than that, it is mutton, less tender but more flavorful. We use lamb for rack of lamb, chops, and leg of lamb. Mutton is used for ground meat. All sheep bones make excellent broth. Lamb is high in protein, and contains cobalamin, selenium, zinc, niacin, phosphorus, and iron.

Lamb (or Beef) Burgers

We like this recipe for ground lamb so much that we use it for beef burgers as well, and often mix the two for a more succulent burger.

1 lb ground lamb (or beef, or a blend)
4 t Worcestershire sauce
1 T dark balsamic vinegar
1 t each garlic granules, pepper, dried thyme
Hamburger buns (we prefer potato buns)
Fixings (details below)

Mix ingredients well and refrigerate for 1 hour. Broil hamburger buns until brown, preferably with butter. Fry burgers, place on buns and garnish with fixings of choice such as pickles, fresh tomato, lettuce, chili sauce, mayonnaise, or mustard. Serve with fried potatoes.

Rack of Lamb

The rack of lamb holds the lamb chops; you can order this cut as individual chops and fry, grill, or broil them. We prefer roasting the whole rack and cutting off the chops when serving; the meat is more flavorful and succulent when roasted on the bone.

Sprinkle the rack with salt, pepper, and garlic granules and top with butter. Place on a wire rack in a shallow pan and roast uncovered at 400 about 1 hour until the meat is done (internal temperature 145). Carve into chops and serve.

Roasted Leg of Lamb (and Soup)
For the Roast:
5 lb leg of lamb, bone in
2 cloves garlic, minced
2 sprigs rosemary, minced
For the Soup:
1 leg of lamb bone
2 cloves garlic, halved
1 each carrot and stalk of celery, halved
1/2 onion
1/2 t each salt, peppercorns, dried or fresh basil, rosemary, and oregano
Fresh or frozen vegetables, as desired

To Prepare the Roast: Pierce the leg every inch or so with a sharp knife. In each slit, place a sliver of garlic and a sliver of rosemary. Place the leg of lamb, fat-side up, on a wire rack, uncovered, in a greased roasting pan. Place in 450 oven and immediately reduce heat to 325. Roast 30 minutes per pound or until the internal temperature reaches 175 to 180 for meat well done. Serve the roast with roasted or mashed potatoes and vegetable of choice.

To Prepare the Soup: The bone of a roasted leg of lamb is so flavorful that we always make soup from it the next day for another complete meal. Cook bone with vegetables, herbs and spices in enough water to cover, until broth is savory. Replace cooked vegetables with peas, corn, carrots, dried tomatoes, as desired. Season to taste, and add rice, noodles, or potatoes.

Baked Lamb Chops
Drizzle olive oil on both sides of chop. Season with salt, pepper, garlic granules and dried thyme.
Heat olive oil in large, oven-proof frying pan. Brown chops in pan, about 2 minutes per side. Roast, covered, in oven at 400 for 20 minutes, until internal temperature is 145 for medium rare, 170 well done.

Curried Lamb
This is a great company meal, served over rice and with peas.

2 lb lamb shoulder or leg
3 T bacon fat or olive oil
1/2 C chopped onion
1/2 T sweet curry powder
1 C homemade lamb, pork, or beef broth
1/2 C chopped celery
2 T chopped parsley

Remove fat and fell from meat, cut into 1-inch cubes, brown in fat or oil with onion and curry powder. Add broth, celery and parsley. Cover meat and simmer until tender, about half an hour.

For Fenalår (dried, salted leg of lamb), see *Keeping the Harvest*.

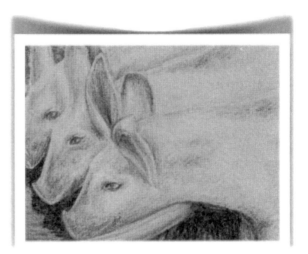

Pork

Pigs are omnivores, and their meat will take on the flavor of whatever they eat. We heard a sad story about a man in Alaska who raised his pigs on rotten salmon. The pork was inedible.

Our pigs are fed on whey from cheesemaking, ground organic barley, chopped apples, cooked potatoes and other vegetables. The idea that pigs will eat anything is incorrect. We have to mash the cooked potatoes and mix them with grain, milk or whey, or the pigs will flip them out of their feed bowls. This may not be everyone's experience, but it is ours.

Our pigs are moved to new paddocks on a weekly basis to give them fresh grass. We provide them with a movable shelter for shade, fresh water for drinking, and a large tub to splash in. Given the chance, pigs are remarkably clean animals and will not smell if fed and housed properly.

We take our pork cuts as chops, country ribs, ground pork, ham steaks, smoked ham, ham hocks, and bacon, but there are other options.

Pork contains iron, magnesium, phosphorus, potassium, zinc, thiamin, riboflavin, niacin, cobalamin, and pyridoxine.

Country Ribs

You can use pork spare ribs for this recipe, but country ribs have more meat. Make the barbecue sauce ahead of time.

Parboil country ribs for 4 minutes to remove excess fat. Place ribs in a 9x13-inch glass baking pan, cover with foil (do not seal) and bake at 450 for 15 minutes.

Reduce heat to 350 and pour the barbecue sauce over the meat. Recover with foil. Bake for an hour, basting as needed.

For the Barbecue Sauce:
1/4 C chopped onion
1 T bacon drippings or olive oil
1/2 C water
2 T dark balsamic vinegar
1 T Worcestershire sauce
1/4 C lemon juice
2 T brown sugar
1 C chili sauce
1/2 t salt
1/4 t each paprika and pepper
1 t dried mustard

Sauté onion in drippings or oil. Add all other ingredients and simmer for 20 minutes.

Pork Chops with Dried Plum Sauce

Sometimes we just rub pork chops with salt, pepper, and garlic granules, brown them in a frying pan, cover and put them in the oven at 350 to finish cooking. If we want something more elegant, we make the following recipe.

1 T olive oil
4 pork chops, seasoned with salt and pepper
2 T minced shallots, onions, or leeks
1 C dry red wine

1 sprig rosemary
1 C homemade pork, chicken, or beef broth
1 C chopped dried plums
2 t brown sugar
2 T dark balsamic vinegar
1 t cornstarch
1 T butter
1 T chopped fresh parsley

Heat oil until simmering. Cook pork chops 2-3 minutes per side. Transfer to a plate and tent with foil. Add shallots, onions or leeks to pan and cook until fragrant, about 30 seconds.

Deglaze pan with wine, add rosemary and bring to a boil. Cook until wine is reduced by half, about 2 minutes. Add broth, plums, brown sugar, and any juices from chops. Bring to a boil, then reduce heat to medium and simmer until plums soften, 2-3 minutes.

Whisk together vinegar and cornstarch and then whisk into sauce and cook until thickened. Off heat, whisk butter into sauce, season with salt and pepper. Return pork to sauce to heat through. Top servings with parsley; serve with rice or potatoes.

Pork Ragù

12 oz dry medium shell or penne pasta (or homemade spätzle)
3 T olive oil
1 C minced onions
1/2 C sliced Kalamata olives
1/4 C diced dried tomatoes, soaked in olive oil
2 T tomato paste
1 T minced fresh garlic
1 t sugar
1 t red pepper flakes
1/2 t dried oregano
1 lb ground pork
3 T dark balsamic vinegar
1 qt home-canned tomatoes
1/2 C chopped parsley
Salt to taste
Grated Parmesan or other hard cheese

Heat oil in a large frying pan over medium. Add onions, olives, dried tomatoes, tomato paste, garlic, sugar, pepper flakes, and oregano. Cook until onions soften. Add ground pork and cook until no longer pink, breaking up chunks. Stir in vinegar, cook until absorbed. Add tomatoes, bring ragù to a simmer, and cook about 10 minutes. Stir in parsley, season with salt.

This dish can also be made with pre-cooked beef, lamb, or Summer Sausage (see below for sausage).

Cook pasta shells according to package directions. Drain and rinse with hot water. Place in bowls and ladle the sauce over the top. Sprinkle with grated cheese. As an alternative, serve *Pork Ragù* over *Spätzle* (see *Bread & Grains*).

Organ Meats

Organ meats, particularly liver, but also hearts, kidneys, and intestines, as well as snouts, ears, and feet, are flavorful, and easy to prepare. They are also the most nutritious parts of the animal.

Beef liver contains vitamin A, riboflavin, pyridoxine, folate, cobalamin, choline, copper, iron, selenium, and phosphorus. Pork liver contains iron, magnesium, phosphorus, potassium, zinc, thiamin, riboflavin, niacin, cobalamin, and pyridoxine.

Tips for Organ Meat
~Beef liver has a thin sheath called the "fell," which should be removed, because it will not break down during cooking. Pork liver does not have a fell.
~To get thin slices, cut the liver partially frozen.
~Cook liver briefly, just until it is still a little pink inside.
~ We use intestines mostly for making sausage (see below).

Baked Stuffed Heart
Beef heart makes a wonderful dish for holidays. Heart is a muscle meat and requires a long, slow cook in liquid. A 4-5 pound beef heart or 3 veal hearts will serve six.

For the Heart:
1 beef heart, cleaned of fat, arteries, veins, washed well and dried.
2 C homemade beef broth
4 slices bacon

Place cleaned heart in a casserole dish, cover with bacon, pour broth over, and bake at 325 for 3-4 hours, depending on size. Remove to a plate, and fill cavity with *Apple and Onion Dressing* (see *Turkey* in *Poultry* for recipe).

Stuff the cavity of the heart with the dressing, (do not pack). Heat the stuffed heart at 400 long enough to warm before serving.

Beef or Pork Liver Creole
1 lb beef or pork liver, thinly sliced
Flour for dusting liver
1 1/4 C sliced onions
1 qt home-canned tomatoes
1/2 C (or more) diced celery
1 thinly sliced green pepper, seeds and membrane removed
A few grains cayenne
1/2 t salt

Dust the slices of liver with flour. In a Dutch oven or other large pot, brown the slices in bacon drippings or olive oil. Add onions, tomatoes, celery, green pepper, cayenne and salt. Cover the pan and simmer about 20 minutes. Serve over rice.

Venetian Beef or Pork Liver with Onions
3 large onions, sliced
1/4 C olive oil
1 apple, diced
3 T grated lemon peel
2 lb liver, thinly sliced
Flour
Salt and pepper

Place onion in frying pan with oil and cook, stirring, over medium heat until onions are soft and golden. Stir in apple and lemon peel, cook briefly, then lift from pan with slotted spoon and set aside. Coat slices of liver with flour, shaking off excess. Lay pieces on waxed paper and sprinkle lightly with salt and pepper.

Return frying pan to burner, and brown floured liver slices in it. Do not crowd. Brown liver until it is done on the outside, a little pink on the inside. Pour onions, apple, and lemon over liver, gently mix and heat, and serve over rice.

Fried Chicken Liver
One of our practices on the sad days when we slaughter our laying hens is to collect their delicate livers and fry them gently in a bit of butter.

12 chicken livers
Flour for dusting
Salt, pepper, and garlic granules

Butter for frying
Half an onion, sliced

Carefully rinse the livers in cool water and pat dry. Dust in some flour, sprinkle with salt, pepper and garlic granules. Fry the onion in butter until translucent, add the liver and fry briefly. Serve with some sourdough rye bread and a glass of beer.

Sausage

Sausage is ground meat combined with fat, herbs, spices, and salt, and is an important part of the culinary tradition of every culture. Sausage making goes back to the beginnings of agriculture in the Near East, when people had enough surplus meat to cut it up, salt it, and stuff it into casings made of animal intestines. When butchering, we routinely combine various cuts of beef, pork, lamb, chicken, and turkey with innards, especially livers, kidneys, hearts, snouts, tongues and tails, to make a variety of sausages.

Fresh sausage can be kept for a few days in the refrigerator or frozen for a year or more before you put it on the grill or in the frying pan. It can be wrapped as patties or stuffed into casings. It can be the star of a meal, or added to beans, soups, stews or casseroles for extra flavor, texture, and protein.

To make sausage at home, we recommend a meat grinder with a sausage-stuffer attachment, or a separate machine for stuffing sausage. Casings for stuffing can be purchased at most grocery stores. On the farm, we retain pork, beef, and lamb intestines, then clean and freeze them for use in stuffing sausages.

Boudin Blanc

This is a white sausage we make at home, cooking some for immediate consumption and freezing the rest for future meals. We combine the chicken breasts of old layers with the occasional wild rabbit and pork. You will need 1-inch-wide sausage casings and cotton string for tying them into 6-inch sections.

1/2 lb leaf lard or hard back pork fat
1/2 lb pork loin
1/2 lb chicken, turkey, or rabbit breast
2 t salt
1 t ground white pepper

1/8 t each of ground cloves, nutmeg, and ginger
1/4 t cinnamon
2 C chopped onions
1/4 C warm cream
1/2 C bread crumbs (see *Bread & Grains*)
3 eggs, beaten

Mince the fat with a sturdy knife. In a meat grinder, use the finest plate to grind the pork, turkey, chicken or rabbit meat. In a bowl, combine the minced fat and the meat. Add salt, pepper, cloves, nutmeg, ginger and cinnamon, and regrind together with the chopped onions.

In a separate bowl, soak the breadcrumbs in the cream, then add the eggs and the reground meat mixture. Mix well with your hands.

Feed the casing onto the stuffing tube on your meat grinder or sausage stuffer, working the casing well to the end of the tube. Begin stuffing the sausage into the casing, twisting the casing every 6 inches and tying it off with cotton string.

When you have the desired number of sausages for a single meal, tie 2 strings 1/2 inch apart, and cut so that each section is tied off.

Put the bundles of sausages into boiling water. Reduce heat to 190 and cook about 20 minutes. If sausages rise to the surface, prick the casing to release air and avoid bursting.

Remove sausages from the water, allow to dry, and freeze what you will not use immediately.

To prepare, brush the sausages with melted butter and fry or grill them until golden brown.

Liver Paté

This rich and delicious spread can be made from any liver. Try using it for crackers or bread, topped with snipped fresh chives or a pickle relish.

4 lb lamb and chicken liver, washed and sliced
About 2 C milk for soaking
4 onions, sliced
1 C butter
2 C heavy cream
1/2 C brandy
1 T salt
1 1/2 t pepper
1 T each ground allspice and fresh thyme

Slice lamb livers 1-inch wide, chicken livers in half. Soak in milk for 1 hour. Give milk to the dog.

Sauté onion slices in butter until soft and deep golden. Add liver pieces. Cook until done in the center, but do not overcook.
Pour all into a food processor. Purée, slowly adding cream for a soft, spreadable texture. Add the brandy, salt and pepper, allspice and fresh thyme. Process and taste, adjusting brandy and spices to your liking. (Have slices of bread and crackers handy so you can taste at the last two stages.)

The paté should be a little salty, very creamy, and a bit rich with just a hint of brandy and herbs. Don't skip the allspice; it really balances the liver flavor.

Scoop into small jars, cover, and freeze until wanted. Let thaw overnight in the fridge and serve at a slightly-warm room temperature, so flavors melt on the tongue.

Pork or Lamb Sausage

This sausage is essentially finely ground meat flavored with herbs and spices. We fry and eat it with potatoes or bread.
1 lb fresh or frozen pork or lamb
3 T yellow onion, minced
2 t Dijon mustard
1 t each parsley, mint, and dill, chopped
1 t dried oregano
1/2 t ground coriander
Salt and pepper to taste
Olive oil for sautéing

Mix ground pork or lamb with the onion, mustard, herbs and spices. Shape into patties and fry until well-browned on both sides. For a variant of this sausage using sage, see *Herbs*.

Summer Sausage

This is not a sausage we make at home, but have made for us when we slaughter an older beef animal. The meat is flavorful, but not tender, so we have it processed into ground meat and then deliver to Del Fox Meats together with enough pork or other fat.

They mix it with spices, herbs and salts, stuff the meat into casings, and smoke them. The salting and smoking are light, and the sausages need to be frozen for long-term storage. Further smoking and drying in natural casings would turn the summer sausage into salami.

Summer sausage tastes fresh even after years in the freezer, and it is an important staple in our diet. We always have a package of it in the refrigerator. We slice it to eat with a little mustard, or put it on bread and butter, or add it to vegetable soups.

Broth & Aspic

Homemade broth is the foundation of much of our cooking. Every time we cook meat that has a bone, we make broth for the meal that day (for example, see *Schnitzel*, above). This practice recalls the tradition of housewives to keep a pot on the back of the wood-burning stove in which they simmered leftover meat, bones, or vegetables. In southern states of the U.S., this was called Pot liquor (or "potlikker"), made from cooking greens, beans, and meats. Pot liquor contains iron and other minerals, vitamins C and K.

We also make broth on a bigger scale by retaining bones from the slaughter animals, cooking them in large pots with carrots, onions, celery, pepper and garlic, and pressure canning the broth for winter storage. Pigs' heads, feet, tails, and snouts, as well as chicken feet, are boiled for broth and for making aspic.

Aspic (Schweinekopfsülze)

This is a traditional recipe from southern Germany:

1/2 pig's head
2 pig's feet, well scrubbed
3 carrots, chopped
1/4 celeriac, chopped
1 leek, chopped
Bundle of 5 sprigs each of thyme and parsley
2 bay leaves
Spice bag: 1/2 t each of juniper and allspice berries, plus 2 t black peppercorns
1 T salt
3 T white wine vinegar
1 T sugar
Gelatin powder or sheets, as needed

Place carrots, celeriac, leek, bundled herbs, bay leaves, spice bag, salt, pig's head and feet in a heavy pot, cover with water and simmer for about 3 hours until the meat is fork-tender. Remove head and feet and discard vegetables, herbs, and spices. Strain broth through a sieve or cheesecloth.

Reduce the broth to about 1/3, about 2 1/2 cups. Chop the meat, fat, and skin, reheat the broth, add chopped meat and season with vinegar, sugar and salt to an intense flavor. Spoon 1 tablespoon of broth on a plate and refrigerate for 10-15 minutes. If the aspic remains soft, soak 2-3 gelatin sheets or powder in cold water for 10 minutes and stir into hot broth. Add more gelatin if needed. Pour the aspic into a mold and refrigerate for at least 6 hours. Slice and serve with roasted potatoes or flavorful bread. Chase with a good beer.

Notes:

Bread &Grains

If you chop your own wood, it will warm you twice; if you bake your own bread, it will sustain you twice. There is aesthetic and spiritual pleasure in baking, and profound satisfaction in eating the delicious, firm, healthy loaves that come out of your oven.

In Europe, bread remains a staple, and in Germany, Austria, and Switzerland, *Butterbrot* (bread and butter) is a main dish, provided the bread is substantial, which usually means a version of long-fermented sourdough rye. It is worth remembering that rye is the oldest grain cultivated in northern Europe because it thrives in cold and wet weather.

Henning remembers an episode in his childhood. One morning, when he came into the kitchen and saw the glistening loaves of new bread lying on the counter, his grandmother told him that the cat had had her litter in the warm, rising dough during the night. But Grandmother had scraped off the mess and baked the loaves anyway. "Bread is the staff of life," she said. "It is sacred!"

Elizabeth remembers a similar story told by a colleague in the English department at the University of Washington. As a child, he had emigrated from Italy, where his mother had always baked their bread at home, a practice she continued in America. While at school in Poulsbo, WA, he was astonished to see his classmates throw away the crusts of their sandwiches. In his home, when a piece of bread fell to the floor, his mother would pick it up, and, making the sign of the cross, put it in his mouth. Bread is sacred!

The making and eating of bread is a cultural practice of deep significance for bodily and spiritual health. Historically, the consumption of bread served as a marker of community identity. The term *companion* literally means someone in your community with whom you share bread.

Some 3000 years ago, the hero in Homer's *Odyssey* anxiously asked his fellow seafarers as they were approaching the land of the Cyclops, "Are they bread eaters?" In other words, are they human? And a millennium later, Christ taught his followers to pray to God to "give us our daily bread" and to celebrate the presence of the divine in the world through eating bread in Holy Communion.

Baking bread does take time, mostly in having to be at home during the rising and the baking. But the time it takes is relative because you can make and freeze multiple loaves. Depending on your family's bread consumption, one baking can provide bread for weeks. You can bake two loaves of French bread in less time than it takes to go to the store to buy them.

Moreover, the process is satisfying. Baking your own bread is part of self-sufficiency. Working with the dough can be a time for meditation. The house

149

smells wonderful, and you produce sandwiches that stand up to mayonnaise.

Baking bread is not difficult, and becomes easier with experience. Henning taught Elizabeth how to bake rye bread. He would say, "Add flour," and when she asked, "How much?" he answered, "Just enough." She soon learned to use her senses instead of measurements: the dough, after kneading, should feel firm and alive, and push back when poked with a finger.

We use organic flour for everything. It is free of pesticides and herbicides, and has a finer texture than non-organic flour containing soy fillers and other additives to promote quick-rising dough. Crepe batter, sauces, and pancakes made with organic flour don't have those annoying little lumps in them. We raise our own rye and wheat, and grind the grain whole for each baking in a counter-top, stone-burr mill. We freeze any ground flour not used immediately.

We use whole grain for the bulk of our bread, because it contains the whole kernel: the bran, the endosperm and the germ.

The fiber-rich bran is the outer layer that protects the seed inside the kernel. It contains B vitamins and trace minerals.

The endosperm is the middle layer that contains the carbohydrates and protein constituting refined flour.

The germ at the tip of the grain is the nutrient-rich core that holds the seed of new life. It also contains antioxidants, vitamins E and B, and healthy fats. Because it is alive, the germ tends to go rancid unless frozen, which is why it is removed in the refinement process.

We purchase organic refined flour to use in small quantities in kneading and shaping the bread. It provides the gluten needed to bind the air spaces created by the yeast in the rising process. The gluten holds the dome shape of the bread.

We use both the natural yeasts harvested from the environment in sourdough starter and granulated commercial yeast. Any yeast is a living organism. A unicellular fungus, it remains dormant in the dry, granulated form of commercial yeast, but you can also buy fresh yeast packed in small cakes. Either

way, keep it in the refrigerator. When sprinkled over warm water sweetened with honey, sugar, or molasses, the yeast organism becomes active. You see the granules sink and start to bloom. When ready, all the granules will be dissolved and the top of the mixture foamy. Whisk gently to encourage this process. Add the proofed yeast to the flour immediately.

Yeast Breads

We distinguish yeast breads made with granulated dry yeast from long-fermented breads made with sourdough starter. A fundamental difference between the two types of bread is that the long-fermented bread will stay fresh much longer without refrigeration and most of the gluten will have been converted to digestible peptides.

Basic White Bread
This bread makes good toast, but Henning thinks it does not have much "staying power." It is a good bread to give to someone who is sick, together with a cup of chicken broth.

1 T granulated yeast
1 1/2 C warm water (115 degrees) for the yeast
1 T sugar
4 C white flour
3/4 C water for the dough
2 t salt
Olive oil for bowl and bread pan

In a small bowl, pour water over the sugar. Sprinkle on yeast, and allow to proof. It will become foamy and triple in size. Whisk the mixture to stimulate proofing. In a large bowl, combine flour and salt. Mix in the water, and add the yeast mixture. Stir until the ingredients are blended and the dough pulls away from the bowl.

Transfer the dough to a flour-dusted countertop. Knead, adding flour to hands, dough, or counter as needed. Knead until dough is firm and comes back when you poke it with a finger. Wash the bowl (we use a scrub brush or a cleaning pad for this — a sponge will be ruined). Dry the bowl and coat it lightly with olive oil.

Place the dough in the bowl and turn to coat with the oil. Cover with a towel and place in a warm, draft-free spot to rise until double in bulk. Rising time will vary with ambient temperature.

Brush a bread pan with olive oil. Remove the risen dough from the bowl, and knead it for a bit. Shape it into a rectangle and drop into the prepared bread pan, pushing the dough into the corners. Cover with a towel and let it rise a second time, until the dough is a bit above the edges of the pan.

Slash the top of the loaf in three or four places to ensure even baking. Bake at 400 for about 45 minutes. When the top is brown and firm, invert the loaf into your hand. If the bottom and sides are soft, place the loaf (without the pan) directly on the oven rack and turn the oven off. When the bread is completely baked, place it on a rack to cool.

French Bread

We thank Debbie Têtu for this and the focaccia recipes that follow. French bread makes a wonderful companion to salads, soups, and pasta. We cover it with butter or dip it in olive oil, garlic and herbs.

2 C warm water (115 degrees)
1 T sugar
2 T granulated yeast
4 C white organic flour, plus some for kneading (you can use whole-wheat flour, but it won't be a traditional French bread in taste or texture)
1 heaping t salt
Olive oil, as needed

In a small bowl, pour water over sugar. Sprinkle on yeast, and allow to proof. It will become foamy and triple in size. Whisk the mixture to stimulate proofing. In another bowl, mix flour and salt. When the yeast has proofed, pour it over the flour and salt, and mix. If the dough seems dry, add a bit of olive oil.

Turn the dough onto a dusted counter, stretch and fold it several times, instead of kneading. The more kneading you do to any bread, the finer the texture. We like our French bread to have that wonderful stretchy quality that invites one to tear it into serving pieces. Folding the dough helps develop the gluten that gives the dough its strength and good volume to the loaf.

Wash and dry the bowl, and lightly coat with olive oil. Place the dough in the bowl, turn to coat with oil. Cover with a towel and place in a warm, draft-free spot to rise until double in bulk. Rising time will vary with ambient temperature.

Sprinkle a baking sheet with cornmeal. Divide the dough into two parts and roll each into a long loaf. Work out any cracks, which will enlarge during baking. Place loaves on the baking sheet. Slash the loaves in several places to ensure even baking.

If you want a crisp crust, spritz the loaves with water, or brush them with a combination of equal parts cold water and egg white, beaten together. Place in a cold oven, and turn the temperature to 400. Bake for 20-30 minutes.

Focaccia

Follow the recipe above, adding olive oil to the dough if needed After kneading, divide the dough into halves. With your hands and a rolling pin spread each half 1/2 inch thick onto baking sheets sprinkled with cornmeal.

Brush the top with olive oil and prick it multiple times with a fork. At this point, you can bake it in a preheated oven at 400 for 20 minutes, and then eat it as bread. You can cover the pieces with cheese, tomatoes, garlic spread, pesto, and anything else to your taste, or eat it plain with a pasta dish.

For a more elaborate focaccia, tuck into the dough your favorite herbs and vegetables, such as diced garlic, halved Kalamata olives, rosemary leaves, and slices of marinated artichoke. Sprinkle with Parmesan or other hard cheese. Bake as above. Cut into squares and serve.

You can use dried tomatoes soaked in olive oil as a topping, but add them or Feta cheese after the focaccia comes out of the oven.

Potato Bread

This recipe makes nice firm loaves, good for toast or at the dinner table, dipped in olive oil with diced garlic and herbs. Shaped into a six-inch round, potato bread also makes a great hamburger bun.

2 C of thoroughly mashed potatoes (perhaps left over from the day before)
2 T granulated yeast
1 T sugar
5 C warm water (115 degrees)
16 C organic white flour
1 T salt
Olive oil, as needed
In a large bowl, combine sugar and 1 cup warm water. Sprinkle the yeast on top. Whisk in 6

tablespoons of the flour. Set aside in a warm place for 30 minutes or until bubbly.

Add a bit of warm water to the potatoes, mash to work out any lumps and to have the potatoes mix with the flour more easily.

To the starter, add the potatoes, 4 cups warm water, and the salt. Stir in the flour 1 cup at a time until the dough coheres. Turn the dough onto a dusted counter and knead, adding flour until the dough is firm and elastic.

Wash and dry the bowl and coat with olive oil. Place the dough in the bowl and turn to coat. Cover and put in a warm place to rise until the dough has doubled in bulk. Rising time will vary with ambient temperature.

Return the dough to the dusted counter and cut into four loaves. Knead and work out any fissures that would become cracks during baking. Place in greased bread pans, cover with a towel, and let rise in a warm place. Slash the tops of the loaves. Bake at 350 for about 35 minutes until tops and bottoms are brown. Remove from bread pans, return to oven racks, and turn the heat off. The bread will finish baking as the oven cools. Cool the bread on racks.

Sunflower and Millet Bread

This recipe produces subtly flavored, firm-textured bread with a wonderful crunch from the sunflower seeds. Millet is a gluten-free whole grain, packed with protein, antioxidants, and nutrients, and it grows in poor soils. We like to eat this bread with soup.

For the Millet:
1 1/2 C water
1 C uncooked millet
4 T melted butter
4 T honey
2 1/2 t salt

For the Sponge:
1 T granulated yeast
1 C warm water (115 degrees)
1 T honey
1 C organic white flour

For the Dough:
1 C or more sunflower seeds
2 C organic whole-wheat flour
2-3 C organic white flour

To Prepare the Millet:
Bring water to a boil in a medium saucepan. Add millet, cover, and turn the heat to very low. Cook for 15 minutes, or until all the water is absorbed and the millet is tender. Fluff with a fork, add the remaining ingredients, and stir until well combined. Let it cool to room temperature.

To Make the Sponge:
Place honey in a large bowl, cover with the water, sprinkle with yeast and whisk to blend. Whisk in the flour, and put the sponge in a warm place for 30-45 minutes until risen and bubbly.

To Make the Dough:
Beat the cooked millet into the sponge, along with the sunflower seeds. Stir in the flour, one cup at a time. Knead on a dusted counter until the dough is glossy and makes a firm ball. Wash the bowl, dry and coat with olive oil. Place the dough in it, turning to coat. Allow to rise until double in bulk. Rising time will vary with ambient temperature.

Oil two bread pans or one cast-iron frying pan, pressing dough to fill the sides. Bake at 350 for 35 minutes. Remove bread from pans, turn the oven off, and return loaves to oven rack to firm, if needed. Cool on a rack.

Whole Wheat Bread

This is a fast bread to make; it requires no kneading and rises only once, in the baking pans. It is more flavorful and has more "staying power" than *Basic White Bread* (above).

7 1/2 C organic whole-wheat flour
1 T salt
1 T sugar
3 T granulated yeast
3 C warm water (115 degrees), divided
4 T molasses

Mix the flour and salt in a large bowl and place in the oven at the lowest setting. Both the bowl and the flour and salt mixture should be warm when you make the dough.

Put the sugar in a medium bowl, add 1 cup warm water, sprinkle on the yeast and whisk to dissolve. Whisk in the molasses and allow the yeast to proof. Stir in another cup of warm water. Combine the flour and yeast mixtures. Stir, adding enough warm water (about 1 cup) to make a wet, sticky dough. Place the dough directly into three greased bread pans. Cover, set in a warm spot, and allow the dough to rise nearly to the top of the pans. (This will happen very quickly.) Bake at 350 for 35 minutes, until the crust is nicely browned. Remove from pans, turn off the oven, and leave loaves on the rack for 20 minutes or more to finish baking.

Gluten Intolerance and Fermentation

Gluten is a natural protein in wheat, rye, barley, and other grains. It helps bread to rise, gives it its chewy texture, and allows pizza dough to stretch. People have been eating grains that contain gluten for thousands of years, mostly with no problem in breaking down the protein and digesting it.

However, since World War II, gluten sensitivity (also called gluten intolerance) has become a problem for 6-7% of the American population, and celiac disease is now four times more common in the U.S. than it was 50 years ago.

We think, however, that the increase in gluten sensitivity is less a problem of personal health than a growing socio-cultural disorder for which producers, processors, distributors, the medical establishment, government agencies, and unwitting consumers, all bear responsibility.

There are three causes for the increase in gluten intolerance since WWII. First, with the invention of the industrial "slurry method," the traditional process of slow bread fermentation was replaced with mass-production methods that require only a couple of hours from flour to finished loaf. This necessitates the addition of more gluten (and other chemical "improvers") to force a quick rise of the dough.

Second, to support bread-production methods requiring higher gluten levels, heritage strains of wheat were replaced with gluten-enhanced varieties.

Third, gluten was now added to many other products that benefit from its structural properties, including processed meats, beer, soy sauce, dressings, gravy, ketchup, canned soups, frozen or canned vegetables, sauces, ice cream, and even cosmetics.

Part of the problem may be simply too much of a good thing, such as eating high-gluten bread products (bread, pizza, pasta, muffins, cakes, cookies, bagels) several times a day.

Eating more fruits and vegetables in place of wheat-based snacks will aid the ability to digest all foods, including those that naturally contain gluten.

Before deciding that stomach pains, bloating, fatigue, and headaches are caused by gluten intolerance, it is advisable to see a health provider. The discomfort may be due to an allergy to wheat, or to a compromised digestive system.

Celiac disease is a disorder that causes genetically susceptible individuals to respond to undigested gluten. If gluten passes from the stomach into the small intestine without being broken down, it can flatten the villi, the tiny finger-like projections that absorb nutrients and deliver them to the bloodstream. Stomach discomfort results when the flattened villi can no longer do their work. When this becomes a chronic condition, celiac disease results.

Many people who are allergic to wheat, or have gluten intolerance or celiac disease, choose to follow a gluten-free diet. They would do well to eat natural foods, such as fruits and vegetables, nuts, fish and red meats. We would not recommend that they turn to packaged foods, such as cake and brownie mixes, granola bars, and breakfast cereals that advertise themselves as "gluten free."

These highly-processed foods often contain added sugars, fats, petroleum-derived additives and chemicals. They are low in dietary fiber and high in sodium. And they are expensive. A loaf of "gluten free" bread can have more than 20 ingredients and cost 2-3 times as much as a traditional loaf.

It is not difficult to find alternative grains and flours, such as rice, millet, buckwheat, quinoa, polenta, cornmeal, and oatmeal, for example. Or better yet, grow your own heritage wheat that contains lower levels of gluten or purchase it from a local gardener or farmer. We grow pre-Green Revolution grains, which have not been bred to produce more gluten. We grind the grains as we need them for bread.

Gluten-free Cereal

Instead of purchasing a ready-made, high-gluten breakfast cereal, make your own granola. Have it for breakfast with milk or yogurt, and give it to the children for a snack.

Granola

3 C regular rolled oats
3 T brown sugar
1/2 t cinnamon
1/4 t salt
1/3 C honey
1/4 C grapeseed oil
1 t vanilla
1 C chopped dried fruit (we use our own dried
pears and plums)
1 C chopped walnuts or almonds

Combine oats, sugar, cinnamon, salt. In a separate
bowl, combine honey, oil, and vanilla, and mix with
oats. Spread mix on a rimmed baking sheet covered
with parchment paper. Bake at 300 for 15 minutes,
then stir by lifting and shifting the parchment paper;
bake 15 minutes more. Add fruits and nuts and toss
to combine. Cool. Store in a glass jar.

Fermented Bread

Gluten is digested in the fermentation process,
which converts the gluten into harmless peptides
easily absorbed in the stomach and intestines.

We developed a demonstration for our farm class,
in which Henning would take a spoonful of
fermented bread dough, put it in a sieve, and run
water through it. It disappeared down the
drain. Then he would repeat the process with white
flour mixed with water to make an unfermented
dough, and wash it in water as above. The result
was a ping pong ball-sized chunk of gluten.

He would hand it off to the students, and they
found that it behaved like Silly Putty®— you could
stretch it, roll it, smear it over any surface, and it
was indestructible. That's what you get with
conventional bread. Fermenting bread breaks down
the gluten into digestible peptides, which are chains
of amino acids that aid in digesting food.

The recipes below require sourdough starter.
Sourdough is a marvelous thing. A starter can be
handed down from generation to generation.
Pioneer women used to tuck it in bed with them on
cold nights to keep the bacteria alive, and it served
as a rising agent for their biscuits and bread.

You can buy packaged sourdough starter and build
it up, or get a cup from a friend or a local bakery

and keep it going. Whenever we use some, we
rebuild it with equal parts of raw milk and white
flour. Be careful not to fill to the top of the
container, lest it overflow during the night.

Whisk flour and milk, a cup each at a time, into the
starter you have, then set the sourdough out on the
counter overnight, with the cover sufficiently ajar to
allow the bacteria and yeasts in the air to enliven the
starter. When it has increased in volume, cover it
tightly and refrigerate. If there is a film of liquid on
the top when you take it out to use it, you can either
pour it off or stir it in.

You can also make your own sourdough. Just place
a mix of equal parts of milk and flour in a
container on your kitchen counter, and yeasts from
the air will culture the mix in a few days. Watch it
carefully. When the mix is bubbly, it is time to
refrigerate it. Otherwise, the yeasts will devour the
starter and you'll have a dead mix.

This process is a good example of just how local
real foods are. A few years ago, there was a big to-
do about San Francisco sourdough bread. What
people didn't pay attention to is that San Francisco
sourdough is possible only in San Francisco — each
locale has different yeasts in the air, and
sourdough imported from elsewhere will soon
take on the qualities of its new location. That's
terroir!

Some people use rye instead of wheat flour because
it absorbs moisture more readily, and it attracts
more wild yeast. Others use water from cooked
potatoes instead of milk.

Sourdough Breads

The bread we eat on a daily basis is mostly long-
fermented in order to neutralize the effects of the
gluten needed to structure the dough.

Rye Bread
This bread requires two steps, but produces four
delicious loaves. It is better to make this bread over
two days, so that it has a chance to "sour"
(ferment) and the result will be more flavorful; but
in a pinch, you can make the whole thing in one
day.

For the Starter:
5 C sourdough

1 bottle dark beer
1 C dark molasses
5 t salt
2 lb dark rye organic flour
2 T caraway seed

For the Dough:
5 C organic white flour
5 T granulated yeast
4 C warm water (115 degrees)
2 T sugar
Olive oil, as needed

The more water you use, the more flour you will need. If you want more rye flavor in your bread, cut down on the water.

To Make the Starter, mix after adding each ingredient. Cover the starter with a towel and leave it overnight.

To Make the Dough. In a small bowl, combine water and sugar, and sprinkle the yeast over the top. Whisk the yeast in briefly, and allow to proof. Pour the yeast mixture into the starter, mix thoroughly, and begin stirring in white flour, cup by cup, until the dough is too stiff to stir any longer. Turn onto a well-floured countertop and knead, adding flour as necessary. Knead until the ball of dough is glossy, firm, and "alive" — when you poke a finger into it, the indentation should spring back.

Wash and dry the bowl, coat with olive oil, place the dough in it and turn to coat. Cover and keep in a warm place until double in bulk. Turn the dough onto the floured countertop and cut into four equal portions. Knead each thoroughly, being sure to work out any fissures that would turn into cracks during baking. Place each loaf in a greased baking pan, cover, and let rise to the tops of the pans. Slash the tops. Bake at 350 for about 40 minutes. If the bread seems soft on the bottom, remove from pans, put on oven rack, turn the oven off and let the bread finish baking. Cool on racks. Freeze extra loaves.

Oh So Sour Dough Bread
This is a variation on the recipe above. It requires more time, which means more fermentation, and the result is a firm, deeply flavorful bread.

Day One:
5 C sourdough starter

1 bottle dark beer
1 C dark molasses
5 t salt
2 lb dark organic rye flour
2 T caraway seed

Add these ingredients one by one in a large bowl, mixing thoroughly after each addition. Cover with a towel, and let it sit on your kitchen counter.

Day Two:
Do nothing. Let the dough sit, sour, and take in all the healthy yeasts from the air.

Day Three:
3 T granulated yeast
1 C warm water
1 T sugar
3 or more C white flour
Olive oil, as needed

Proof the yeast in warm water and sugar. Stir it into the dough, which will have developed a nice dark crust. Stir in additional white flour, one cup at a time. Turn the dough onto a floured countertop, knead briefly, and form it into a ball. Wash and dry the bowl and coat with olive oil. Return the dough to the bowl, turn to coat, place it on the counter, and cover with a towel.

Day Four:
When the dough has doubled in bulk, place on a floured countertop, divide into quarters, and shape into loaves. Knead as little as possible. Place loaves in pans that have been coated with olive oil, put them in a warm spot, and allow to rise. It will rise more while baking.

Bake at 350 for 40 minutes. If the bottom of the bread seems soft, remove from pans, turn oven off, and put loaves on racks for final firming.

Whole Wheat Sourdough Pancakes
These pancakes are wholesome, delicious, and filling. They have a nut-like flavor, and we like to top them with strawberry jam and yogurt.

3 eggs
1 C milk
2 C sourdough
1 T baking soda
2 t baking powder
1/3 t salt
1 T grapeseed or other vegetable oil

1/4 C sugar
1 3/4 C whole wheat flour

Mix all ingredients thoroughly, cook in a non-stick pan, and enjoy! We find these keep beautifully for next-day breakfasts or snacks.

Wood-Fired Oven Pizza, Bread and Roast

About ten years ago, we built a wood-fired oven on our deck. We cut alder wood from the forest to heat it, because alder has little sap that would coat the baking surface in the oven.

We start the fire early in the morning, monitoring the heat with a handheld temperature gun, and adding wood during the morning as needed. When the temperature reaches 1000 degrees, we sweep the burning wood to the back of the oven, then sweep the floor of the oven with a stiff broom to clean away ashes. We check the temperature and bake the pizza.

By the time the pizza is done, the oven is at about 500 degrees, and it is time to put in rounds of bread, which take about 60 minutes to bake. The size of our oven allows us to bake up to twenty 1-pound loaves at a time.

When the bread is out and cooling, we put in a roast in a cast iron pot, and let the meat cook until it is fork-tender. We remove the roast, place carrots and potatoes and other root vegetables in the pot and let them cook until done. The process creates an all-day feast.

At the end of the day, the internal temperature is about 70 degrees, and we place cultured milk in the oven to turn into yogurt or quark over night. We love to have gatherings: summer parties are always celebrated with wood-fired pizza.

Mary's Farm Pizza

We found that because the dough was fermented, our interns or farm guests who were gluten intolerant could eat this pizza without any discomfort. For convenience, we make pizza using our usual sourdough starter. However, a better pizza is made with a special starter prepared just for pizza (see below). We usually make more dough than we need for one meal and freeze the rest.

For the Dough:
1 1/2 C sourdough or special pizza starter
1 1/2 C flour, including some whole grain flour if you like
1 T olive oil
1 t salt

For the Special Pizza Starter:
1 1/4 C room-temperature water
1 t granulated yeast
1 small t honey
1 3/4 C flour

To Make the Special Starter:
Mix water, yeast, honey and flour in a lidded container, leave on the counter for several hours, then refrigerate overnight.

To Prepare the Dough:
Mix starter of your choice with all the other ingredients in a bowl to form a ball. Cover and let rest for two hours to rise and ferment. Divide into small rounds, each weighing about 4-5 ounces, wrap individually in plastic wrap, and let rest in the refrigerator for 24-48 hours.

Remove from refrigerator and let warm for two hours. If using the home oven, place a pizza stone in the oven and preheat it to 500 degrees. If using a gas- or wood-fired pizza oven, heat the oven to an internal temperature of 700-800 degrees.

Place a ball of dough in a bowl of flour, turn to coat, then put on a floured work surface. With your fingers, press the dough from the center outward to make a round, lift it up by the edge and let gravity extend the dough as you turn it. Then use a rolling pin to flatten the dough to about 1/2 inch thick, rotating it frequently.Transfer the finished dough to a well-floured pizza peel (or, in a pinch, a baking sheet).

If using your home oven, slide the dough onto the preheated pizza stone (or baking sheet) sprinkled with cornmeal. Bake about 10 minutes, or until golden brown.

If using a pizza oven, slide pizza from the peel directly onto the baking surface. In either case, it is helpful to use a second peel to slide the pizza dough into the oven. Rotate the pizza as it bakes to ensure even browning. In a 700-800 degree pizza oven, the pizza will bake in a minute or two.

Toppings can be added before or after baking, depending on the recipe. Brush the crust with olive oil. We use homemade basil and tomato sauce, homemade mozzarella, and fresh basil.

We have also used spiced hamburger, sautéed red onions, Kalamata olives, thinly sliced garlic, pesto, and fresh or dried tomatoes.

We believe that "less is more" — with a really good crust, tomato sauce and cheese are enough. A good tomato sauce can be made by puréeing a quart jar of home-canned tomatoes with an immersion blender and adding salt, pepper and fresh herbs, plus a squirt of olive oil, to taste.

To Freeze the Pizza Dough:
When the dough has been divided into 4-5 ounce rounds, but has not yet fermented and risen, place rounds in a baking pan with a 2-inch high edge, leaving a space two fingers wide between them. Wrap the whole pan with plastic wrap and place in the freezer for a couple of hours. When frozen, use a spatula to remove the rounds from the baking pan, put them in separate zip-lock bags and return to the freezer for up to four months before using.

Take the dough rounds out of the freezer the day before making pizza and place them in a baking pan dusted with semolina, and sprinkle a few grains of semolina on top of each round. Wrap the whole pan with plastic wrap and place in the refrigerator to thaw. Remove from the refrigerator an hour before making the pizza.

Neapolitan Pizza
This is a more ambitious pizza with a crusty raised edge, well worth the extra time it takes to make it.

For the Dough:
5 1/2 C warm water
7 t sea salt
12 C organic flour
Grated Parmesan, as needed
Fresh mozzarella, cut into 1-inch slices and cubed to 1/2 inch, as needed
Basil leaves, torn

For the Special Pizza Starter:
1 1/4 C room-temperature water
1 t granulated yeast
1 small t honey

1 3/4 C flour

To Prepare the Starter:
Mix water, yeast, honey and flour in a lidded container, leave on counter for several hours, then refrigerate overnight.

To Prepare the Dough:
In a bowl, mix the Special Starter with the water, stir in half the flour and the salt and then the other half of the flour.

Scrape the dough from the bowl onto a dusted work surface, press with one hand, fold over, repeat several times, then cover (with a bowl) and let rest for 15 minutes.

Put some drops of olive oil on your hands, then with a scraper circle the dough. Make a ball by lifting the dough from two sides and letting it fall over itself. Repeat, always leaving the top on top, to make a soft, tender ball.

Put some oil in a bowl, slide the ball into the bowl, cover, and let rest for 20 minutes.

Turn the dough onto a dusted work surface, and with the scraper cut into three elongated sections. Turn the edges under to make into three rolls.

Taking a roll of dough in one hand, squeeze out eight to ten 4-inch rounds above your fist, each weighing about 4-5 ounces. Place the rounds in a floured baking pan with a raised edge, two fingers apart. Wrap the pan with cellophane and let the dough rise for 2 hours at room temperature, or freeze (see above).

The dough is ready for making the pizza when the rounds attach to each other in the pan. Coat the edge of the scraper by dipping it into semolina, lift a round from the pan and place on a dusted work surface.

With your fingers press the dough from the center outward to the sides, leaving a raised edge. Flip it over and back again, so the top of the round ends up back on top. If sticky, add a little more semolina.

Pressing the dough with one hand, pull it sideways with the other to enlarge the round to 8-10 inches. Repeat, turning the round.

Then, placing both open fists underneath the round, pull it apart while turning the pizza, with the top staying on top.

Spread the tomato sauce (see above) on the pizza, and with the peel place it in the 700-800 degree pizza oven to bake for 1-2 minutes, until golden.

With the peel, remove the pizza from the oven, generously sprinkle with Parmesan, the cubed mozzarella, and a little olive oil.

Return pizza to oven and bake until crusty, rotating it so it browns on all sides. Remove from oven, add torn basil leaves and serve.

Pasta

Traditional pasta is made from hard wheats, particularly semolina, which contains high levels of gluten, the protein that gives pasta its desired texture. In Mediterranean Europe this has not been a problem historically because the genetic vulnerability to gluten intolerance and celiac disease is a characteristic of northern Europe, where 30-40% of the population carry the predisposing gene. By contrast, in southern Europe (as well as Africa and most of Asia) the vulnerability rate is negligible.

Given the nomadic lifestyle and ethnic blending in the modern world, however, celiac disease has become ubiquitous, exacerbated by a general decline in nutritional quality of foods due to their denaturing by processing and long-distance shipping.

In Italy, the traditional home of pasta, and in Canada, food researchers have taken note of this shift, and long-fermented pasta has emerged in response to gluten intolerance. A Canadian company, Kaslo Sourdough, now markets *Pasta Fermentata,* the first commercial sourdough pasta that "brings a delicious and healthy solution for your gastronomic difficulty."

However, we often make our own, as time allows, simply because homemade pasta, made and eaten immediately, is superior in flavor and digestibility.

We make spaghetti, linguini, lasagna and fettuccini from semolina flour by using a simple Italian-made pasta machine. We also like spätzle, the southern German or Austrian equivalent of pasta, made by various methods.

Fermented Pasta
1/2 C sourdough starter
1 1/2 C semolina flour
2 eggs, beaten
Milk, as needed
2 T olive oil
Cornmeal for dredging the pasta

Mix the sourdough starter and flour in a bowl, cover and let ferment on the counter overnight.

The next day, pour the fermented mixture and the eggs into the bowl of a mixer with a dough hook and mix until it forms a ball. Or, if you prefer to do this by hand, mix the ingredients in a bowl and knead 10 minutes or more until the dough is elastic, and then shape it into a ball.

Wrap the dough in plastic and let it rest for 30 minutes.

On a dusted work surface, briefly knead the dough and cut into 1/2-inch slices, and pass each slice several times through the flat rollers of the pasta machine set at positions 1-5 until desired thickness is achieved. Attach the fettuccini, spaghetti, or other cutters to the machine and cut the dough slices into the long ribbons of finished pasta.

Alternatively, roll out the dough with a rolling pin to desired thickness and cut into noodles by hand.

Layer the noodle ribbons in an oblong dish dusted with cornmeal to keep the pasta from sticking. When all the pasta is cut, drop into boiling salted water with a little olive oil added; cook to desired tenderness.

Find various sauces for pasta in the *List of Recipes.*

Spätzle

Spätzle is made from bits of dough cut with a knife, made with a spätzle maker, or pressed through a ricer. The spätzle maker consists of a perforated grater topped with a cup-sized funnel into which you ladle the soft batter. As the funnel slides back and forth across the grater, the batter falls into the boiling water and cooks in a couple of minutes. The ricer is a perforated cup with a plunger to push the dough through the perforations.

We have tried all three methods of making spätzle with fermented dough. The simplest, which calls for only three ingredients for the dough (sourdough starter, flour and a little warm water) makes a stiff dough that is best cut into small pieces with a knife and cooked.

Knife-Cut Fermented Spätzle
2/3 C sourdough starter
2 cups organic flour
1/3 C warm water, as needed

4-5 T butter
1/4 t each salt, pepper, and garlic granules
4 T minced parsley

Mix sourdough starter, flour and enough water to make a stiff dough. Knead briefly, coat lightly with oil, wrap loosely in plastic wrap, place in a bowl and and let ferment on the counter overnight.

The next day, briefly knead and roll out into long 1/2-inch thick rolls. Cut into 1/4-inch pieces and drop into boiling salted water. Cook for about 15 minutes until firm but tender. Stir occasionally to keep spätzle from sticking together.

Drain, place in a bowl, stir in butter, salt, pepper, garlic granules, and parsley.

Fermented Spätzle Made With Spätzle Maker or Ricer
2/3 C sourdough
2 C organic flour
4 eggs, beaten
Warm milk as needed
Butter and spices as above

Mix sourdough with beaten eggs and flour to make a soft batter. Place in a covered bowl and ferment on counter overnight.

The next day, stir the batter, add milk or additional flour as needed to make a thick batter. Pour the batter one large ladle at a time into the funnel of the spätzle maker on top of a pot of boiling salted water, and cook the spätzle for 1-2 minutes, stirring occasionally. Remove the cooked spätzle, set aside, and repeat until all the batter is used.

Mix with butter, parsley and spices, and serve. To make the spätzle with a ricer, add enough additional flour to make a soft dough and press through a ricer into the boiling water. Cook as above, mix with butter, parsley and spices, and serve.

Spätzle Frittata
Freshly-made spätzle, with butter, spices and parsley added (as above)
4 eggs, beaten
1 C sliced mushrooms
1/2 C minced onion

Sauté the onions and mushrooms in olive oil and butter in a non-stick pan. When the onion is translucent, add eggs and cook until set. Spread the spätzle over the top and gently lift the egg mixture to test for brownness. Serve at once.

Notes:

Keeping the Harvest

There are many good reasons for preserving food. First, you know what is in those jars, freezer bags, or sausages, because you put it there; no need to be concerned about can liners or lists of un-pronounceable chemicals on the labels (see *Why Avoid Commercially Canned Foods* below for a discussion of commercial can liners).

Second, you help mitigate climate change. 40% of all the food raised in this country never reaches the home table. Instead, it it is scraped off plates in restaurants, or disposed of by grocery stores as blemished or out of date. If food is fed to animals or put on the compost pile, the captured carbon turns into a source of fertility; if it is put into a landfill wrapped in plastic, anaerobic decomposition turns the food into methane, a greenhouse gas whose warming effects are fifty-six times those of CO_2. The U.S. has higher levels of climate-changing emissions from landfills than any other country, putting out the equivalent of the emissions from thirty-seven million cars on the road each year.

Third, by preserving the harvest of spring, summer, and fall, you will have the fruits of the growing season available in winter when garden and field are dormant. Pull a jar of home-canned tomatoes off the shelf, add some herbs and spices, heat it and pour over homemade pasta. A nutritious meal in minutes!

We can, dry, ferment, freeze, juice, pickle, salt, and dry-store foods to be consumed during the non-growing season. All of these methods are safe if you pay attention to cleanliness, acid levels, temperature, processing time, and appropriate equipment and methods.

Besides making foods available during the time of year when you cannot grow them, many processing methods enhance the flavors and digestibility of foods and allow them to be stored for a long time. A pickle, for example, is a cucumber that provides flavor for years, and a good cheese unlocks the potential of fresh milk. Dried fruits are a wonderful snack for children after school or on a camping trip. A slice of long-fermented sourdough rye bread with homemade butter is a meal in itself.

Canning

Canning is a form of pasteurization. As we noted in *Dairy*, pasteurizing milk dramatically reduces its vitamin content and the availability of its minerals, and it destroys the enzymes that metabolize the life in the food. Put plainly, a food without enzymes is dead. This is why processed foods are on some level nutritionally deficient.

We nevertheless recommend canning foods because they supply flavors and fibers we crave in winter. Furthermore, the minerals, along with some fat-soluble vitamins, proteins, fats and carbohydrates remain relatively unchanged by the process of canning.

High-acid foods, such as fruits, can be safely preserved by using a water-bath canner. Foods need to have a pH level of 4.6 or lower for water-bath canning without an acidifier. Low-acid foods, as, for example, most vegetables, have pH levels from 4.6 to 6.9 and require an acidifier, either lemon juice or vinegar.

Plan your garden according to your needs for preserved as well as fresh foods. How many tomatoes will you need for canning and saucing in addition to fresh tomatoes? How many cucumbers will you need for pickling? If you do not have a garden, local farmers can supply you. Imperfect fruits and vegetables that cannot be sold to restaurants, grocery stores, or at the farmers market will be excellent for home preserving.

Water-Bath Canning

There are many good canning books available: our standbys are Rodale's *Stocking Up*, Ferrari's *Canning and Preserving*, and Ball Blue Book's *Guide to Preserving*. Do not use old canning books: today's vegetables, especially hybrids, may be lower in acid than vegetables grown even ten years ago, which means you will need an acidifier for safe canning. Older books also often recommend undesirably long blanching times. If in any doubt about safety, equipment, or procedures, call your local extension agent or the producers of your canning jars.

Before you start, consult any good canning book for a complete description of the canning process and safety procedures. Here is a summary of the steps we have learned to follow (sometimes the hard way) over time:

Use a standard water-bath canner with a stainless steel rack (aluminum racks will rust). Use only Mason or Ball jars, made to withstand high heat. Use only new metal lids; screw bands, however, if clean and rust-free, can be used multiple times.

To sterilize jars, wash them in hot, soapy water, rinse, and then place them in warm water in the canner. Add a splash of vinegar to the canning water to prevent calcium deposits on the jars or the canner. Bring the water to a boil, and boil jars 10 minutes.

Using a jar lifter, drain each jar into the canner and place on a clean towel. Place rings and lids in a small pan, and cover with boiling water (do not boil them on the stove). Let them sit in the water until ready to use, at least 5 minutes.

Have the food, jars, and water about the same temperature. This prevents breakage from temperature change. Fill the jars with food, remove air pockets with a plastic spatula, and pay attention to the recipe's required headroom (the space between the food and the rim of the jar).

Clean the rim of each jar with a clean paper towel, cover with a lid and a band you make fingertip tight. Place the filled jars in the warm water in the canner, being sure the top of the jar is covered by at least two inches of water.

Turn the burner to high, and when the water begins to boil, turn the heat to medium — the water will keep boiling for the recommended time. When the time is up, turn the burner off and let the jars cool in the canner until you can comfortably lift them out with your hand.

To remove the jars while still hot invites breakage and overflow because of temperature change. Allow 12 hours for a complete seal. If you press the lid and it pops up again, the seal is incomplete and the jar must be reprocessed or the food used right away. When you store the jars, remove the band. It is no longer necessary, and will rust if left on the jar.

Water-Bath Canning for Fruit

Fruit is sufficiently high in acid that bacteria is destroyed in a water-bath canner. For some fruits, you can use a light or medium syrup as a sweetener. A light syrup contains 2 1/2 cups sugar and 5 1/2 cups water; the yield is 6 1/2 cups. A heavy syrup contains 3 1/4 cups sugar and 5 cups water; the yield is 7 cups.

Applesauce

Applesauce is easy to make. You can spice it up with sugar, cinnamon, nutmeg, and salt, but we find that flavorful apples are fine without the additions. Just wash, core and chop the apples (no need to peel), put them in a large pan with a little water, and start cooking them gently. Stir frequently, adding more chopped apples until you have the desired texture. Follow canning procedures using a spatula to push apples down into jars and eliminate air pockets. Leave 1/2 inch head room. Process pint or quart jars for 20 minutes.

Canned Cherries

6-7 lb cherries
Water, light or heavy syrup, as desired

Wash and stem the cherries. Sweet or sour cherries can be canned in water, or covered with a light or heavy syrup. We prefer to process the cherries whole, but you can pit the fruit, using a chopstick to remove the pits.

Pack the fruit into sterile jars and cover with liquid, leaving 1/2-inch head room. Clean rims and seal. Process 25 minutes. Makes 6 pints.

Canned Peaches

We prefer to eat our peaches fresh; however, if there is a large harvest, we process them. You can make all kinds of jams and chutneys with peaches. We like the simplest recipe, which calls for 2-3 pounds of peaches per quart, with light or heavy syrup.

Wash peaches; dip briefly in boiling water, place immediately in cold water and slip off the peel. Cut in halves or quarters, remove pit. Make a light or heavy syrup and keep hot. Pack peaches cavity-side down in hot jars and ladle hot syrup over, leaving 1/2-inch headroom. Remove air bubbles. Clean rims and seal. Process pints 25 minutes, quarts 30 minutes.

Canned Pears

We like to eat pears fresh, and will store them for a time layered in newspaper in a cool place.

Be aware that since pears mature from the inside out, they can look and feel fine on the outside but be too soft on the inside. Dry (see instructions in this section) or can them while they are still firm. Canning books have recipes for mincemeat or brandied pears.

6-9 lb pears (18-27 medium-size pears)
Light or medium syrup (see under *Water-Bath Canning for Fruit*).

Wash and peel pears. Cut in halves or quarters and core. Prepare syrup. Place pears, cut-side down, overlapping, in hot, prepared jars. Pour syrup over, leaving 1/2-inch headroom. Remove air bubbles. Clean rims and seal. Process pint jars 20 minutes and quarts 25 minutes. Makes 6 pints or 3 quarts.

Tomatoes

Tomatoes make wonderful canned foods. They are medium on the scale of acidity, so should always have an acidifier. We use 1 tablespoon bottled lemon juice for pints, and 2 tablespoons bottled lemon juice for quarts.

Basil and Tomato Sauce

This is the sauce we use for spaghetti, pizza, lasagna, and other pasta dishes.

3 T olive oil
3 onions, minced
3 garlic cloves, minced
2 T fresh basil, chopped, or 1 T dried basil
3 T minced parsley
4 lb tomatoes (25-30 tomatoes), cored and chopped
2 t each salt and pepper
1 1/2 t sugar

Add oil to 6-quart pot. Mince onions and garlic in a food processor and sauté in oil until transparent. Process tomatoes to the consistency of juice. Add to pot with onions and herbs. Add the rest of the ingredients and blend well. Cook on low heat for 1 1/2 hours, stirring often. When sauce is done, ladle into hot jars, and add 2 tablespoons lemon juice per quart, leaving 1/2-inch headroom. Clean rims and seal. Process 45 minutes. Makes 6 quarts.

Canned Tomatoes

Canned tomatoes are a part of our weekly menu. We use them in chili, casseroles, and in some fish and meat dishes.

3 lb tomatoes per quart jar
Bottled lemon juice

Clean, core, and chop tomatoes. Pack tomatoes into hot jars, pressing them down until liquid covers the tomatoes. Add 2 tablespoons lemon juice per quart, leaving 1/2-inch headroom. Remove air bubbles, clean rims and seal. Process 45 minutes.

Chili Sauce

We use chili sauce on meat dishes, such as pork ribs, and on wraps, tacos, eggs, rice, and in casseroles.
4 quarts chopped fresh tomatoes (about 24 large)
2 C each chopped onions and sweet red peppers
1 hot red pepper, seeded and diced
1 C sugar

3 T each salt and mixed pickling spices
1 T each celery seed and yellow mustard seed
2 1/2 C vinegar (no need to use lemon juice)

Combine tomatoes, onions, peppers, sugar, and salt in a sauce pot. Cook gently 45 minutes. Tie spices in a spice bag or cheesecloth and add to mixture. Cook until mixture is reduced by one half, about 45 minutes. Stir as sauce thickens. Add vinegar and cook slowly until as thick as desired. Remove spices. Ladle hot sauce into hot jars, leaving 1/4-inch headroom. Clean rims and seal. Process 15 minutes. Makes about 6 pints.

Canned Tomato Soup

6 onions
1 bunch celery
1 head garlic
2 medium zucchini
4 T olive oil (for sautéing)
1 large bowl tomatoes (about 25 tomatoes)
1 large handful fresh basil leaves
4 bay leaves
1 large sprig oregano (6 inches long)
1 medium sprig rosemary (4 inches long)
Salt, pepper, sugar or honey, to taste

Chop onions, celery, garlic and zucchini in food processor. Sauté in olive oil in a large pot. When vegetables are soft, puree tomatoes and basil in the food processor and add to the pot. Let simmer several hours until thick and smooth. Toward the end of cooking, add the bay leaves and sprigs of oregano and rosemary and let simmer.

Check the taste after 20 minutes and remove the bay leaves and sprigs or let simmer a little longer to strengthen the herbal flavor. Season to taste with salt, pepper, sugar or honey.

Add 2 tablespoons lemon juice to each sterilized quart jar. Fill to 1/2 inch from top, remove air pockets, clean rims and seal. Process 50 minutes, following protocol for water-bath canning, above. Let cool in the canner, then remove the jars from the canner. Remove rings when the jars are cool and ready to store.

This soup is a concentrate, and can be thinned with milk. We find that adding a little cream at the table smooths the flavor and texture wonderfully.

Ketchup

4 qt chopped tomatoes (about 24 large)
1 C chopped onion
1/2 C chopped sweet red pepper
1 1/2 t celery seed
1 t each whole allspice and mustard seed
1 stick cinnamon
1 C sugar
1 T each salt and paprika
1 1/2 C vinegar

Cook tomatoes, onion and pepper until soft; puree in a food processor. Cook pulp until thick and reduced by 1/2, about an hour. Tie whole spices in a spice bag or cheesecloth. Add spice bag, sugar, salt and paprika to tomato mixture. Cook gently about 25 minutes, stirring frequently. Add vinegar; cook until thick, stirring as needed. Remove spice bag; adjust seasoning to taste.

Ladle into hot, sterile jars, leaving 1/4-inch headroom. Clean rims and seal. Process 10 minutes; let cool in canner.

Salsa

As well as all the other uses for salsa, we add it to cooked beans.

3 1/2 lb tomatoes (16-17 medium) diced
2 onions, diced
2 t salt
1 t pepper
2 T each lemon juice and chopped cilantro
1/2 C vinegar
1 1/2 t cayenne pepper

Combine all ingredients and mix well. Heat salsa until just hot. Ladle into hot jars, leaving 1/2-inch head room. Clean rims and seal. Process 45 minutes.

Pressure Canning

Pressure canning is necessary for low-acid foods, such as meat, poultry, and seafood. We use the pressure canner to make pork, beef, chicken, lamb, and turkey broth, and canned beans. Every year, we check the ring and plug (the rubber parts of the canner) and the pressure gauge. Some hardware stores or county extension agents will check the pressure gauge for you. Never immerse it in water. Be sure to read the instruction book before using the canner.

Broths

To make broth, simmer bones in a large pot for about three days in order to extract the marrow and attain flavor. Add half an onion, several cloves of garlic, a carrot, a stalk of celery with leaves, several peppercorns, and herbs such as basil, bay leaf or sage. Do not add salt until using the broth, because salt added during simmering over long periods of time will turn the broth bitter.

When the broth is cooked and flavorful, strain out the solids and ladle the broth into prepared jars. Follow the instructions that come with your canner regarding the amount of water, vinegar, headroom, pressure, and time. As with water-bath canning, turn the burner off when the time is up and let the jars sit in the canner until cool. Remove from water, clean jars as necessary, check for seal, remove rings, label, date, and store.

You can pressure-can many low-acid foods, such as green beans. Consult your canning book.

Why Avoid Commercially Canned Food

Many conventional recipes call for canned beans. We do not purchase them or any commercially canned food, because the liners in the cans, intended to reduce corrosion and keep food fresh, usually contain BPA.

BPA (bisphenol A) is an industrial chemical used to make certain plastics and resins. Polycarbonate plastics are used to line tin cans and other food containers, such as water bottles. BPA, which can seep into the food, is a hormone disruptor, and contributes to cardiovascular problems, endocrine dysfunction, cancer, and diabetes.

In 2010, Canada declared BPA toxic, and banned it from baby bottles, baby drinking containers, and food products sold across the country. In 1998, Japan phased it out from food containers, and in 2012, Sweden did the same. It is still used in the U.S.

There are companies in America (names available on line) that use alternative can liners in order to avoid BPA, but it remains unknown if those substitutes are any safer. We prefer to can our own food not only to avoid toxic can liners, but because we can avoid additives to the food itself. We find home-canned food safer, fresher and better tasting.

Can Your Own Dried Beans

You can process dried beans in a pressure canner, using water or broth. We like to use these for chili; all we have to do is cook hamburger and pull a couple of jars of beans and a quart of canned tomatoes off the shelf.

Per pint:
1/2 C dried beans
1/2 t salt
Boiling water or broth to cover beans

Leave 1-inch headroom. Process at 10 pounds pressure for 75 minutes. This recipe makes a pint of beans and can be doubled for quarts. Process for 90 minutes.

Drying

It is possible to dry foods in the sun, in the oven, or in a dehydrator. Dried vegetables and fruits lose little of their nutritional value. They do lose volatile nutrients like vitamin C and beta carotene, but retain most of their minerals and vitamins A and B.

Each drying process has special requirements. We prefer our dehydrator. There are many kinds of dehydrators, and it's good to do some research to find the one that suits you. We use one that allows us to set temperature and time, and add or subtract trays.

We dry apples, pears, plums, and tomatoes every year, and find the fruit wonderful for snacking or in granola, and the tomatoes useful in a number of dishes. All foods should be thoroughly dried, but leathery rather than desiccated. Follow the directions about temperature and time that come with your dehydrator.

Freeze dried fruits and tomatoes in ziplock bags; residual moisture will cause the food to develop mold if kept on a shelf.

Apples
Core and slice apples thinly. No need to peel. Dip slices in lemon juice to prevent oxidation. Place on dehydrator racks, keeping the slices from touching.

Herbs

We dry many herbs for teas: calendula, catnip, chamomile, marshmallow, mint, nettle (leaves or seeds), rose hips, and sage. These can be placed in the oven on low heat (watched carefully), on a screen in a greenhouse, or on trays in a food dehydrator. Once dried, they can be stored in glass jars.

Pears

Core and slice firm pears thinly; no need to peel. Place on dryer racks, keeping slices from touching.

Plums

The plums you dry should be freestone (the pit comes away from the flesh easily). Wash, pit, and cut thinly. Place on dryer racks, keeping the slices from touching.

Tomatoes

Dried tomatoes are a mainstay in our winter diet, added at the last minute to soups and stews, and used for pizza and focaccia. Steep briefly in olive oil for dishes that require oil-soaked dried tomatoes.

Choose meaty rather than juicy tomatoes, such as Marzano or plum or any other saucing tomato. Slice tomatoes thinly, place on dryer racks over the sink, and sprinkle with dried basil before dehydrating.

Fermentation

Before refrigeration, canning, and freezing became widely available, people preserved meat, fish, fruit, milk, and vegetables by drying, salting, and fermenting. Most people are familiar with fermentation in beer, wine, cheese, sauerkraut, and yogurt, to name the most common examples, and know that it is a process highly beneficial to health.

Fermentation preserves nutrients and breaks food down into more digestible forms. For example, people who cannot drink fresh milk because they are lactose intolerant can digest it in fermented forms, such as quark, yogurt, and kefir.

Some fermenting agents act as antioxidants that remove free radicals from human cells and thereby help prevent cancer.

Fermentation also removes toxins from foods that contain them. For example, all grains contain phytic acid that block the body's absorption of some minerals. Soaking grains before cooking neutralizes the acid. For example, the night before serving oatmeal for breakfast, soak it in water and a tablespoon of whey. The phytic acid will be neutralized and the oats predigested, and will need only warming the next day.

The importance of fermented foods in the diet is appreciated by physicians who use foods to treat or prevent illness. An article in *The Lancet*, the largest medical journal in the English-speaking world, reported on a study done on school children in Sweden. Half attended a Waldorf school, half did not. The researchers found that the children in the Waldorf school had 30-40% fewer allergies, ear infections, asthma, dermatitis, and other skin ailments. The two most important differences between these groups of children were that the Waldorf students regularly consumed raw milk and ate fermented foods.

Do not worry about botulism in fermented foods. Lacto-fermentation is a biological process that creates an environment in which the botulinum bacteria cannot grow.

For more information about the benefits and methods of fermenting foods and a number of easy recipes, see *Wild Fermentation* by Sandor Katz and *Nourishing Traditions* by Sally Fallon. Anyone wishing to reconsider the industrialized diet will find these books thought provoking and useful.

Bean Dip

This was fun to make with students in the Ecological Food Production class that met on the farm. They got to eat the fresh and fermented results, and enjoyed both.

2 C dried black beans
2 T whey or lemon juice
4 cloves garlic, diced

For the Fresh Dip:
Boil beans in water for 1 minute, and let stand off-heat for one hour. This removes the sugars from the beans that make them "gassy." Drain and rinse thoroughly. Place beans in a pot, cover with water, 1 tablespoon whey or lemon juice, dried basil,

chopped garlic and onion, and cook gently until beans are tender. Drain, reserving liquid. When beans are cool, process in a food processor, adding liquid through the feeding tube as necessary until you have a nice paste. Enjoy with chips as a snack or make a burrito by heating bean paste and rolling it up in a tortilla with desired meats and/or vegetables to make a meal.

To Ferment:
Place the prepared bean paste in a glass container, cover securely, and let sit out for three days, then refrigerate. Fermentation adds all of the benefits noted above, and gives the bean paste a pleasant acidic flavor. Eat with chips or tortillas.

Sauerkraut — To Make

Making sauerkraut is a yearly tradition in our household. In Germany it is still considered a superfood, much like daily doses of fermented vegetables in Asian countries. At 27 calories per cup, sauerkraut is loaded with folate, vitamin B6, riboflavin, thiamin, and vitamin K. It provides one third of recommended vitamin C and is rich in minerals such as iron, potassium, and magnesium. Fermentation increases the nutritional benefits of cabbage, making it more digestible and creating probiotic effects in the gut. It is also reported to lower the risk of breast cancer.

It is also disarmingly simple to make. We use a 5-gallon ceramic crock and make a year's supply at a time, but you can make smaller amounts, as well. (See method for Kimchi, below.) You will need six heads of white cabbage, canning or pickling salt, a 5-gallon crock, a large stainless-steel bowl, a scale large enough to hold the bowl, a large cutting board, a good sharp knife, and two turkey-roasting bags with ties.

Soak the cabbage in cold salted water to remove dirt and critters. Remove outer leaves and any parts of the cabbage that have spots. Quarter the cabbage and cut out the core. Slice the cabbage fine, about 1/2-inch thick. Strands that are too thin will become mushy in storage; large chunks will not absorb the liquid.

Place mixing bowl on the scale. For each pound of cut cabbage, add 2 teaspoons of salt and mix well with your hands. Place cabbage in the crock and press it down with your fist, being careful not to bruise the cabbage. Continue until the crock is

nearly full. By the time you are finished, the salt will have begun to draw liquid from the cabbage.

Place the filled crock on a thick folded towel or newspaper in a place where it will remain cool. Temperature is important. The best sauerkraut is made at a temperature below 60 degrees, and takes at least a month of fermentation. It may be cured at higher temperatures in less time, but the kraut will not be as good. We put ours in a storage room in the barn kitchen.

Put one turkey-roaster bag inside another (we use these because they do not leak) and fill with enough water to expand the bag to cover the top of the kraut. Tie them firmly and place over the kraut until the surface is covered.

The next day, check to see if the brine has covered the cabbage. If not, add a brine made of 2 tablespoons salt to 1 quart water, until cabbage is covered. Check the kraut periodically to remove any scum that might have formed on the sides of the crock or the bottom of the bags. The kraut will stay good for nearly a year.

Sauerkraut — To Prepare

When we want sauerkraut for a meal, we use a fork or slotted spoon to remove the desired amount from the crock, carefully replacing the water bags to preserve the anaerobic environment.
To retain the enzymes, warm as little as possible as you prepare sauerkraut for the table. Rinse thoroughly to remove salt.

Sauté a diced onion in olive oil or butter. Add a quart of kraut and sauté briefly. Add a diced apple, a little caraway seed, and white wine (you can use water or broth instead, but the wine lends a subtle taste to the dish). Simmer briefly. We serve sauerkraut with meat that will stand up to its flavor — beef roast or pork chops or homemade Boudin Blanc sausages, for example.

Kimchi

We knew about kimchi as a traditional Asian food, but had never tried it because of its reputation of being spicy-hot. Since we eat northern European foods because we grow them here, we did not think that kimchi would be part of our regular fare, even though sauerkraut, its milder cousin, is a common dish on our table. Then Jesse Pizzitola, one of our apprentices, gave us a jar of kimchi he had made. It was so flavorful, without being too spicy for our palates, that it became a favorite condiment.

For nutritional information and general guidelines to fermenting cabbage, see *Sauerkraut*.

The lovely thing about making kimchi is that you can vary it as you like — more garlic, hotter peppers, less onion, more cabbage — it all depends on your taste. This is the recipe Jesse passed on to us:

1 head white cabbage, finely chopped
2 t salt for every pound of cabbage
1 inch or more of fresh ginger peeled and diced
4 cloves garlic, diced
1 Anaheim pepper, seeded and diced
1 large onion, minced
Ground black pepper, to taste

Chop the cabbage, mix with salt, and let it sit until the salt begins to draw liquid from the cabbage. Add the rest of the vegetables and the pepper, mix well, and put into a half-gallon glass jar. Depress the vegetables to immerse them in liquid. Place a half-pint, lidded jar filled with water on top of the vegetables to immerse them, and screw a lid on top of the half-gallon jar.

Place newspapers under the jars in case of overflow. Store in a cool spot for a week or more, until the vegetables have a mellow taste, then remove the small jar and refrigerate. Before serving, rinse with cold water to get rid of the salt. Enjoy with meat and potatoes, sandwiches, or hamburgers, for example.

Kimchi with Red Cabbage

3 lb red cabbage, finely chopped
1 each red, yellow, and green pepper, plus 1 Anaheim pepper, seeds and membrane removed, chopped
Various hot peppers, seeded and minced, if you want the mix to be spicy
5 small carrots, scrubbed and chopped
1-2 onions, chopped
5 cloves garlic, chopped
Fresh ginger root, 1-2 inches, peeled and minced
Sea or kosher salt

For the Brine:
Use enough water to cover vegetables in quart jars, and use 1 tablespoon salt for every cup of water. Mix to dissolve salt.

Mix vegetables, pack into jars, and cover with brine, leaving two inches of headroom. Cover with lid and place in a cool area for a week or more to ferment. Place newspapers under the jars in case of overflow. If making Kimchi from red instead of white cabbage, it is advisable to open the lid every day to release CO_2. Store in refrigerator after a week or so.

Rinse well to remove salt before serving.

Freezing

This is one of the best ways to keep vegetables and berries because it preserves all the nutrients, including the enzymes. However, we blanch the vegetables in order to slow enzyme action for longevity of the frozen food and prevent loss of flavor, color, and texture. We freeze berries, broccoli, cauliflower, corn, leeks, garlic, peas, pumpkins, rhubarb, spinach, squash, tomatoes, and zucchini every summer for winter consumption.

Almost all vegetables should be blanched before freezing by brief immersion in boiling water. Blanching time is very important and varies with the kind of vegetable and the size of the pieces. Too little blanching stimulates the activity of enzymes and is worse than no blanching. Greens, such as spinach, can be stir-fried rather than blanched for a better product. Leeks and peppers can be frozen without blanching; they are the exception, although leeks will last longer in the freezer if briefly blanched, and their texture will be softer.

Berries
We freeze strawberries, blackberries, raspberries, blueberries, gooseberries, and black and red currants right after picking, just removing the stems and any dirt. Berries are frozen without blanching, which would destroy their texture. They can be defrosted to eat over yogurt or by themselves, served over desserts, juiced, or made into jam.

Broccoli & Cauliflower
Soak the heads in salted water. Cut stalk and break florets into small pieces. Blanch for three minutes or steam for five; plunge into cold water to stop

cooking process. Drain, let dry, and place into freezer bags. Use for soup or casseroles.

Corn

Freezing corn should be done in a single process to preserve the sugars. Pick and shuck the ears, removing silk. Place the ears in boiling water until a kernel can easily be pierced with a knife — about 3 minutes. Using tongs, remove ears from the water and immerse in cold water so that cooking action is stopped. Holding the ear on a cutting board, remove kernels with a sharp knife, and place in a colander to drain liquid. Place in freezer bags and enjoy all winter.

A really nifty alternative to this method is to roast the corn on the cob, in the husks. Remove outer leaves from the fresh corn, retaining only the leaves closest to the cob. Place in a single layer on a baking sheet, and roast at 400 degrees for about 30 minutes. Remove cobs from oven, cool, and peel off remaining leaves. Cut kernels from cob, and place into freezer bags.

Leeks

In mild winters, we keep leeks in the soil because they are not subject to predation by rodents or worms. However, leeks can also be frozen to use as a side vegetable or for soup. Trim and clean them, using white and light green parts only. Cut thinly, blanch briefly (no more than 50 seconds) and put in freezer bags.

Peas

Pick peas every day so you can shell and freeze them as soon as you have a good quantity. Place peas in a colander immersed in boiling water. When they pop to the surface, place them in another colander immersed in cold water. When they are cold, put them to drain in a third colander and when they are dry, pour them into freezer bags and freeze for winter consumption.

Garlic

You can store garlic in a braid in the kitchen, snipping off heads as you want them. You can also roast and freeze garlic for adding to soups and stews. Wash and peel several heads of garlic. Place in an oven-proof pot, such as a Dutch oven, lightly cover with olive oil, cover the pot, and roast at 400 degrees until the garlic cloves are soft. Remove, cool, mash, and spoon into ice-cube trays. When

they are frozen, place them in freezer bags to be used in soups, stews, and casseroles.

Rhubarb

Rhubarb, a vegetable that is used as a fruit, can be frozen just by cutting the stalks into 1-inch pieces, and putting them in freezer bags. They maintain their texture so well that we steam them a little before using them in pies.

Spinach & Other Tender Greens

We grow kale, chard and mâche all year long in the garden, and tender greens such arugula, lettuce and mustard in the greenhouse. All can be eaten fresh or frozen (except lettuce which will turn to mush by freezing). Kale is best after a frost which accelerates the sugars in the leaves. Other greens such as spinach and Asian greens need to be blanched or steamed for 2 minutes, followed by soaking in cold water for the same amount of time. Drain, dry and put into freezer bags.

Squash

Cut squash or pumpkins in halves or quarters, and remove seeds. Bake at 400 until you can slide a knife through the flesh easily. Slip off the peel, and cut flesh into chunks and freeze, or process it for pies or soups and freeze in desired amounts.

Zucchini

Zucchini does not need to be blanched. We shred the zucchini and freeze it in ziplock bags to use for soups or breads all winter.

Juicing

Apples and pears should be processed in a cider press. Many communities gather around a single press, bring their fruit, help with the pressing, and take away a share of the juice. The juice needs to be processed in a water-bath canner for 10 minutes for storage, or refrigerated if you will use it right away. Juice can also be frozen in plastic food-grade jugs.

Apple Cider & Vinegar

We have fermented apple juice into fizzy light wine by adding a few grains of salt to juice that has been separated from the solids by siphoning it off with a rubber tube. Place the juice in a wide-mouth wine bottle, cover with cheesecloth, and refrigerate for several days until the juice clarifies to a golden color.

You can make hard cider by placing siphoned juice into a carboy jug topped with an airlock or cheesecloth folded into several layers to keep out fruit flies. The longer you let the cider sit, the more alcohol it will develop.

Vinegar is basically hard cider that has been allowed to ferment longer. To accelerate the process you can add a starter, called a "mother," (also known as "SCOBY," the acronym for symbiotic culture of bacteria and yeast) by either using the dregs from last year's vinegar production or making it new by fermenting whole apples.

Whole Apple Vinegar

35 fresh apples
1 t raw sugar per apple, dissolved in filtered water
2-gallon sterilized glass jar

Cut the apples into chunks including cores and peels. Place in the glass jar, add dissolved sugar, and fill jar with filtered water to cover the apples. With a wooden spoon, push the apples below the surface of the liquid. Repeat daily to prevent mold. Cover the jar with several layers of cheesecloth or a paper filter held tightly with rubber bands. Ferment for 4-6 weeks, depending on ambient temperature.

Decant by pouring the contents of the jar through a cheesecloth. Squeeze the pulp gently to extract all the vinegar, and discard the remains (we give it to the chickens or pigs). In 2-3 weeks, the vinegar will clarify, leaving behind a cake of "mother" at the bottom of the jar. Siphon vinegar into separate bottles and cover with tight lids. The vinegar will keep on the shelf indefinitely. Store the "mother" in a tightly lidded jar and submerged in vinegar.

Grapes, Currants

There are several ways to make juice from grapes or currants. Elizabeth's mother used to squeeze Concord grapes through a jelly bag, using her hands. Other folks use a blender or food processor to break down the fruit, and then drain the juice to extract skins and seeds. We prefer using a stainless-steel steamer juicer that originated in Germany and became an essential tool in Scandinavia, where people relied on juiced berries to supply them with vitamin C during the winter. Steaming retains higher concentrations of vitamin C than boiling because

of the reduced contact with water at relatively low temperatures.

Juicers have three sections. First, there is a large pot that sits on the burner. Fill it 3/4 full with water and a splash of vinegar to prevent scaling. On top of that sits a second pot containing a funnel and an outlet for a plastic hose, where the juice is accumulated and from which it is drained. On top of that sits the third part, a colander, into which the berries go. In organic production, you do not need to wash the berries, which can include stems, seeds, even leaves. The steam from the bottom pot will clean the berries. If the fruit, such as currants, is acidic, sprinkle sugar over the fruit as you place it into the colander.

Turn the burner to high until the water begins to boil, then turn the heat to medium. Steam will rise into the colander and extract the juice that dribbles down into the second pot. When enough juice has accumulated, decant it. Elizabeth finds it safer to pour juice from the side of the pot into a batter bowl with a lip than to use the plastic hose for decanting. Pour the juice from the batter bowl into sterilized pint or quart jars. Leave 1/4 -inch head-room. Clean rims and seal. Process in a water-bath canner for 10 minutes. Juice will be concentrated, so that 1 quart of canned juice provides 2 quarts of drinking juice. When serving, dilute as desired.

Pickling

Pickling is the process of preserving or extending the shelf life of food by anaerobic fermentation or by immersion in vinegar.

Pickling cucumbers differ from slicing cucumbers in size, shape and texture. Use small pickling cucumbers from the vine and pick them in the morning when the sugars are up. Immerse in cold water, slice off both ends and rub off the spines before processing. Pickles require several weeks on the shelf before they are actually finished.

Bread & Butter Pickles

These sweet pickles are used for hamburgers and sandwiches.

6 lb pickling cucumbers
4 large onions
1/2 C pickling salt
4 C each vinegar and sugar

1 T celery seed
2 t turmeric
2 T yellow mustard seed
1 T mixed pickling spices
Ice cubes

Slice cucumbers and onions and alternately layer in a large strainer, covering each layer with salt. Cover the top with ice cubes and let drain 3 hours in a sink. Add ice as needed. Drain and rinse thoroughly. Combine vinegar, sugar, and spices, and bring to a boil. Boil 10 minutes. Add cucumbers and onions to the pot and bring to a boil again, stirring to mix. Fill hot, sterilized jars with cucumbers and onions. Add hot liquid to within 1/2 inch of the tops of the jars. Release air bubbles, clean rims and seal. Process for 10 minutes. Makes 7-8 pints.

Dill Pickles

5 lb small pickling cucumbers
1 gallon each vinegar and water
3/4 C pickling salt
Put into each quart jar:
1 clove garlic
1 T pickling spice
Several sprigs fresh dill
1 T dill seed

Wash cucumbers, rub off spines, and cut off ends. Bring water, vinegar, and salt to a boil. Have hot jars ready, and put garlic, pickling spices, dill sprigs, and dill seed in each jar. Pack with prepared cucumbers. Ladle the hot vinegar to within 1/2 inch of the tops of the jars. Remove air bubbles, clean rims, and seal. Process in a water-bath canner for 10 minutes. Makes 7 quarts.

Zucchini Pickles

These are our pickles of choice for salads and hamburgers, and for spicing up egg salad.

6 C each sliced green zucchini and yellow summer squash
2 large onions, thinly sliced
1 each yellow, red, and green peppers, thinly sliced
1/2 C pickling salt
2 C sugar
4 C each water and vinegar
2 T each yellow mustard seed and celery seed
2 t turmeric
Cover zucchini, onions, and pepper with water to which salt has been added. Let stand for 2 hours.

Drain and rinse the vegetables. Combine the sugar, water, vinegar and spices and bring to a boil. Add the vegetables and cook 2 minutes. Pack vegetables into hot jars and fill with the hot liquid, leaving 1/2-inch headroom. Release air bubbles, clean rims and seal. Process in a water-bath canner 10 minutes. Makes 6-7 quarts.

Dilled Green Beans

Dilled green beans are an excellent side dish with any food for a crowd. On a platter, arrange lettuce leaves, sauerkraut, cooked black beans, slices of boiled or pickled eggs, smoked fish, olives, and dilled green beans, and let people take their pick.

2 lb green beans
2 1/2 C each water and vinegar
1/4 C salt
In each jar, put:
1 garlic clove
1/8 t dried dill weed
Small sprig of fresh dill weed
3-4 peppercorns
1 bay leaf
1/4 t red pepper flakes

Cut ends off beans and wash thoroughly. Bring water, vinegar, and salt to a boil, then add beans and cook 2 minutes. Remove beans to a strainer, reserving liquid. Add the spices to each hot jar. Put in beans. Fill with liquid, leaving 1/2-inch headroom. Remove air bubbles, clean rims and seal. Process in water-bath canner 10 minutes.

Pickled Eggs

In the winter, we give our laying hens time off, not turning on a light in the hen house to provide the required 14 hours of light per day to keep their egg laying at maximum. Come spring, they lay up to a dozen eggs per day, more than we can consume. So we pickle the extra eggs, which will last up to three years in the refrigerator. We use half-gallon jars to pickle and store the eggs in.

In each jar, place:
2 C vinegar
2 T salt
1/2 T each yellow mustard seed and pickling spice
1/2 bay leaf
For perfect cooked eggs, place them in a steamer basket or pot and turn the heat on high. When the water starts boiling, turn heat to medium, and steam

eggs for 20 minutes. Put eggs in cold water; when they are cool, the peels will come off readily. Place eggs in the jars with pickling ingredients. It takes three days for the eggs to pickle. They are wonderful sliced over salads, or just eaten on their own.

Pickled Shallots

Shallots, fresh out of the ground, chopped into salads or sautéed with onion and garlic are wonderful. Dried, they can be used the same way, although the older they get, the more difficult they are to peel. Or you can pickle them and keep them close to the table for a spicy condiment, or served, as you would dilled beans, in a free-choice salad.

2 lb shallots, peeled but left whole
7 C water, enough to cover the shallots
1 lb coarse sea salt
8 whole cloves
10 whole allspice
2 whole cinnamon sticks
8 white peppercorns
10 black peppercorns
4 bay leaves
12 coriander seeds
4 small dried hot chiles
4 C each malt and white wine vinegar

Make a brine with the salt and 7 cups of water, enough to cover the shallots. In a glass jar, leave the covered shallots in the refrigerator for a week.

Drain and rinse the shallots. Heat the malt and wine vinegars in a stainless-steel pan together with the spices. When this comes to a gentle boil, add shallots and simmer for 5 minutes. Remove from heat, put the shallots in jars and cover with the spiced vinegar. Mature for a month in a cool place. They are now ready to use and will keep for a long time in a cool, dark place.

Salting

Before refrigerators and freezers, people would ferment, brine or salt foods to keep them through the winter. The results are delicious and versatile.

Corned Beef

This salted beef actually has nothing to do with corn but got its name in Anglo-Saxon times when a granular salt the size of a wheat kernel— "corn" to a Briton — was used to process it.

A 5 lb cut of beef; we like brisket best, but tongue or hanging tender work well, too.
4 quarts hot water
2 C pickling or kosher salt
1/4 C sugar
2 T pickling spice
Cloves of one head of garlic, peeled

To Corn:
Combine hot water, salt, sugar, pickling spice. When cool, pour over the beef, which has been placed in a deep enameled pot or ceramic crock. Add the cloves of garlic.

Put a plate on top of the meat to keep it submerged, and cover pot. Cure in a cool place for three weeks, turning meat every five days; be sure it stays submerged.

To Cook:
Cover the meat with boiling water and simmer, allowing about 1 hour per pound, or until a fork can penetrate to the center. Slice it very thinly across the grain. Serve on dark rye bread or with cabbage wedges simmered the last 15 minutes with the meat.

Fenalår — Dried Leg of Lamb

Fenalår is a traditional Norwegian cured meat made from salted leg of lamb. It is a very popular food in Norway and often served with other preserved food at Christmas or on holidays. It was also a meat that could be carried by people working away from home, such as hunters, woodsmen, or fishermen.

Today, it is usually carved off the finished leg and eaten like beef jerky (it has the same texture but a richer taste) or chopped and added to dishes like scalloped potatoes or split pea soup.

Henning brought this particular recipe from Norway, and we have found the process to be successful and the results delicious.

1 leg of lamb, bone in

Thick Brine:
3 lb pickling or kosher salt
1 heaping T sugar
1/2 C honey
1 C water

Mix ingredients. Put the meat in a glass, stainless-steel, or ceramic bowl and cover with the brine. Turn the meat and rub it several times a day for one week. As the meat juices come out, the brine will thin and redden — continue to rub it in.

Salt Brine:
9 quarts water
6 lb kosher or pickling salt. (You may use a lesser amount: mix salt into water until the salt will float a potato — that's enough.)
1 lb sugar

Mix ingredients. Put the meat into the salt brine so that the flesh is completely covered (the bone may stick out). Let sit in a cool place for a week. No need to rub any more!

After a week, wrap the leg in layers of cheesecloth, tie securely, and hang to dry in a cool, well-ventilated place for three to four months or more. In the old days, people would hang the fenalår for up to two years to allow the meat to achieve a dense texture and full flavor. Check periodically to be sure the cheesecloth is secure and no insects have gotten in.

When serving, cut the meat perpendicular to the bone. Sliced fenalår dries quickly, so slice only what you will consume that day.

Storing

Dry storage of potatoes, squashes, onions and shallots, rutabaga, turnips, parsnips, and beets requires a cool, dry place that is safe from rodents and from extreme temperature changes. In the barn we have constructed bins (from recycled pallets) that are lined with hardware cloth to keep out rats and mice, and we cover them with old blankets when the temperature drops below freezing. In the garden we constructed clamps, which are shallow trenches lined with straw or hay and topped with a lidded cold frame. In these we store sugar beets for the dairy cows.

To avoid early sprouting, potatoes are stored separately from apples, alliums, or other vegetables and fruit exuding ethylene gas. Potatoes have a special bin with a sloping base and a wire-covered frame at the bottom which can be lifted when retrieving potatoes. When you gather potatoes from the bin, the ones from above will roll to the bottom, keeping the potatoes aerated.

Garlic is also stored dry by braiding and hanging in a cool, dry place.

Notes:

Local Resources

The islands have fed themselves in the past and they can today. You can grow your own fruits, berries, and vegetables, and raise whatever poultry and meats you have room and heart for. What you can't raise yourself, you can find locally.

The following list of farms offering different products comes from the 2019-2020 *Farm Products Guide*, published by the Lopez Community Land Trust, and is available online. While the farms and products listed in this guide have been pretty constant over the years, it is best to call the purveyors to see if information is still current; things can change from year to year. The list is for Lopez Island only; the other islands in the San Juans have a number of farms, farmstands, and locally grown products. Consult the website *Island Grown Products* for more information. There are other farms and individuals who produce food, hay, composts, seedlings, firewood, lumber and other products not listed in the *Farm Products Guide*. You can find several advertised on *Lopez Rocks* and local bulletin boards.

Beef

Local beef, sold by the side, the quarter, or the cut, is readily available on Lopez Island, and some is carried by Blossom Grocery. Lopez Island farms producing beef for the local market include Double R Bar Ranch, Horse Drawn Farm, Jones Family Farms, Midnight's Farm, S&S Homestead Farm, Stonecrest Farm, and Sweet Grass Farm.

Bread

Barn Owl Bakery, run by Sage Anne Dilts and Nathan Hodges, produces wonderful breads baked in wood-fired ovens. Their breads and pastries are made from wild leavened or sprouted grains, many of which come from Lopez Island. Their products are sold at their farmstand at Grayling Farm, and are carried by the Southend General Store, Lopez Village Market and Blossom Grocery. They sell out quickly. Barn Owl also offers pre-ordered baked goods for pickup, and their bread is featured at several local restaurants. S&S Homestead Farm has provided long-fermented rye bread as part of their weekly CSA shares.

CSA

CSA stands for "Community Supported Agriculture." People subscribe for a season, and receive vegetables (sometimes other products, such as fruit, bread, cheese, meat, and eggs as well) throughout the season. Offerings vary, as do the months produce is provided. The cost for a season varies, and some farms offer a sliding scale. Currently, there are several CSAs on Lopez, including Goosefoot Produce and Lopez Community Farm CSA at S&S Homestead Farm. Others exist, but are not listed in the Farm Products Guide.

Cheese

Lopez Island has two licensed cheese makers: Sunnyfield Farm, which produces goat cheeses, raw milk yogurt, and soap; and S&S Homestead Farm, which produces raw milk cheddar cheese. Sunnyfield sells its products on-farm, at the Farmers Market, at Lopez Village Market, at Blossom Grocery; S&S sells through the Southend General Store and Blossom Grocery, and through CSA shares. There are many other cheesemakers, who star at community dinners and potlucks on the island.

Eggs & Poultry

You can procure organic eggs from many farms on the island, such as Danah Feldman, Double R Bar Ranch, Flint Beach Ohana LLC, Fork in the Road, Jones Family Farms, Midnight's Farm, S&S Homestead Farm, which also occasionally grows turkeys; Stonecrest Farm, Super Natural Farm, which grows chickens; T&D Farms, and Windy Bottom Farm. Drive on almost any road on Lopez, and you will see "Eggs for Sale" advertised. Some folks put out eggs and you leave money.

Farmstands

There are many local farmstands, most of them unadvertised. There is one, for example, on School Road, one on Shark Reef Road, and a seasonal seedling stand at the Southend General Store. Better known are those at Horse Drawn Farm, Lopez Island Farm (featuring pork and lamb),

Midnight's Farm (featuring pork and beef), and Stonecrest Farm. The farmstand at Fork in the Road will be up and running by 2021.

Feed and Fertility Products

Hay, haylage, straw, and compost can be obtained from Midnight's Farm, Sweet Grass Farm, T&D Farms, and Lopez Farm Center.

Fiber Art

All kinds of handmade fiber products are produced on the island. Island Fibers, specializing in Lopez-grown wool, provides products from yarn to shawl. Sheila Metcalf weaves one-of-a-kind garments; both studios are regularly featured on studio tours held in the fall. Some fiber crafts, such as beautiful dish towels, are available at Chimera Art Gallery. One Clay Hill Farm produces heritage Navajo Churro breeding rams, ewes, lambs, fleeces, yarn and tanned hides.

Flowers

Flowers are available from Horse Drawn Farm, and from Arbordoun by subscription, for weddings and special events, and usually sold through Blossom Grocery, the Southend General Store, and the Farmers Market. Arbordoun also produces two excellent herbal products, calendula cream and lotion, sold from the farm and from Blossom Grocery. Jones Family Farms offers flowers for sale at their seasonal farmstand.

Fruits and Berries

Tree fruits and berries are available from Chickadee Produce, Fruit City, J&M Occasional Fruit, Midnight's Farm, T&D Farms, Fork in the Road, and S&S Homestead Farm.

Food Hubs

Food Hubs coordinate the sales and distribution of products: consumers order the foods they want, the Hub contacts the farmers who can provide them, and consumers pick up their order at the Hub, rather than going to different farms for plant starts, vegetables, fruit, meat, cheese, and other island-made products. The Food Hub on Lopez Island is at Taproot Community Kitchen, and is open Tuesdays from 12:00-1:00 pm. For more information or to create an account, go to *San Juan Islands Food Hub, Lopez Island,* on the Web.

Grain

Barn Owl Bakery grows landrace and heirloom grains; Fork in the Road produces wheat; Steve Lillestol is growing wheat for the 2021 Grain CSA. He also offers milling. The Locavores and Lopez Community Land Trust offer the use of two small stone mills in the seed library located at 25 Tuatara Road. Ron Norman grows various grains on a number of island farms. S&S Homestead Farm grows heirloom grains for its own use and to preserve heritage seeds.

Hay & Straw

Hay and straw are produced for sale on the island by Ron Norman, Horsedrawn Farm, Jones Family Farms, Midnight's Farm, and T&D Farms. Hay from other producers is available at Lopez Farm Center.

Herbs

Danah Feldman grows herb starts. Horse Drawn Farm produces herbs for sale through their farmstand. Herb starts from T&D Farms are available at Sunset Builders and by subscription. Whispers of Nature provides "herbs and healing services used by ancient traditions," and has a labyrinth with flowering plants and herbs where one can walk for reflection and meditation.

Lamb

Grass-fed lamb is available from many Lopez farms, including Carter Farm, Double R Bar Ranch, Flint Beach Ohana LLC, Hill Farm, Horse Drawn Farm, Jones Family Farms, Lopez Island Farm, Lucky Ewe Farm, One Clay Hill Farm, S&S Homestead Farm, and Stonecrest Farm.

Pork

Pork is available from Horse Drawn Farm, S&S Homestead Farm, Lopez Island Farm, Midnight's Farm, Stonecrest Farm, and Jones Family Farms, which also provides goat meat. Jones Family Farms meats are available from the farm, in restaurants, and local stores.

Processing Kitchens

For many years, local producers who wanted to sell value-added products made them in restaurant kitchens after closing hours. Now, people can process the products they want to sell or donate in two locations: Taproot, and Fork in the Road Farmstand and Kitchen. Taproot is a nonprofit, shared-use certified, commercial food-processing facility with commercial-grade food-processing equipment. It is used, for example, by the Locavores, who process gleaned fruit for distribution to community organizations such as Meals on Wheels, Lopez Island Schools, the Senior Center and Lopez Fresh. Fork in the Road, located on Fisherman Bay Road, has a fully equipped and certified kitchen that will soon be available for people wanting to process locally-grown farm produce, meat, and ingredients for their own use and for sale. S&S Homestead Farm has a certified processing kitchen used for workshops and demonstrations.

Seafood

There are local fishers who bring in salmon, halibut, and cod in season. Word of mouth (or local social media) will tell you who they are and when their fish is available. Lopez Island Shellfish Farm & Hatchery produces shellfish, including oysters, mussels, clams, and scallops, and local fish in season. Lopez Village Market has wild-caught fish for sale every week.

Seedlings and Plants

Sunset Builders carries seedlings and plants grown by T&D Farms. The Southend General Store has seedlings in the spring from Skyriver Ranch. Seedlings are seasonally offered by various gardeners on Lopez Island (consult the Lopez Island Garden Club).

Seeds

As noted in a previous chapter, vegetable seeds have diminished in quantity and variety as commercial seed companies have merged and eliminated heirloom seed. Fortunately, most local farmers and gardeners grow out a few plants and save their own seed from year to year, exchanging seed in co-ops or informally. Saving seeds is not difficult, but it helps to know how. Saving tomato seeds requires a different process from saving melon seeds, for example, but there are excellent resources available to show you how it's done. A good place to start is *From Seed to Seed: Seed Saving and Growing Techniques For Vegetable Gardeners* by Suzanne Ashworth.

Lopez Community Land Trust (LCLT) maintained a seed library, where people could pay $10 a year for the privilege of taking donated seed, or could donate their own saved seed. All seeds were free. Unfortunately, the seed library is currently deactivated because of a lack of current seed stock. LCLT provided free classes on seed-saving, seed-cleaning equipment, and access to many educational resources. They have a very informative page on-line about protocol in using the seed library. (See *LCLT Seed Library and Seed Exchange Catalog*). They await someone with the interest and expertise to get the library active again.

Sheepskins

Sheepskins are available from the Carter Farm, One Clay Hill Farm, and S&S Homestead Farm. Raw wool is available from many farms during shearing season.

Wine

Lopez Island Vineyard produces excellent wines available at all three grocery stores on the island, and has tasting rooms in the village and at the winery. They are also a presence at the local Farmers Market.

Vegetables

Seasonal vegetables are grown by Chickadee Produce, Danah Feldman, Goosefoot Produce, Horse Drawn Farm, Jones Family Farms, Lopez Harvest, Midnight's Farm, Stonecrest Farm, T&D Farms (available through subscription and in local restaurants). Many growers sell through Lopez Village Market, Blossom Grocery, and local restaurants. S&S Homestead Farm sells vegetables at the farm gate and through their CSA.

Notes:

Recommended Reading

Asher, David. *The Art of Natural Cheesemaking: Using Traditional, Non-Industrial Methods and Raw Ingredients to Make the World's Best Cheeses.* Chelsea Green Publishing. 2015.

Ashworth, Suzanne. *Seed to Seed: Seed Saving and Growing Techniques for Vegetable Growers.* Seed Savers Exchange. 2002.

A Taste of Oregon. Junior League of Eugene. 1980.

Ball Blue Book Guide to Canning and Preserving. Jarden Home Brands. 2014.

Barnett, Tanya Marcovna. "Gratia Plena: Full of Grace," *The Earth Letter.* 2003.

Berry, Wendell. *What Are People For?* North Point Press. 1990.

Bounty: Lopez Island Farmers, Food, and Community. Lopez Community Land Trust. 2016.

Carroll Ricki. *Home Cheese Making.* Storey Publishing. 2002.

Coleman, Eliot. *Four Season Harvest: Organic Vegetables from Your Home Garden All Year Long.* Chelsea Green Publishing. 1999.

Fallon, Sally. *Nourishing Traditions: The Cookbook that Challenges Politically Correct Nutrition and Diet Dictocrats.* New Trends Publishing. 2001.

Ferrari, Linda. *Canning and Preserving.* Crescent Books. 1991.

Gussow, Joan Dye. *This Organic Life: Confessions of a Suburban Homesteader.* Chelsea Green Publishing. 2001.

Howell, Edward. *Food Enzymes for Health and Longevity.* Lotus Press. 1994.

Hupping, Carol. *Stocking Up: America's Classic Preserving Guide.* Simon and Schuster. 1990.

Jeavons, John. *How to Grow More Vegetables Than You Ever Thought Possible on Less Land Than You Can Imagine.* Ten Speed Press. 1974.

Katz, Sandor. *Wild Fermentation: The Flavor, Nutrition, and Craft of Live-Cultured Foods.* Chelsea Green Publishing. 2003.

Kingsolver, Barbara. *Animal, Vegetable, Miracle: A Year of Food Life.* Harper Collins. 2007.

Pellegrini, Angelo. *Lean Years, Happy Years.* Madrona Publishers. 1983.

Pollan, Michael. *In Defense of Food: An Eater's Manifesto.* Penguin Books. 2008.

Pollan, Michael. *The Botany of Desire.* Random House. 2002.

Pollan, Michael. *The Omnivore's Dilemma: A Natural History of Four Meals*. Penguin Books. 2006.

Prentice, Jessica. *Full Moon Feast: Food and the Hunger for Connection*. Chelsea Green Publishing. 2006.

Rodale's *Basic Organic Gardening*. Rodale Press. 1947.

Schlosser, Eric. *Fast Food Nation: The Dark Side of the All-American Meal*. Perennial. 2002.

Smart by Nature —Schooling for Sustainability. U. of California Press. 2009.

Smith, Alisa, and J. B. Mackinnon. *Plenty: One Man, One Woman, and a Raucous Year of Eating Locally*. Three Rivers Press. 2008.

Spurlock, Morgan. *Don't Eat This Book: Fast Food and the Supersizing of America*. G.P. Putnam's Sons. 2005.

Tisdale, Sallie. *The Best Thing I Ever Tasted: The Secret of Food*. Riverhead Books. 2000.

Van Loon, Dirk. *The Family Cow*. Garden Way Publishing. 1976.

Vileisis, Ann. *Kitchen Literacy: How We Lost Knowledge of Where Food Comes from and Why We Need to Get it Back*. Sheerwater Books. 2008.